Waldorf Early Childhood Education:
An Introductory Reader

Edited by Shannon Honigblum

Waldorf Early Childhood Education: An Introductory Reader
First English Edition
© 2017 Waldorf Early Childhood Association of North America
ISBN: 978-1-936849-37-6
Editor: Shannon Honigblum
Editorial Consultant: Lory Widmer
Copy Editor: Donna Lee Miele
Graphic Design: Sheila Harrington, Studio Five
Cover Art: Sheila Harrington

Published in the United States by the
Waldorf Early Childhood Association of North America
285 Hungry Hollow Road
Spring Valley, NY 10977

www.waldorfearlychildhood.org

Visit our online store at
store.waldorfearlychildhood.org

This publication is made possible through a grant
from the Waldorf Curriculum Fund.

All rights reserved.
No part of this book may be reproduced without
the written permission of the publisher, except for brief quotations
embodied in critical reviews and articles.

Table of Contents

Introduction *by Shannon Honigblum* 1

The Essentials of Waldorf Early Childhood Education
by Susan Howard 3

I. History of the Waldorf Early Childhood Education Movement in North America 15

    The Beginnings of Our Waldorf Early Childhood Movement
    by Susan Howard 17

    The Waldorf Kindergarten Movement in North America *by Joan Almon* 23

    The History of the Waldorf Kindergartens and the International Waldorf
    Kindergarten Association *by Helmut von Kügelgen* 25

    Rudolf Steiner Asks for Kindergartens *by Helmut von Kügelgen* 29

II. The Developing Child 31

    Stages of Development in Early Childhood *by Freya Jaffke* 33

    The Significance of Imitation and Example for the Development of the Will
    by Freya Jaffke 41

    Thinking and the Consciousness of the Young Child
    by Renate Long-Breipohl 51

    The Development of Memory and the Transformation of Play
    by Louise deForest 61

    School Readiness and the Transition from Kindergarten to School
    by Claudia McKeen 67

III. The Rhythm of the Day 75

A Day in the Life of the Kindergarten *by Ingeborg Schöttner* 77

Kindergarten Education with Mixed-Age Groups *by Freya Jaffke* 81

Creating a Flow in Time *by Barbara Klocek* 87

Sailing Our Ship in Fair or Stormy Weather *by Tim Bennett* 93

Working with the Will *by Rune Bratlann* 99

Rhythm and Time in the Child's Daily Routine
by Eldbjørg Gjessing Paulsen 101

Finding Your Rhythm
by Nancy Macalester, Susan Weber, and Kimberly Lewis 115

IV. Activities 119

Handwork in the Kindergarten *by Dora Dolder* 121

Practical Activities with the Young Child *by Stephen Spitalny* 125

About Painting and Human Development Through Art
by Freya Jaffke 131

Music in the Waldorf Kindergarten *by Margaret Constantini* 137

The Mood of Early Childhood *by Nancy Foster* 141

Circle in the Kindergarten *by Nancy Foster* 149

Understanding and Fostering Healthy Creative Play *by Joan Almon* 155

The Healing Power of Play *by Joan Almon* 159

V. Language, Storytelling, and Puppetry 169

Fostering Healthy Language Development in Young Children
by Susan Weber 171

Story-thread and Language for the Toddler *by Daniel Udo de Haes* 177

Fairy tale Language and the Image of the Human Being
by Helmut von Kügelgen 183

What to Do about Witches *by Ruth Pusch* 187

Choosing Fairy Tales for Different Ages *by Joan Almon* 193

Marionette Theater *by Helmut von Kügelgen* 199

The Pedagogical Value of Marionette and Table Puppet Shows
for the Young Child *by Bronja Zahlingen* 203

VI. Working with Parents 207

Reflections on Working with Parents *by Kimberly Lewis* 209

Working with Parents *by Louise deForest* 213

Conscious Connections *by Lauren Hickman* 217

A New Vision for Creating Partnerships with Parents *by Margaret Ris* 221

Working with Parents: Ideas for Parent Meetings
by Ruth Ker and Nancy Blanning 229

Creating Partnerships with Parents in First Grade Readiness Decisions
by Ruth Ker 239

VII. The Young Child and the Spiritual World 247

Spiritual Foundations of Waldorf Education *by Michaela Glöckler* 249

Festivals of the Year *by Joan Almon* 253

The Name of "John" and the Fairy Tales *by Stephen Spitalny* 257

Finding the Realm of the Spirit of Humanity *notes by Nancy Foster
from lectures by Michaela Glöckler* 263

Contributors 267
Recommended Further Reading 273

Introduction

Shannon Honigblum

This book brings together a sampling of essays on a wide range of topics that are of interest to the Waldorf early childhood educator and to all caregivers of young children.

These essays have been selected from the resources created over the last thirty-five years by the Waldorf Early Childhood Association of North America, starting with the Waldorf Kindergarten Newsletter (now *Gateways*) and the two collections compiled from it, *An Overview of the Waldorf Kindergarten* and *Deeper Insights into the Waldorf Kindergarten*. From these humble beginnings has grown a rich array of publications that deepen our understanding of the young children in our care, and provide practical and artistic approaches to our work with them. This volume can offer only a small portion of all that is available, and is meant to serve as a starting point for your own explorations.

"The Essentials of Early Childhood Waldorf Education" by Susan Howard provides an overview. Subsequent essays are organized under seven key topics: The History of the Waldorf Early Childhood Movement; The Developing Child; The Rhythm of the Day; Activities; Language, Storytelling, and Puppetry; Working with Parents; and The Young Child and the Spiritual World.

The task of an early childhood educator is important. It is also of lifelong significance for the young child in his or her care. We hope this book will provide interest, inspiration, and insight to teachers meeting the day-to-day joys and challenges of working with groups of young children.

The essays in this book speak to the practical side of teaching in a Waldorf kindergarten—ideas about how to structure a day, what kinds of activities can be healthful, and so forth—as well as to child development and the spiritual core of Waldorf education.

Waldorf education is a spiritually based education, and the task of a teacher is a spiritual task. Rudolf Steiner spoke of the reverence, love, devotion, and gratitude that the teacher must have for the child in his or her care. "Gratitude must permeate teachers and educators of children throughout the period up to the change of teeth, it must be their fundamental mood."[1]

Rudolf Steiner urges teachers to surround the young child with love and happiness, and speaks to the significance these gifts of love and happiness will have for the children in their lives: "…we can bestow upon (the individual) no more signal benefit than a suitable educational influence in the first period of his life (the first seven years). Everything in the nature of joy and love centering upon the child from its immediate environment, plenishes the forces of the physical body, rendering it supple, plastic and amenable to formative influences. The more love and happiness we can ensure for the child in this period, the fewer obstacles later in life…"[2]

Again, in another lecture, Rudolf Steiner emphasizes the importance of love in education. "In a Waldorf school, what a teacher is, is far more important than any technical ability he may have acquired in an intellectual way. The important thing is that the teacher should not only be able to love the whole child, but to love the method he uses, to love his whole procedure. Only to love the children does not suffice for a teacher. To love teaching, to love educating, and to love it with objectivity—this constitutes the spiritual foundation of spiritual, moral, and physical education. And if we can acquire this right love for education, for teaching, we will be able to develop the child up to the age of puberty that by that time we can really hand him over to freedom, to the free use of his own intelligence."[3]

Not only must this love and gratitude be a part of the teacher's attitude toward the children, but the teacher must also, through wonder, observation, and meditation, develop a deep, priest-like devotion: "…the teacher, inasmuch as he gazes at the wonders that are going on between birth and the change of teeth, develops into a religious attitude of the priest. The office of teacher becomes a priestly office, a kind of ritual performed at the altar of universal human life, not with the sacrificial offering that is to be led to death, but with the offering of human nature itself that is to be awakened to life. For it is our task to give over to earthly life what in the child has come to us out of the divine-spiritual world, what with its own forces builds up a second organism out of the being that has come to us out of the divine-spiritual life. If we ponder on these things there awakens within us something like a priestly mood in education."[4]

It is a tall order. However, each striving teacher can meet this challenge with joy. It is our hope that this collection of essays will be of help along the way.

Notes

1   Rudolf Steiner, *The Spiritual Ground of Education,* Lecture 1 (Great Barrington: SteinerBooks 2004).

2   Rudolf Steiner, "The Mission of Religious Devotion: Human Character, Part II" in *Transforming the Soul Volume I* (Great Barrington: SteinerBooks 2004).

3   Rudolf Steiner, *The Spiritual Ground of Education,* Lecture 1.

4   Rudolf Steiner, *The Essentials of Education* (Great Barrington: SteinerBooks 1998).

The Essentials of Waldorf Early Childhood Education

Susan Howard

From *Mentoring in Waldorf Early Childhood Education* (WECAN 2007)

Is there a Waldorf early childhood "curriculum?" Are there specific activities—puppet plays or watercolor painting, for example—that are required in a Waldorf program? Are there certain materials and furnishings—lazured, soft-colored walls, handmade playthings, natural materials, beeswax crayons—that are essential ingredients of a Waldorf setting? What is it that makes Waldorf early childhood education "Waldorf?" Rudolf Steiner spoke on a number of occasions about the essentials of education and of early childhood education. His words shed light on what he considered fundamental:

> *Essentially, there is no education other than self-education, whatever the level may be. This is recognized in its full depth within anthroposophy, which has conscious knowledge through spiritual investigation of repeated Earth lives. Every education is self-education, and as teachers we can only provide the environment for children's self-education. We have to provide the most favorable conditions where, through our agency, children can educate themselves according to their own destinies. This is the attitude that teachers should have toward children, and such an attitude can be developed only through an ever-growing awareness of this fact.*[1]

Thus the essential element in early childhood education is actually the educator, who shapes and influences the children's environment, not only through the furnishings, activities, and rhythms of the day, but most important, through the qualities of her own being and her relationships: to the children and other adults in the kindergarten, to the parents, to daily life in the kindergarten, and to living on earth.

These qualities, which include attitudes and gestures both outer and inner, permeate the early childhood setting and deeply influence the children, who take them up through a process of imitation. The results of such experiences appear much later in the child's life through predispositions, tendencies, and attitudes toward life's opportunities and challenges.

Viewed in this way, early childhood education demands an ongoing process of self-education by the adult. If we again ask, what makes a Waldorf program "Waldorf," the answers might be sought less in the particular activities or rhythms or materials and furnishings, and more in the extent to which these outer aspects are harmonious expressions of inner qualities, attitudes, capacities, and intentions of the teacher—all of which can have a health-giving effect on the children, both in the moment and for the rest of their lives.

Those of us who are committed to this path of Waldorf early childhood education, whether as early childhood teachers or mentors, may actively ask ourselves how qualities essential to the healthy development of young children are living in our own early childhood groups, in our own daily lives, and in our own inner practice.

Rudolf Steiner spoke on a number of occasions about experiences essential for healthy early childhood education, including the following:

- Love and warmth
- Care for the environment and nourishment for the senses
- Creative, artistic experience
- Meaningful adult activity as an example for the child's imitation
- Free, imaginative play
- Protection for the forces of childhood
- Gratitude, reverence, and wonder
- Joy, humor, and happiness
- Adult caregivers on a path of inner development

The following brief descriptions of these qualities and related questions are intended to serve the self-reflection of the individual teacher, the observations of the mentor, and the process of helpful, open dialogue between mentor and mentee.

Love and Warmth

Children who live in an atmosphere of love and warmth, and who have around them truly good examples to imitate, are living in their proper element.[2]

Love and warmth, more than any programmatic approach to early education, create the basis for development. These qualities are expressed in the gestures that live between adult and child, in the children's behavior toward one another, and also in the social relations among the adults in the early childhood center. In other words, they form the social community of early childhood education. When Rudolf Steiner visited the classes of the first Waldorf school, he was known to ask the school children, "Do you love your teacher?"

Questions we can ask ourselves and discuss in mentoring conversations include the following:

- Are love and warmth living in the atmosphere?
- How are they expressed in the gestures that live between adult and child?
- How are they expressed in the children's behavior toward one another?
- How are the social relations among the adults caring for the children?
- What hindrances exist to creating a loving atmosphere?
- How is love expressed in the teacher's response to "inappropriate" behavior (excessive noise, aggression, disruptions, conflict)?

Less apparent within the day, but also of great significance, are these same qualities of love and warmth in relations with colleagues outside the classroom, with the parents, and with the wider community:

- How are the relations between the early childhood educators and the parents?
- How are the relations with the other colleagues in the early childhood groups and in the rest of the school?
- How does the teacher work with conflict and difficulties with adults?
- Are the children surrounded by a community which offers love and warmth and support?

Care for the Environment and Nourishment for the Senses

The essential task of the kindergarten teacher is to create the "proper physical environment" around the children. "Physical environment" must be understood in the widest sense imaginable. It includes not just what happens around children in the material sense, but everything that occurs in their environment, everything that can be perceived by their senses, that can work on the inner powers of children from the surrounding physical space. This includes all moral or immoral actions, all the meaningful and meaningless behaviors that children witness.[3]

Early learning is profoundly connected to the child's own physical body and sensory experience. Thus the physical surroundings, indoors and outdoors, should provide nourishing, diverse opportunities for the child's active self-education. By integrating diverse elements and bringing them into a meaningful, understandable and harmonious order, the adult provides surroundings that are accessible to the young child's understanding, feeling, and active will. Such surroundings provide the basis for the development of a sense of coherence. The child unconsciously experiences the love, care, intentions and consciousness expressed through the outer furnishings and materials of the classroom.

The inner qualities offer a moral grounding for the child's development; the environment is "ensouled" and nurturing.

The adult shapes not only the spatial environment, but also the temporal environment, creating a loving, lively yet orderly "breathing" through rhythm and repetition. Through this healthy breathing process, the child gains a sense of security and confidence in his or her relationship with the world.

Here we can ask:

- Does the environment of the early childhood program offer these qualities of order, care, transparency, and meaning? What is expressed through the outer furnishings and materials?
- Does the space offer diverse opportunities for nourishing experiences in the realm of touch, self-movement, balance, and well-being?
- Are the activities of the day integrated in time into a healthy flow, in which transitions are as smooth and seamless as possible?
- Are there opportunities for lively, joyful physical movement as well as for more inward, listening experience? For large-group, small-group, and solitary experiences?

Creative, Artistic Experience

...[I]n order to become true educators, the essential thing is to be able to see the truly aesthetic element in the work, to bring an artistic quality into our tasks... If we bring this aesthetic element, we then begin to come closer to what the child wills out of its own nature.[4]

In the early childhood class, the art of education is the art of living. The teacher is an artist in how she perceives and relates to the children and the activities of daily life. She "orchestrates" and "choreographs" the rhythms of each day, the week, and the seasons in such a way that the children can breathe freely within a living structure. In addition, the teacher offers the children opportunities for artistic experiences through song and instrumental music, movement and gesture (including rhythmic games and eurythmy), speech and language (including verses, poetry, and stories), modeling, watercolor painting and drawing, puppetry and marionettes.

Here we may ask:

- How do the arts live in the kindergarten, in the teacher, and in the children?
- How is the rhythmic flow of time formed?
- Is the teacher engaged artistically in the domestic arts and work processes?
- How is creative, artistic experience of the child fostered through the furnishings and play materials of the kindergarten?

- Is the play of the children creative and artistic in its imagery, its social interactions, its processes?
- Is the teacher's work with individual children both practical and imaginative? What kinds of imaginations inform her work?
- Is the teacher herself engaged in creative artistic endeavors? Is she striving to deepen her own understanding and experience of what it means to be artistic?

Meaningful Adult Activity as an Example for the Child's Imitation

The task of the kindergarten teacher is to adapt the practical activities of daily life so that they are suitable for the child's imitation through play... The activities of children in kindergarten must be derived directly from life itself rather than being "thought out" by the intellectualized culture of adults. In the kindergarten, the most important thing is to give children the opportunity to directly imitate life itself.[5]

Children do not learn through instruction or admonition, but through imitation.... Good sight will develop if the environment has the proper conditions of light and color, while in the brain and blood circulation, the physical foundations will be laid for a healthy sense of morality if children witness moral actions in their surroundings.[6]

Real, meaningful, purposeful work, adjusted to the needs of the child, is in accordance with the child's natural and inborn need for activity and is an enormously significant educational activity. Thus, rather than offering "thought-out," contrived projects and activities for the children, the teacher focuses on her own meaningful work through activities that nurture daily and seasonal life in the classroom "home": cooking and baking, gardening, laundry and cleaning, creating and caring for the materials in the surroundings, and the bodily care of the children.

This creates a realm, an atmosphere, of freedom in which the individuality of each child can be active. It is not intended that the children copy the outer movements and actions of the adult, but rather that they experience the inner work attitude: the devotion, care, sense of purpose, intensity of focus, and creative spirit of the adult. And then, in turn, each child is free to act as an artist-doer in his or her own right, through creative free play and active movement, according to his or her own inner needs and possibilities.

As we observe a class we may ask ourselves:

- How does meaningful adult activity live in the group, both indoors and out?
- Does the caregiver seem able to devote herself inwardly and outwardly with enthusiasm, in an artistic way, to real life activities and adult work?
- Does she appear engaged artistically in a creative process?

- ✦ Are her work activities truly meaningful and purposeful, in a logical sequence that the child can grasp?
- ✦ Do the children imitate the adult's work through their play (not necessarily her outer actions, but perhaps more important, through the inner gesture of her work)?
- ✦ What qualities are expressed in the children's play?

Free, Imaginative Play

In the child's play activity, we can only provide the conditions for education. What is gained through play stems fundamentally from the self-activity of the child, through everything that cannot be determined by fixed rules. The real educational value of play lies in the fact that we ignore our rules and regulations, our educational theories, and allow the child free rein.[7]

And then, a seemingly contradictory indication:

Giving direction and guidance to play is one of the essential tasks of sensible education, which is to say of an art of education that is right for humanity... The early childhood educator must school his or her observation in order to develop an artistic eye, to detect the individual quality of each child's play.[8]

Little children learn through play. They approach play in an entirely individual way, out of their own unique configuration of soul and spirit, and out of their own unique experiences in the world they live in. In addition, the manner in which each child plays may offer a picture of how he or she will take up his or her destiny as an adult.

The task of the kindergarten teacher is to create an environment that supports the possibility for healthy play. This environment includes the physical surroundings, furnishings, and play materials; the social environment of activities and social interactions; and the inner/spiritual environment of thoughts, intentions, and imaginations held by the adults.

We may ask the following questions relating to the children's play in the kindergarten:

- ✦ What is the quality and duration of the children's play? Is it active, dynamic, healthy, creative? Are the children self-directed and deeply engaged, socially and individually?
- ✦ How does the early childhood teacher reconcile these two seemingly contradictory challenges: to give free rein to the child at play, and to guide and direct and provide the conditions for healthy play to develop?
- ✦ What are the themes and images of free play in the kindergarten?
- ✦ Do the play materials offer diverse and open-ended possibilities for creativity, social interaction, and bodily movement?

✦ Are there opportunities for a wide range of play activities outdoors? How are the children active outdoors, compared with indoors? How much time is there for indoor vs. outdoor play?

Protection for the Forces of Childhood

Although it is highly necessary that each person should be fully awake in later life, the child must be allowed to remain as long as possible in the peaceful, dreamlike condition of pictorial imagination in which his early years of life are passed. For if we allow his organism to grow strong in this non-intellectual way, he will rightly develop in later life the intellectuality needed in the world today.
—Rudolf Steiner, *A Modern Art of Education*

The lively, waking dream of the little child's consciousness must be allowed to thrive in the early childhood group. This means that the teacher refrains as much as possible from verbal instruction; instead, her gestures and actions provide a model for the child's imitation, and familiar rhythms and activities provide a context where the need for verbal instruction is reduced. Simple, archetypal imagery in stories, songs, and games provides "digestible" experiences that do not require intellectual or critical reflection or explanation.

Here we may ask ourselves as educators:

✦ Does the atmosphere in the room foster an imaginative, not-yet-intellectually-awakened consciousness in the children?

✦ Are the children allowed to immerse themselves fully in play without unnecessary instruction and verbal direction from the adults?

✦ Are play processes allowed to run their course, or are they interrupted?

✦ Does a "group consciousness" prevail in group activities, or are children singled out for special privileges and "turns" and offered choices?

✦ Do the sequence and rhythms of the day carry the children along, or do the children ask what is coming next?

✦ Does the teacher invite children to participate in activities such as rhythmic circles or finger games through her own activity, or does she wait to see if children are "ready" or verbally explain what is coming?

An Atmosphere of Gratitude, Reverence, and Wonder

An atmosphere of gratitude should grow naturally in children through merely witnessing the gratitude the adults feel as they receive what is freely given by others, and in how they express this gratitude. If a child says "thank you" very naturally—not in response to the urging of others, but simply through imitating—something has been done that will greatly benefit the child's whole life. Out of this an all-embracing gratitude will develop toward the whole world. This cultivation of gratitude is of paramount importance.[9]

Out of these early all-pervading experiences of gratitude, the first tender capacity for love, which is deeply embedded in each and every child, begins to sprout in earthly life.

If, during the first period of life, we create an atmosphere of gratitude around the children, then out of this gratitude toward the world, toward the entire universe, and also out of thankfulness for being able to be in this world, a profound and warm sense of devotion will arise... upright, honest and true.[10]

This is the basis for what will become a capacity for deep, intimate love and commitment in later life, for dedication and loyalty, for true admiration of others, for fervent spiritual or religious devotion, and for placing oneself wholeheartedly in the service of the world.

And so we may ask:

- How do gratitude, reverence, and wonder live in the kindergarten?
- Do they come to natural expression from adults and children?
- Are they spontaneous and sincere, or sentimentalized?
- Or if these qualities seem to be missing, how does their absence manifest?

Joy, Humor, and Happiness

The joy of children in and with their environment must therefore be counted among the forces that build and shape the physical organs. They need teachers who look and act with happiness and, most of all, with honest, unaffected love. Such a love that streams, as it were, with warmth through the physical environment of the children may be said to literally "hatch out" the forms of the physical organs.[11]

If you make a surly face so that a child gets the impression you are a grumpy person, this harms the child for the rest of its life. What kind of school plan you make is neither here nor there; what matters is what sort of person you are.[12]

Here we may explore the following questions as educators:

- Do happiness and joy live in this group of children and their teachers?
- What are the most joy-filled aspects of the work?
- Which aspects of the work are least permeated with joy?
- How is the teacher's earnestness and serious striving held in a dynamic balance with humor, happiness, and "honest, unaffected love?"
- Are there moments of laughter and delight in the room? How does humor live in the community of children and adults?

Adult Caregivers on a Path of Inner Development

For the small child before the change of teeth, the most important thing in education is the teacher's own being.[13]

Just think what feelings arise in the soul of the early childhood educator who realizes: what I accomplish with this child, I accomplish for the grown-up person in his twenties. What matters is not so much a knowledge of abstract educational principles or pedagogical rules... [W]hat does matter is that a deep sense of responsibility develops in our hearts and minds and affects our world view and the way we stand in life.[14]

Here we come to the spiritual environment of the early childhood setting: the thoughts, attitudes, and imaginations living in the adult who cares for the children. This invisible realm that lies behind the outer actions of the teacher has a profound influence on the child's development.

The spiritual environment includes recognition of the child as a threefold being—of body, soul and spirit—on a path of evolutionary development through repeated earth lives. This recognition provides a foundation for the daily activities in the kindergarten, and for the relationship between adult and child.

In addition to the questions we have already pondered above, we may ask:

- How is the adult actively engaged in inner development as an early childhood educator, and as a human being?
- How is she cultivating a relationship to the children on a spiritual basis?
- How is the educator working with her colleagues to foster an environment of spiritual striving and a deepened study of child and human development?
- Does she strive to approach her work in such a way that the children in her care are not burdened by unresolved issues in her personal life?
- Do goodness and moral uprightness stream from the being of the teacher? Is her inner and outer activity in coherence with healthy social and ethical values? Is she striving to be an example worthy of the children's imitation?

- Does the educator love the children? Does she work to create healthy, caring relationships with their parents, with colleagues, and with the community? Does she love the earth, as well as the world into which the children are incarnating?
- How does she see her relationship to the past, the present, and the future of our human journey?

This is the very challenging realm of self-knowledge and the activity of the individual ego of the adult—a realm where it is difficult to be objective in our observations. Yet ultimately it is this realm that may affect the development of the children most profoundly. It is not merely our outer activity that affects the developing child; it is what lies behind and is expressed through this outer activity. Ultimately the most profound influence on the child is who we are as human beings—and who and how we are becoming.

Conclusion

The so-called "essentials" described here are qualitative in nature. For the most part, they do not characterize a body of "best practices"; instead, they describe inner qualities and attributes of the adult that foster healthy development in young children. These qualities can come to expression in a wide variety of ways, according to the age range and particular characteristics of the children in a particular group; the nature of the particular program (a kindergarten or playgroup or extended care program, for example); or the environment and surroundings (urban or rural, home or school or child care center, for example).

Many practices that have come to be associated with Waldorf early childhood education—certain rhythms and rituals, play materials, songs, stories, even the colors of the walls or the dress of the adults or the menu for snack—may be mistakenly taken as essentials. The results of such assumptions can be surprising or even disturbing: a "King Winter" nature table appearing in a tropical climate in "wintertime," or dolls with pink skin and yellow hair in a kindergarten where all the children in the school and the surrounding culture are brown-skinned and black-haired. Such practices may express a tendency toward a doctrinal or dogmatic approach that is out of touch with the realities of the immediate situation and instead imposes something from "outside."

There is a parallel concern at the other end of the spectrum from the doctrinal or dogmatic. The freedom that Waldorf education offers each individual teacher to determine the practices of her early childhood program can be misinterpreted to mean that "anything goes," according to her own personal preferences and style. Here too, there is the danger that the developmental realities and needs of the children are not sufficiently taken into consideration.

Each of these one-sided approaches may be injurious to the development of the children. As Waldorf early childhood educators we are constantly seeking a middle, universally human path between polarities. Rudolf Steiner's advice to the first Waldorf kindergarten teacher, Elizabeth Grunelius, in the early 1920's, could be paraphrased as follows: Observe the children. Actively meditate. Follow your intuitions. Work out of imitation.

Today we are challenged to engage in a constant process of renewal as Waldorf early childhood educators, actively observing today's children in our care, carrying them in our meditations, and seeking to work consciously and artistically to create the experiences that will serve their development. Our devotion to this task awakens us to the importance of self-education and transformation in the context of community. Our ongoing study of child and human development, our own artistic and meditative practices, and our work with anthroposophy, independently and together with others, become essential elements for the practice of Waldorf early childhood education. Here we can come to experience that we are not alone on this journey; we are supported through our encounters with one other and with spiritual beings who offer support toward our continued development and toward the renewal of culture Waldorf education seeks to serve.

Notes

1. Rudolf Steiner, *The Child's Changing Consciousness* (Great Barrington: SteinerBooks 1996).
2. Rudolf Steiner, *The Education of the Child* (Great Barrington: SteinerBooks 1996).
3. Ibid.
4. Rudolf Steiner, *A Modern Art of Education* (Great Barrington: SteinerBooks 2004).
5. Rudolf Steiner, *The Child's Changing Consciousness*.
6. Rudolf Steiner, *The Education of the Child*.
7. Rudolf Steiner, *Self-Education in the Light of Spiritual Science* (Spring Valley: Mercury Press 1994).
8. Rudolf Steiner, untranslated lecture, Utrecht, Feb. 24, 1921.
9. Rudolf Steiner, *The Child's Changing Consciousness*.
10. Ibid.
11. Rudolf Steiner, *The Education of the Child*.
12. Rudolf Steiner, *The Kingdom of Childhood* (Great Barrington: SteinerBooks 1995).
13. Rudolf Steiner, *The Essentials of Education* (Great Barrington: SteinerBooks 1998).
14. Rudolf Steiner, "Education In the Face of the Present Day World Situation," lecture given on June 10, 1920.

I. History of the Waldorf Early Childhood Education Movement in North America

The first Waldorf school, based on the teachings of Rudolf Steiner, was founded in 1919 in Stuttgart, Germany. Steiner envisioned a healing education. He envisioned an educational system that was deeply aligned with the development of the human being and that would help individuals take hold of their destinies and to be able to think freely and clearly.

Steiner developed an educational philosophy that pays attentions to and educates the whole child: head, heart, and hands; or thinking, feeling, and willing. The Waldorf school movement has grown to over two thousand Waldorf schools with kindergartens worldwide and many more freestanding kindergartens.

As Susan Howard describes in this section's first essay, Rudolf Steiner spoke extensively about the development of the young child and the importance of kindergartens. He urged schools to open kindergartens, recognizing the significance of providing healthful early childhood education. "It would be very nice if we could bring in some children in the first seven years of early childhood education. In the end, we must have them somewhat younger" (see Note).

The history of the Waldorf early childhood movement is further explored in this section by Joan Almon and Helmut von Kügelgen.

Note

See *An Overview of the Waldorf Kindergarten* (Waldorf Kindergarten Association of North America, 1993), p. 6. Nora was a eurythmist and Waldorf teacher who lived and worked in Austria, Germany, and the Netherlands from the pre-World War I years through the 1960s.

The Beginnings of Our Waldorf Early Childhood Movement

Susan Howard

From *Gateways* Newsletter Issue 49 (WECAN 2005)

2005 was the eightieth anniversary of the Waldorf kindergarten movement. This brought an opportunity to reflect back on the origins of our work, to consider how this work had developed over the course of eight decades, a rich lifespan in human terms, and to ponder its renewal in the twenty-first century in light of the current needs of the child and cultural conditions around the world.

The first "official" Waldorf kindergarten opened at the first Waldorf School in Stuttgart in 1926, a year and a half after the death of Rudolf Steiner. However, there was actually an early first attempt that is less known. I have looked through various articles, unpublished manuscripts and notes from conversations to piece together the following story of the very beginnings of our Waldorf early childhood movement.

Even before the opening of the first Waldorf School in 1919, Rudolf Steiner had spoken about the importance of the first seven years of life and his regret that the class teachers would receive the children only after this formative period was complete.

> *The teachers will take on children to educate who are already at a certain age; and they must consider thereby that they are taking on these children after they have already experienced the education or perhaps the miseducation of their parents in the very first stage of their lives. What we are striving for will only be able to be accomplished completely when humanity has progressed so far that parents understand that even in the first period of upbringing, modern humanity has special educational needs.*[1]

Five years earlier, in 1914, Rudolf Steiner had met Elisabeth Grunelius, a nineteen-year-old from the Alsace region of Germany, who had just completed her state kindergarten training in Bonn. Elisabeth had read *Theosophy*[2] by Steiner, and decided to help with the building of the Goetheanum in Dornach, Switzerland. She joined a group of artists working under Steiner's direction on wood relief sculptures for the new building. Elisabeth stayed in Dornach for eighteen months, working on the woodcarvings and attending lectures by Rudolf Steiner, before resuming her early childhood studies at the Pestalozzi-Froebel Seminar in Berlin. Afterwards, she was drawn to the newly developing Waldorf school in Stuttgart.

Once the first Waldorf School opened in 1919, Rudolf Steiner asked the teachers to free up a room for a kindergarten, but it was not possible. Finances were strained, and the faculty chose to use every available space for additional grade-school classes. Later, in 1920, Rudolf Steiner spoke again with the faculty about the importance of the kindergarten:

It is true that it would be better if you could have the children in kindergarten. The longer you have them, the better. Thus you could admit children who are not yet old enough to come to school. …It would be very nice if we could bring in some children in the first seven years of early childhood education. In the end, we must have them somewhat younger; it is much less important when they are older.[3]

After a visit to an elementary class, he was heard to exclaim, "We need kindergartens! We need kindergartens!" He asked the teachers to free up a classroom for a kindergarten, but again they said it was not possible. According to a later comment by Elisabeth Grunelius, the teachers did not seem to grasp the importance of the kindergarten.

Steiner remembered Elisabeth from Dornach, and asked her to write a sixty-page proposal for how one would work with three- to five-year olds. She tried, but felt she could not do it, since she had not had any direct experience with young children.

I felt I had to have experience first. One could not sit at a table and figure it all out. Today it is perhaps difficult to imagine a time when no one had worked consciously with the imitative capacities of the child. We need to remember that class teachers teach, but the kindergarten teacher must show what should be done through her life and being.[4]

Then, in the spring of 1920, a new government regulation changed the beginning of the school year from Easter to September. This meant that the children who would have begun first grade at Easter now had no teacher until September. On Good Friday, 1920, Rudolf Steiner asked Elisabeth Grunelius if she would take on a kindergarten group from Easter to September. She later described this moment as follows:

I was now finished with my (state) training and was very certain that on no account did I want to work with children! I wanted to study medicine. I answered Rudolf Steiner, "I must think about that further," and stood there looking down in thought. As I stood there, he also remained standing, as if he was waiting for an outer answer from me. When I looked up, I was puzzled that he was still there. I thought, well, if Rudolf Steiner is there and helps, then perhaps I can carry this out! And I answered, "If you will stand behind me, then I can."[5]

A week later, they began. But it was hardly an ideal beginning! She met for three hours each afternoon with about twenty pre-first-graders. The room was used for the eighth grade in the morning, with fixed benches running along the walls and heavy table-desks that could not be moved, and the floor was painted black! Luckily, it was spring and summer time, and she could be outdoors with the children most of the time. She had no toys or play materials. She had only Rudolf Steiner's statements that meditation should be the basis of life in the kindergarten, and that she was to work out of imitation—two entirely radical thoughts that she had never encountered before in her training for early childhood education!

She later remembered one little girl who slammed the door each day very hard. She had asked her several times to do it nicely, to no avail. On the third day, Elisabeth realized that she herself did not close the door completely. So when the little girl was watching, Elisabeth closed the door "nicely," and after that, the little girl also closed it nicely every time. This was an incredible experience for Elisabeth at that time.

Once she showed Rudolf Steiner crayon drawings the children had made, and he said it would be even better to let them do watercolor painting with good, large brushes and flowing colors. "It is not the picture that is important," he said, "but the children should imitate your 'noble attitude,' they will want to dab around (*nachpatschen*) with the color, rather than exactly copy your gestures."[6]

She also did clay modeling—"the children could hardly wait to plunge their hands into this sculptural material and start forming it," she later wrote—and she told fairy tales.

The kindergarten continued until the end of the summer holidays, but then there was no real possibility to go on in that unsuitable room. There was also "an overflowing deficiency of money," and still no real support from the class teachers. Elisabeth Grunelius joined the College of Teachers and worked as a handwork teacher and substitute for class teachers until 1926. She returned to Dornach from time to time to work with artistic activities, eurythmy, speech, clay modeling, painting, and anthroposophical studies. These experiences were her Waldorf kindergarten training.

During these years Rudolf Steiner continued to urge the teachers to open a kindergarten, and gave lectures such as *The Roots of Education* and the *Essentials of Education*,[7] where he spoke of the work of the early childhood educator. Finally, in 1924, one of the teachers, Herbert Hahn, heard Rudolf Steiner's call and decided to take up the challenge of having a kindergarten built on the school grounds.

The new kindergarten was finished in 1926, nearly eighteen months after Rudolf Steiner's death. It was described as a "barracks" with three rooms, one a eurythmy room painted "bluish pink like rose mallow," a color Steiner had indicated for eurythmy. The room for painting was a dark blue, "darker than the sky," and the playroom was carmine red. Rudolf Steiner had expressed how different color experiences for the children, according to whether they were restless, slow, etc., would provide inwardly arising complementary color experiences to meet their different needs. For children with sleeping problems, for example, Steiner had suggested deep orange curtains around the bed. Outdoors there was a sandpit and a garden.

Elisabeth tried to build up kindergarten activities out of sensing in her fingertips what the children needed, working meditatively, and aspiring to work with imitation rather than "pulling things out" of the children.

Once she invited a basket maker to come and work in the presence of the children.

He was a young man, and he had his shirt sleeves rolled up so that the children could see how strong he was. He had a big basket, and he finished it with large branches. On the next day, in the cloak room, I saw reeds hanging from the coat hook of one of the children, a very inhibited girl. I asked her why she needed the reeds. "To make baskets," she replied. Then I immediately went out and bought reeds and bottoms for baskets and on the next day, all the four-year-olds made baskets. I wanted to help them, but they could do it themselves. They never could have done that if they had not seen the basket maker at work.

Three years later, Klara Hatterman, a young woman from Hannover, Germany, who was eager to learn to be a Waldorf kindergarten teacher, approached Elisabeth Grunelius and urged her to offer a training course. Elisabeth felt too inexperienced but, reluctantly, she agreed to meet with a small group of four to five interested people. When they arrived, she asked them all to leave, saying that she was not ready. They all left except Klara, who became her intern and later her friend and colleague for life. One could say that these two were the pioneers of our movement.

In 1931, Klara founded a small kindergarten in Hannover. The new Hannover Waldorf School was struggling spiritually and financially to establish itself, so the kindergarten had to be independent. Klara rented a two-room apartment and transformed one of the rooms into a space for the children each day. Here the work blossomed. For ten years, as many as twenty children visited the kindergarten each day.

In 1938, the Stuttgart and Hannover Waldorf schools were closed by the Nazis. Klara's home kindergarten, less visible, continued until 1941. When the Nazis closed it, she fled to Dresden and opened a small kindergarten in a cellar there. It was the only remaining Waldorf initiative until it too was discovered and closed by the National Socialists.

In 1940, Elisabeth sailed from Genoa to the United States at the invitation of friends. In 1941, she opened a kindergarten at the Myrin farm in Kimberton, Pennsylvania, as the foundation for a new Waldorf school. In 1948 she went on to found a kindergarten at the new Waldorf school on the campus of Adelphi University in Garden City, Long Island. It was here that she wrote and published her book, *Early Childhood and the Waldorf School Plan*,[8] which was translated into many languages, including Japanese.

In 1946, after the war, Klara Hatterman returned to Hannover and started a kindergarten again under very primitive circumstances, with a tar paper roof and umbrellas to provide indoor shelter from the rain. Grass grew through the floor, and in winter there were snow crystals on the walls. In the beginning, outdoor free play consisted of playing in the post-war rubble and discovering a spoon or a nail or something to help build up the kindergarten.

For seven years, the kindergarten, now a part of the school, took place under these difficult circumstances, until the "ugly duckling" became a "swan." The woodwork teacher developed the architectural plans and built the furniture, and the school's business manager devoted himself to creating the social and financial basis for a kindergarten building. At Christmas, 1953, the new kindergarten building was dedicated.

Beginning in 1950, at the age of forty-two, Klara Hatterman invited other kindergarten teachers to come together each year for several days during the Holy Nights, to deepen their anthroposophical study of the young child. They asked, "How can we develop ourselves so as to be able to receive the being of the young child from the spiritual world? What activities and approaches can we develop for work in the kindergarten? How can we provide real support for parents in the upbringing of children?" They struggled to deepen their understanding of the power of imitation, of the child as a sense organ, of the thought of reincarnation in relation to early childhood development. They committed themselves to founding and developing kindergartens, working out of an anthroposophical view of the human being.

We could say that these gatherings were the beginnings for what eventually incarnated in 1969 as the International Association of Waldorf Kindergartens. Today, there is truly a worldwide movement that includes over two thousand kindergartens, home and center-based child care, parent-child groups, and family centers.

We can look back with gratitude to Elisabeth Grunelius and Klara Hatterman for their courage, their tireless enthusiasm for their work in the face of adversity, their heartfelt love and warmth for the little child, and their profound devotion to ongoing deepening of their work through study and inner development. They were researchers, intuitively feeling their way through exact observation of the children in their care. They were visionaries, able to see far beyond their own immediate surroundings, and able to consciously work with the reality of the spiritual nature of the child.

Today, we carry forward the work of these pioneers, exploring new approaches to meeting the needs of the young child in a new century. What are the needs of the incarnating spiritual beings in our care today? How can we grow and deepen so that we can be worthy of their imitation? What is it that lies at the core of our work spiritually?

The early gatherings at the Holy Nights in Hanover grew into large international kindergarten conferences held each year at Whitsun. For many years, Klara Hatterman opened each conference with the following verse, "Whitsun Mood," by Rudolf Steiner, which reminds us of the spiritual context out of which our work can grow and flourish in times to come.

Being aligns with being in widths of space.
Being follows being in rounds of time.
When you, O Man, remain in widths of space, in rounds of time,
Then you are in realms that fade and pass away.
Yet mightily your soul rises above them,
When you divine or knowingly behold the Eternal,
Beyond the widths of space, beyond the rounds of time.

Notes

1. Rudolf Steiner, *The Foundations of Human Experience*, Lecture 1 (Great Barrington: SteinerBooks 1996).

2. See Rudolf Steiner, *Theosophy* (Great Barrington: SteinerBooks 1994).

3. "Rudolf Steiner Asks for Kindergartens: Elisabeth Grunelius" in *An Overview of the Waldorf Kindergarten* (Waldorf Kindergarten Association of North America, 1993) p. 6.

4. Elisabeth Grunelius, "Rudolf Steiner Asks for Kindergartens," unpublished.

5. Ibid.

6. From a conversation between Elisabeth Grunelius and Ingeborg Brochmann at the World Kindergarten Conference in Dornach, 1984.

7. See Rudolf Steiner, *The Essentials of Education* (Great Barrington: SteinerBooks 1998) and *The Roots of Education* (Great Barrington: SteinerBooks 1998).

8. Elisabeth Grunelius, *Early Childhood Education and the Waldorf School Plan* (Fair Oaks: Rudolf Steiner College Press 1991).

The Waldorf Kindergarten Movement in North America

Joan Almon

From *An Overview of the Waldorf Kindergarten* (WECAN 1993)
Updated for this publication

By the 1980s a new situation was developing in the North American Waldorf kindergarten movement. Many of the original teachers were retiring, and they were a group of wonderful women who had drawn heavily on their own rich childhoods along with their studies of anthroposophy and Waldorf education to create unique kindergartens. Many of the next generation of teachers had had fine childhoods but found themselves without the background in gardening, housekeeping, arts and crafts that had come so naturally to the earlier teachers. This next group needed courses and books to develop the missing skills and the soul qualities that they awaken.

Fortunately, in the mid 1970s Werner Glas had already recognized this need and had begun a kindergarten training program at the Waldorf Institute, bringing experienced teachers from Europe to offer courses. The North American teachers were grateful for this impulse and took it a step further in 1983 by forming an Association that would focus on publications, courses, and conferences for Waldorf kindergarten teachers. The first challenge was to help fifty teachers from North America attend the 1984 International Kindergarten Conference in Dornach. We took an active role in that conference and were invited to participate on the Board of the International Kindergarten Association. The North American Association thus became part of the worldwide Waldorf kindergarten movement.

Starting at that time the Kindergarten Association organized a North American kindergarten conference, participated actively in the 1991 International Kindergarten Conference in Dornach, organized many regional conferences, and helped organize introductory and advanced courses. It began publishing the Kindergarten Newsletter (now *Gateways*) and worked with publishers on other publications.

It grew even more active as a rapidly growing number of communities began founding Waldorf kindergartens. Public school districts were also taking an active interest in Waldorf education, and university professors were interested in including Waldorf education in courses and research projects. To meet these challenges the Kindergarten Association worked closely with the Waldorf Schools Association through the 1990s. It also worked actively with the International Kindergarten Association in an effort to help build Waldorf kindergartens and training seminars in eastern Europe, in the black townships of South

Africa, in South America, and in other countries. The 1990s mood of new freedom went hand in hand with an awakening interest in Waldorf education, and the starting point of such awakenings is nearly always with the kindergarten.

At the same time that the kindergarten movement expanded outwardly, it also strove to grow deeper in its anthroposophic understanding of the young child. Courses and conferences for deepening the work developed, and the Kindergarten Association worked closely with the Anthroposophical Society and its Pedagogical Section on many issues. With this growth of activity that reaches both inward and outward, the 1990s proved to be a challenging but richly rewarding decade for the kindergarten movement and its teachers.

At the end of the 1990s the US Alliance for Childhood was founded and Joan Almon became its Director; as its advocacy activity grew, Joan stepped back from her leadership role.

The Waldorf movement continued to expand its work, during the mid-to-late nineties, with younger and younger children in parent-child and parent-infant classes, toddler programs and all-day child care. The name "kindergarten" seemed too small to encompass the fullness of our Association and its membership, and in the late nineties the Waldorf Kindergarten Association changed its name to Waldorf Early Childhood Association of North America (WECAN). In 2002, WECAN hired a part-time Coordinator, Susan Howard.

Also during this time and into the early 2000s, the expansion and diversification of early childhood work continued worldwide. The International Waldorf Kindergarten Association became the International Association for Steiner Waldorf Early Childhood Education (IASWECE).

In recent years, collaborative research groups have been formed to explore areas that needed to be deepened and extended—the work with the older child in the kindergarten and the transition into the grades, the care and education of the child from birth to age three, diversity and multiculturalism, therapeutic education, working with parents, the training and ongoing professional development of educators, and most recently, public policy and advocacy. Out of this research, WECAN Publications has offered a growing array of books and other resources. WECAN conference activity has also continued to grow.

Membership, too, has grown. In 2016, WECAN had nearly five hundred individual members and two hundred organizational members here in North America; worldwide there were approximately two thousand Steiner/Waldorf kindergartens in more than seventy countries. The most exponential growth has been taking place in China, where more than three hundred Waldorf kindergarten initiatives have been founded in the last ten years. A number of experienced North American Waldorf early childhood educators now act as mentors, advisors, and trainers in Latin America, Africa, and Asia.

The History of the Waldorf Kindergartens and the International Waldorf Kindergarten Association

Helmut von Kügelgen

From *Love as the Source of Education* (WECAN 2016)
Originally published in *An Overview of the Waldorf Kindergarten* (WECAN 1993)

Rudolf Steiner saw the educational question as a part of the moral responsibility of mankind and therefore central to all social problems. The forming of the social life could, in turn, only be a part of an encompassing cultural renewal, which begins from the foundation of human self-knowledge. What is the task, and what is the meaning of human existence on earth and in the cosmos? How do the destinies of individuals, of nations, and indeed of all mankind weave in and out of one another? With an eye to what lay ahead in the twentieth century—the unparalleled development of technological civilization and the huge abysses of human and inhuman relationships—his work had to bind together the widest perspectives of worldly and human development with the deepest questions of incarnation, of the education and self-education of humanity.

Each of Rudolf Steiner's statements about education is drawn from a knowledge of man and the world which awakens a love for self-determined action and an awareness of the meaning of existence and, indeed, of difficult destinies. Thereby they lead from these into a daily practice of education dealing with details on such matters as age differences, nutrition, toys, etc. In addition, the science of the physical world, the amazing science with its child technology, must be supplemented by a science of the soul and spiritual reality of man and of the divine spiritual being of the ensouled and spirit-filled cosmos. In this way, anthroposophical spiritual science, which looks at humanity in its totality of body, soul and spirit, brings together and reconciles the spheres of cultural life—science, art, and religion. They should interpenetrate one another and unite themselves in humanity. "Science should become alive, art should become alive, and religion should become alive—that is, in the final analysis, true education and instruction." Rudolf Steiner spoke these words at the birth of the first Waldorf school, on the opening day of the Free Waldorf School in Stuttgart.

In his lectures, "The Study of Man as the Foundation of Pedagogy," a study which paints a picture of humanity from the spiritual, soul and physical points of view, he laid the foundation for Waldorf education. Already in the introduction of the first lecture, Rudolf Steiner commiserated that at first only children could be admitted to the school who were already beyond the age of imitation, who had already lived through the first seven years which make such a decisive impression on one. "We will only completely achieve what we are undertaking when we are so far advanced as human beings that even the parents understand that the first years of education present a special task for modern man." A broad cultural work with the parents and the pressing desire to absorb, even in the earliest phases of life, the healing effects of an education appropriate to our times, are the first and enduring impulses for the founding of the kindergartens and for the development of an early childhood education which does justice to the worth of man and supports development through a gradual incarnation.

In the last years of his life, Rudolf Steiner called Elisabeth von Grunelius to the kindergarten work. He was able to add to the indication he has given in 1907 when he gave a lecture entitled "The Education of the Child from the Viewpoint of Spiritual Science" (now available in book form as *The Education of the Child*). He added to these indications in many more lectures, not only on pedagogical subjects, but also when he addressed matters of pure spiritual science. But he did not live to see the actual foundation of the first Waldorf kindergarten. This took place in 1926, just one year after his death, when Elisabeth von Grunelius began the first kindergarten. A few additional Waldorf kindergartens followed this example in the years before World War II.

The War broke out over humanity in 1939, just twenty years after the founding of the first Waldorf school. We must look at is as a sign of the decline of human culture, given its destruction of the spirit and cultural life of middle Europe through the deeds of National Socialism. It has changed the world, which since then has not come to peace but to further cultural disintegration—the tensions between east and west, between industrial states and developing countries, the social polarization which has weakened the middle, and the exploitation of the ecological life systems of the earth. Because of the disintegration itself, there has arisen a demand for Waldorf education more and more often in western countries.

By the end of the 1960s a slogan rang forth around the world that education of the young child makes a life-long impression on the human being's destiny, and educational issues became the headlines of the newspapers. Among parents, one could see an unprecedented uncertainty because of the prevailing opinion of educational theorists who could only envision a cognitive education for the future supported by audio-visual media. The opposite extreme, an antiauthoritarian education, in which the children did not work on the necessary conditions for life and development, soon showed its destructive effects. This challenged Waldorf education to work for a healthy education, for a sheltered and guided childhood, and also to work against early cognitive education in the first seven years. Waldorf preschool educators discussed in the press and at meetings of representatives of the new pedagogy what they had been practicing in Waldorf kindergartens for many years. In many lectures, meetings and conferences, kindergarten teachers, school teachers, doctors, and scientists worked together to set forth the conditions of childhood. Brochures and leaflets were printed in which the developmental stages of the child were presented and learning through imitation was described. Such imitation assumes that the kindergarten teacher is doing sensible, practical life activities in the kindergarten. Themes were discussed such as free play, simple toys, speech development through the example of the educators, storytelling and puppet plays, and artistic activities in music, movement, and handwork; there were also discussions about the social and moral qualities in the group of children and in the work with parents.

Out of this work there came together in 1969 twenty-four German institutions which formed an Association of Waldorf Kindergartens. Already with the effort to create the legal papers for this Association, whose greatest concern is to struggle responsibly for the rights of children to a human education, there arose the necessity to work together with Waldorf kindergartens in other countries. So the Association soon expanded with the agreement of the Waldorf and Steiner kindergartens of many lands. From its very founding, one of its purposes was to intervene on an international scale against educational theories which still today seriously threaten the healthy development of the young child through one-sided, cognitive pedagogy. This union named itself the "Internationale Vereinigung der Waldorfkindergaerten" (the International Association of Waldorf Kindergartens). Its board of directors consists of members of many countries, and it provides a continuing exchange of experiences across the borders. It is concerned with establishing and developing a kindergarten education and the corresponding work with the parents, which suits the human being's development and preserves the creative forces found in the growing child and allows them to ripen.

At this writing there are 66 member kindergartens in the USA, Canada and South America; there are eight in Australia and New Zealand, and 320 in Western Europe, of which 180 are in Germany where the headquarters of the Association are located. Each year new kindergartens spring up in each land, for the initiatives or parent groups in many places are directed towards Waldorf kindergartens.

Editor's Note: Due to the tremendous growth of Waldorf early childhood education worldwide, the original International Association of Waldorf Kindergartens separated into two organizations in 2006: the International Association for Steiner/Waldorf Early Childhood Education (IASWECE) with thirty-two member country associations and active internationally, and the Association of Waldorf Kindergartens, which is responsible for the Waldorf kindergartens in Germany and is a member country association in IASWECE.

Today there are 188 member Waldorf kindergartens and early childhood programs in North America, 550 in Germany, and more than 2100 worldwide in sixty-five countries in Asia, Africa, Australia/New Zealand, Europe, and North and South America.

The name "Kindergarten" was replaced by "Early Childhood Education" in the name of the International Association, in order to include the diversity of programs for the child from pre-birth to school entrance, including a growing number of programs for children under the age of three and their parents.

The most important task of the Association is to look after the development of Waldorf kindergarten teachers and watch over the founding of new kindergartens. The Association works with the parents and initiative groups to set forth the pedagogy of Rudolf Steiner and to encourage patience so that they will prepare a foundation and wait until a teacher is found who wishes to work out of an understanding of Rudolf Steiner, and who is, above all, capable of doing so. For this reason, conversations take place between the instructors in the existing kindergarten seminars and the specialty schools, and experienced kindergarten teachers travel to the United States and other lands all over the world to support the good training programs with their advice and example. In countries where there are a number of Waldorf kindergartens and where distances permit, the teachers come together in regional meetings during the year to work with one another on basic questions of education. The Association supports this regional cooperation, for it does not attempt to lead the kindergarten movement from the center, but is rather concerned with the exchange of the fruits of the work.

In order to contribute to the substance of the kindergarten work, study materials are published by the Association and further writings are made available by a wide variety of publishers. An annual conference takes place in Hannover with a rich offering of educational courses. This conference began in 1955 as a small circle. In recent years 700 or more kindergarten teachers attended from all countries in which Waldorf kindergartens exist. At the conference more courses are being offered in a variety of languages so that the conference can also be fruitful for those who do not speak—or do not yet speak—the language of Rudolf Steiner. The impulse for this conference arose from Klara Hatterman, who had the opportunity to work together with Elisabeth von Grunelius, and who built up the large Waldorf kindergarten in Hannover after World War II.

It is precisely in the education of the young child, with which the understanding and cooperation of the family is so important, that the work out of the folk awareness, the social, religious, and cultural bonds, receives its unique character. This makes the exchange of experiences on an international level infinitely fruitful. On the other hand there also lives in the young child the purely human experience. Thus a foundation can be laid in the kindergarten for a human culture which can tie together human beings beyond the limits of boundaries. Through our children and their education, there can arise on our time an impulse for peace and humanitarianism embracing all human relationships. To work for this is one of the deepest concerns of the International Waldorf Kindergarten Association.

Rudolf Steiner Asks for Kindergartens

Helmut von Kügelgen

From *Love as the Source of Education* (WECAN 2016)
Originally published in *Erziehungskunst*, Number 7/8 (1979)

Rudolf Steiner laid the intellectual/spiritual foundation for Waldorf education through his series of lectures known as *The Study of Man*.[1] In the very first lecture he said that each epoch of human evolution must demand its own unique form of education. He said that the gift offered to education by the Waldorf school could only be fulfilled in the "present and near future" if parents and, especially, teachers of children up to age seven, were to accompany the school with understanding:

> *You will be asked to take over the education of children who are already of a certain age and you will need to remember that in the very first epoch of their lives, these children have received education (or often perhaps mis- education) from their parents. That which we wish to accomplish can only be completely fulfilled when humanity has progressed to the point that parents also understand that people of today are faced with special tasks when it comes to education in the first seven-year epoch of a child's life. We will still be able to make improvements in many areas that were lacking in the first years of a child's life once we have the child in school.*[2]

The extent to which Rudolf Steiner understood the problem of the loss of healthy instincts in child rearing, as well as the loss of healthy environments, is illustrated in a report by Nora von Baditz, who heard Rudolf Steiner say the following after visiting a classroom: "We need kindergartens! We need kindergartens!"

He said something similar in a teacher's conference:

> *It is really better if you have the children in kindergarten, don't you agree? The longer you have them, the better. That way, we could have the children who are not yet in school. Up to now, we have essentially enrolled the children in the same way as a public school; we can begin when a child's imitative stage is coming to an end. It would be very nice if we could contribute something to a child's upbringing in the first seven years of life. We need to offer something for the preschool years; later years are much less important.*[3]

Shortly after this, Rudolf Steiner spoke of the founding of the Waldorf school in Stuttgart, and talked about the Waldorf educational method in light of his experiences during the school's first two years, in the so-called Christmas course for teachers (published in English as *Soul Economy*[4]). Other pressing tasks, as well as concerns about finances, prevented him from establishing a kindergarten at that time, even though he had had conversations with Elisabeth von Grunelius, who was slated to be the kindergarten teacher and was already a member of the teacher's college. On December 29, 1921, he said:

If you have the task of approaching a very young child in the capacity of a parent or guardian, you will feel an extraordinarily strong responsibility to commit yourself to understanding the whole of the child's existence up to now. For this reason, it has always been especially painful for me that we are only able to enroll children into the Stuttgart Waldorf School once they have reached Central Europe's compulsory school age. It would be a source of deep satisfaction for me if younger children could also be enrolled in the Waldorf School. But, over and above any other difficulties, the biggest hurdle we face in establishing a kind of school for very young children is an extraordinarily pronounced lack of funds, as with all our other endeavors in the anthroposophical movement. Considering the lack of finances, the most we can hope for is that if the Waldorf School is not too negatively perceived in the future, we will also get to the point of being able to enroll younger children.[5]

In 1926, soon after Rudolf Steiner's death, Elisabeth von Grunelius started the first Waldorf kindergarten that was fully integrated into the Waldorf School. Today, a worldwide Waldorf kindergarten movement has grown from it. It is considered part of Rudolf Steiner's great impulse for education. Waldorf schools grow from kindergartens and parent initiatives, and they "need kindergartens"; even more today than in 1919 and 1921.

Notes

1   See Rudolf Steiner, *The Foundations of Human Experience* (Great Barrington: SteinerBooks 1996).

2   Ibid, Lecture 1.

3   Rudolf Steiner, *Faculty Meetings with Rudolf Steiner* (Great Barrington: SteinerBooks 1998), meeting of June 23, 1920.

4   Rudolf Steiner, *Soul Economy* (Great Barrington: SteinerBooks 2003).

5   Ibid.

II. The Developing Child

The following essays outline various aspects of early childhood development, including sense impressions as they concern the young child, imitation, rhythm, meaningful work and will development. Additional essays illuminate the issues surrounding first grade readiness.

Freya Jaffke, in her essays titled "Stages of Development in Early Childhood" and "The Significance of Imitation and Example for the Development of the Will," writes about how the young child is extraordinarily open to sense impressions—soaking up the atmosphere that surrounds him or her. Protection of these senses is important in order for a child to develop in a healthy way.

Rudolf Steiner said in a lecture in 1924: "…during the first period of life, the child is in the highest degree, and by its whole nature, a being of sense. It is like a sense organ. The surrounding impressions ripple, echo, and sound through the whole organism because the child is not so inwardly bound up with its body as is the case later in life, but lives in the environment with its freer spiritual and soul nature. Hence the child is receptive to all the impressions coming from the environment.[1]

Another aspect of early education is the ability of a child to imitate and to learn from imitation. The individuals that stand around a young child must work and interact with the world in such a way that they are worthy of imitation. Through imitation, creative play, and meaningful work—the child develops the joy, strength, and enthusiasm for life and learning.

Regarding imitation, Rudolf Steiner said: "The whole point of a preschool or kindergarten is to give young children the opportunity to imitate life in a simple and wholesome way. This task of adjusting life as one carries it out in the presence of the child in a meaningful, purposeful way, according to the needs of each child, is in accordance with the child's natural and inborn need for activity and is an enormously significant educational task."[2]

Later that same year Rudolf Steiner reiterated these ideas about imitation being of primary importance for the young child: "…Education in the kindergarten would therefore never depend on anything other than the principle of imitation. The teacher must sit down with the children and just do what she wishes them to do, so that the child has only to copy. All education and instruction before the change of teeth must be based on this principle."[3]

Rudolf Steiner stressed the importance of imitation in early childhood teaching again and again during his lectures, also noting the significance of the inner being of the teacher in relation to imitation: "What matters in a kindergarten is that the children should have a harmonious relation to those who are in charge of them and that people should behave quite naturally, so that the children are naturally led to imitate."[4]

Renate Long-Breipohl writes in her essay about the link between imitation and the ability to think, quoting Rudolf Steiner: "The child learns to think because it is an imitative being, wholly given up to its environment. It imitates what happens in the environment under the impulses of thoughts."

Rhythm is also of utmost importance in early childhood education. Healthy predictable rhythm helps to educate a child's will forces in an orderly and harmonious manner. Strong will forces will help the individual in his or her ability to do good work, to get things done, and to take hold of his or her destiny.

Another important aspect of childhood development for educators is the question of first grade readiness. How can we discern the correct time for a child to leave the kindergarten and enter into first grade? Essays by Louise deForest and Claudia McKeen address these questions. Their essays speak to the importance of creative play in developing the foundation for thinking and learning as well as to the importance of giving children the proper space to allow for their bodies to develop and mature before focusing their forces on learning and thinking. These essays describe the development of the young child as he or she transitions from kindergarten to school readiness and provides educators with insights into discerning whether a child is ready for school.

Notes

1 Rudolf Steiner, *The Essentials of Education* (Great Barrington: SteinerBooks 1998).

2 Rudolf Steiner, from an unpublished lecture given on April 18, 1924.

3 Rudolf Steiner, *Human Values in Education* (Great Barrington: SteinerBooks 2002).

4 Rudolf Steiner, *The Child's Changing Consciousness* (Great Barrington: SteinerBooks 1996).

Stages of Development in Early Childhood: Tasks and Goals for Parents and Educators

Freya Jaffke

From *The Developing Child: The First Seven Years* (WECAN 2004)
Originally published in *A Deeper Understanding of the Waldorf Kindergarten* (WECAN 1993)

Editor's Note: Freya Jaffke, author of a large number of books and articles, has provided insight and encouragement to early childhood teachers and caregivers for many years. In addition to this essay, you will find several other contributions by her in this book, including the next piece in this section.

While sometimes dated in style and in regards to family constellations and current technological advances, these pieces continue to ring true and provide inspiration.

In this essay, she describes Rudolf Steiner's insights about early childhood development, using Rudolf Steiner's *Soul Economy* as a reference. She writes about how we can protect the young child in order for the child to be able to take up his or her initial tasks of growing and learning in a healthy way. She also describes here the development of play, with insights about independence, fantasy and spontaneous play, and imaginative and planned play.

An introductory note to this essay when first published in *A Deeper Understanding of the Waldorf Kindergarten* read: "To be able to foster a child's development rather than disturb or hinder it through faulty behavior, we must become familiar with and understand these stages of development. [Ms. Jaffke] is a seasoned kindergarten teacher who through long years of work has been able to condense her observations into a picture of the developmental stages of early childhood. Her starting-point is based on the fact that has been proven by anatomical research that a child's body inherited from her parents does not represent a smaller form of the adult. The child's body is being metamorphosed toward its own goal. One can clearly see that a Will, an individuality is at work here which is not identical to the body that has been inherited. Three different stages of development during the years before a child is ready for first grade—up to the seventh year—are described in Rudolf Steiner's *Soul Economy*, Lecture VII."

II. The Developing Child

Steiner observed that the human organism is divided into three areas. Since the sense perceptions are conducted through the nerve system to the brain, he called this association of head-centered functions the "Nerve-Sense System." It is the physical basis for thinking. A second larger area consists of the connection between the rhythm of breathing and the heartbeat, in whose subtle variations the feeling life is manifested. This is called the "Rhythmic System" and has its center in the chest area. The organs of metabolism perform their work deep in the unconscious. If their activity is injured, then the human will is weakened or even disabled. In no other area does the will impulse live more fully and with greater strength than in the movement of the limbs—the spontaneous, willful joy of movement in young children is a good example of this. Thus Steiner defined this "lower" region and called it the "Limb-Metabolic System."

The life processes of the organism and its formation cannot be adequately explained by the chemical reactions of physical processes. Expert anthropologists acknowledge the workings of formative forces. Rudolf Steiner calls them the "formative or life forces." Their effects in shaping the organism and in the physiological processes are evident. However, what exactly is at work is invisible to the external eye and is revealed only through "supersensible" methods of observation, as Steiner describes in the fourth and fifth lectures of *Soul Economy*[2].

He describes how the formative forces are completely occupied at the beginning of human life with the forming of the organism. As the organs draw nearer to their final form, these forces are gradually freed up from this task and metamorphose into spirit-soul forces: those of memory, imagination, fantasy, and the power of thought. They all point to a spiritual shaping and forming. Thus childhood development consists essentially in the birth and gradual unfolding of these forces.

If we wish to understand a child in the first seven years of life, we must look very closely at the individual steps of development. Before we do this though, let us keep in mind the whole situation of the young child at the beginning of life.

Three things must coincide if a birth is to happen. First the two streams of inheritance from the parents unite to give the new body. A soul-spirit being, a human individuality, then joins with the body.

In spite of its outer completeness, this physical body remains unfinished in many ways. The individual inner organs have not yet attained their final, differentiated forms. In the limb system, we see a lack of differentiation—chaotic, involuntary movements. In the nerve-sense system, the child is still totally open.

The child's task in the first six to seven years—years that are his by right for this purpose—is to take hold of his inner body and to develop its differentiation until he is ready for school. Then—when the process of forming the organs is largely finished and only growth is still taking place—his body stands prepared as a useful "instrument." The soul-spirit individuality that joined the physical body at birth can, after further steps of development, begin to manifest itself fully in an external way through this body without being hindered by it.

How can we observe the joining of the individuality to the body? We see how the child's involuntary movements of kicking about gradually become more ordered and directed through his tireless will to be active. We see how he acquires the upright position and how he develops a relationship to the world's equilibrium in learning to walk. We observe how from the worldwide language of babbling a young child finds his way ever more surely and with greater control to the exact sound of his regional language. We see how a much more strongly differentiated and more meaningful activity develops from the early toddling about after adults and the beginning imitation of their behavior.

We can see through all these processes how the individuality is endeavoring to work itself into the body and to make it its own. All the impressions from the environment that meet the child also work very closely in this process of shaping the inner human being.

The impressions work in from the outside through the senses. In the young child these are digested inwardly by the core of his being, the individuality, in two ways: through the imitated behavior and in the development of the yet unfinished organs.

The young child is born unprotected into its new environment. His whole body acts as a single sense organ serving in an indiscriminate way to join the outer world with the inner one. We can compare it to the eye. The eye itself does not see, it only transmits. We see through the eyes. Thus the child's body is a sense organ for the individuality, for the spirit-soul being of the human.

The outer impressions come into the child through the senses, while the inner activity of shaping the organs moves outwards. This working together of the outer impressions and the inner shaping manifests itself in that wonderful power of imitation with which each healthy child is born. Every observation is first taken in deeply, grasped by the will and then, like an echo, comes forth again in a child's behavior.

Two significant tasks result for parents and educators. The first is a gesture of protection. Wherever we are able to do so, we ought to choose carefully out of the environment the impressions that meet the child. The child is best surrounded by happy family sounds of normal speaking and singing rather than those of uproar and quarreling. We also ought to protect the child from every type of technical apparatus such as radio, television, cassettes, videos, etc.

> *Editor's Note*: These days it is also important to note that protecting the child includes mindfulness with regards to our own use of smartphones in the presence of young children (not to mention protecting young children from using smartphones themselves).

In a child's room and for cradles and walls, one soft color provides a soothing effect and is preferable to the well-meant "children's" fabrics and wallpaper which are covered with flowers and animals. When riding in the car, let's make sure that the child can be seated to have a view of mother rather than overstimulating the senses by exposing him to the street traffic.

II. The Developing Child

Editor's Note: Riding in the car is almost always a daily reality for young children. Bringing peace to a frustrating commute may not be easy, but we can strive to keep car rides media free.

The second great task consists in guiding the child step by step into life, allowing him to learn about life for his whole life. This happens chiefly by meaningfully and methodically paying attention to the capability that the child has brought with him—that of imitation—rather than by means of clever teaching.

When we as grown-ups make the effort to be good "examples" of human beings, we will have the effect of awakening impulses in the child through our activities. For we cannot teach a child to imitate. This is a matter of the will and must be grasped by the child's own will. We can be aware of our own behavior: how we go about our work in the home and garden, how we speak with other people, how we care for others, how we arrange and care for our environment. The child takes everything deeply into his own bodily formative processes. Without being able to discriminate between meaningful and foolish behavior, he brings to his own activity what he sees in us as his representatives of life.

The imitative behavior of the child goes through three different stages in the first six to seven years. It is subject to the forces forming the organs, beginning in the head area and working through the whole body right down to the tips of the toes. In the first stage of life, from birth to about two-and-a-half years of age, these formative forces concentrate on the Nerve-Sense System. During this time the child acquires three of the most important human capabilities: gaining uprightness in the face of gravity, walking, and then speech, which is a prerequisite for thinking. All these capabilities the child learns exclusively through imitation. Tragic examples in history have shown that children do not acquire these human capabilities when they grow up surrounded only by animals. This shows clearly that humanity can be learned only from human beings.

From the Age of Crawling to the Awakening of the "I" in the Age of Independence

In what ways are children active in this first stage of life? As soon as they can barely crawl or propel themselves forward, they begin to explore their home environment, and it becomes unsafe. They follow the parent and want to do everything that he or she is doing. With the greatest enjoyment they clatter together the cooking pots, covers and spoons, put their hands into the wash water, pull out the wash and stick it in again, spreading puddles about. They bustle about with the broom, dispersing the dirt rather than gathering it into the middle in a small pile; they eagerly carry things that have just been placed in a certain spot to some other spot. And all this is done with the motto, "Johnny, too," or "me, too!" They take great joy in moving and busying themselves as much as possible with real household items, yet without insight into the purpose and goal of the adult's work—which, of course, progresses very slowly. Without such "willing helpers" the adult work would be done much sooner. However, this is true only from one point of view, for the parent has taken care not only of the house, garden, or handwork, but at the same time she has also accomplished educational work. This should become recognized again much more in today's educational awareness.

Along with their impulsive engagement with the environment, there are also moments when children linger devotedly near parents—for example, when one is peeling apples or working with needle and thread. There are times when they busy themselves in the play area—filling up baskets and emptying them, building towers and knocking them down, singing and pushing a doll carriage. Here it is important to pay close attention to the quality of the play materials. The best objects are those found in nature or which have been only slightly shaped by hand.[3] In their close connections with these objects, the impressions made upon children will be natural, organic shapes, and this works to stimulate their inner organ-forming processes. "Toys with dead mathematical forms alone have a desolating and killing effect upon a child's formative forces."[4]

Children pass through a first real crisis point when for the first time the feeling of "I" is awakened during the Age of Defiance. They experience their own will more and more, but must now learn to bring it into harmony with the environment. Whereas earlier a child always called out "me, too," now he says, "I don't want to."

From the Third to the Fifth Years: Fantasy and Spontaneous Play

Let us now take a look at the second stage, the time between about the third to fifth years. The life or formative forces, which until now have been at work chiefly in the head region, concentrate in this second stage on the middle part of the body, where most importantly the rhythmical organs, the heart and lungs, are located. At this time, two quite new capabilities appear in the child which give him a new relationship to his environment. These are a childlike fantasy and memory.

Here are some examples of play in children who have developed in a healthy way:

- ✦ A four-year-old has small round pieces of real tree branches in front of him on the table and he asks me, "Do you want soda, beer or apple juice?"
- ✦ A four-year-old girl takes a piece of bark, lays two stones upon it and says, "I have a ship with a man at the wheel." Then she comes to my table and asks, "I have brought you some pieces of chocolate, do you want them?" and she lays the stones in front of me. And now the bark becomes a roof for a small dwarfs house.
- ✦ A small bench was first a doll's stove, then laid on its side became an animal's feeding trough, and upside down it was first a doll's bed, and then part of a train.

II. The Developing Child

These examples show that children of this age are capable of changing things in their environment, using them for different purposes in certain cases, and, with the help of fantasy, making them into new things. Children see objects, perhaps remembering them only vaguely, and their imagination fills in all the other necessary details. The prerequisite is that children have already experienced such things before. If a child has never seen a ship, or only seen one in a picture book, he cannot bring it into his play.

A characteristic of play at this age is that it is stimulated by external causes. For this reason, it is best if the available play materials are capable of transformation. They should be incomplete and simple enough so that a child's imagination, remembering the details, can transcend the available objects and "fill them in." The imagination needs this type of activity in order to avoid becoming stagnant. Everything depends on the inner work.

As the muscles of the hand grow firm and strong in performing the work for which they are fitted, so the brain and other organs of the human physical body are guided into the right lines of development if they receive the right impression from the environment.[5]

It is immediately striking that the play is full of change. There are always daily events that are imitated and there are many spontaneous changes—often without any connection. The children continuously think of something new. Many adults who see this may despair and believe the children are unable to concentrate in their play. Concentration at this age level, however, lies in the continuity of play which between three and five years old is characterized in this way. To be sure, quite a bit of disorder and even chaos arise now and then. But it can be called meaningful chaos, for it continuously affects the children in such a way that they remain stimulated and interested. By the fifth year, this changes on its own. Of course, after playtime, the adult will plan sufficient time to clean up, participating herself to set an example so that it becomes an indisputable and joyful habit rather than a sporadically ordered, almost overwhelming burden which one faces alone.

From the Fifth to the Seventh Year: Pictures from the Imagination and Planned Play

The third big developmental step of the first seven years begins around the fifth year. The forces that have been used to form the organs are being freed more and more from the Rhythmical System and are now working in the Metabolic-Limb System. The children are increasingly capable and dexterous right down to their fingertips.

Many children—especially those who were able to play in a rich and creative manner—go through a second crisis in the fifth year. For the first time they experience a real boredom. They can stand before you and say, "I don't know what to do." It is as if their fantasy has left them and suddenly they have no more ideas. The fantasy needs a rest now and ought not to be called upon by reminding the child of yesterday's fine play. We can help to strengthen it much more by having the child participate in our own work—for example, peeling apples, drying dishes, sweeping, baking, sewing. After a while, sometimes after only a few days, new impulses for play arise in the child. A change has taken place. The stimulus for play no longer comes so much from external objects, but it comes now more and more from inside. This means that now the children have an inner picture, a picture from their imagination of past events, and they can bring these up in their play independent of place, time or people.

Five- and six-year-old children love to crouch together talking and making plans for their play. For example, they are building an inn and folded cloths become napkins, menus and purses. A cold buffet is set up and little woolen sheep are offered as fish. One child who is selling drinks has a large log with small branches on it standing before him (it is his "real beer keg"), and he is able to fill an order for any kind of drink with it. Another time they set up a doctor's office with needles, stethoscopes, bandages, and a waiting room, where the folded cloths serve as magazines.

Other typical themes of play are: trash truck, ambulance with a red light, school, carpentry shop, fire engine, cable-railway, telephone installation, deep sea diver and much more. Their play becomes more and more planned. This does not mean, however, that it can't be suddenly changed in the middle if one of the children comes up with a rousing idea.

Children of this age do not need fancier, more detailed playthings. Play materials that can grow with them are better. Their relationship to the materials is changing. Before the fifth year an idea would be stimulated by the materials. After the fifth year an imaginative idea comes first, then the effort to find and make something acceptable from the play materials that corresponds to the imagination. Now the fantasy, which had been so richly developed before, begins to function again.

Nowadays it is no longer a matter of course that children can play so spontaneously and enthusiastically at their corresponding level of development. This is due less to the children than to the immense influence from all sides upon them from earliest childhood on. For example, fully detailed, technically exact toys make it difficult for children to be satisfied with such outwardly simple things as objects from nature, cloths, wooden branches, etc. A healthy child would rather be right in the middle of play than outside as an observer of perfect, technical instruments. The fascination for such toys is soon past and leaves behind an emptiness and longing for more.

One of our most important tasks is to arrange the space—at home and in the kindergarten—to guarantee the needs of creative play. Above all this means creating a world suitable for imitation with adults who are active in a purposeful way, who like to do their work, and who, at the same time, accompany the children in their play in a quiet way. Creative play depends more on a calm, joyful atmosphere of work than on many clever words, suggestions for play, or instructions of any kind. The children must be "lifted up" by the adults' work. They must have a place in it in the broadest sense, even if they are not directly involved. This seems like a contradiction, but it can be experienced by every mother who brings her mending basket or ironing board to the children's room and who radiates calm and interest while working, or by every father who goes about his work in the garden, yard or cellar. The most important thing is the people who surround the child, that they make life rhythmical and ordered, that they like to work and are ready to take on a large part of the work themselves. The young child is an imitator!

The unspoken reward and thanks for such efforts come to the adult through children who are able to play in a fulfilling way and who are building the basis for later life in these early stages.

The tasks of the educator can be discovered easily from all the above descriptions. If we look at the goals, we can summarize by saying that nothing more wonderful can happen in childhood than that a child is able to grasp completely each developmental step and pass though it in a healthy way, and that he is able to practice and gain strength during each particular challenge. When the body is completely formed and accomplishes its first change around age seven, the child may turn to his schoolwork with the same joy, strength and enthusiasm for learning that he showed earlier for play, and be equal to its demands.

Notes

1   See Steiner, *Soul Economy* (Great Barrington: SteinerBooks 2003).
2   Ibid.
3   See Freya Jaffke, *Toymaking with Children* (UK: Floris Books 2010).
4   Steiner, *The Education of the Child* (Great Barrington: SteinerBooks 1996).
5   Ibid.

The Significance of Imitation and Example for the Development of the Will

Freya Jaffke

From *A Deeper Understanding of the Waldorf Kindergarten* (WECAN 1993)

Based on a lecture presented at the North American Kindergarten Conference at High Mowing School in August, 1989

Today we will talk about the development of the will, and we will see how important it is that the child has an example to imitate. We all know that the child has a great openness and is entirely a sense organ. All of his sense impressions go deeply into his body. He can't defend himself from the sense impressions which flood into him.

But a sense organ is only an instrument which can be used by someone. The eye itself, for example, does not see. Someone must look through the eye to see. The eye is only an instrument for seeing. In order to see, the will within the human being must be at work. The whole physical body is one great sense organ for the spiritual and soul being of the child, which came from his pre-earthly existence.

Now we can see two phenomena: First the child is totally a sense being, and second, the child is totally a will being. With the will and through the senses, all the impressions from the environment are grasped and taken deeply into the body where they leave their marks upon the organs. The synthesis of these two phenomena is seen in the wonderful forces of imitation, which every child brings with him as a gift from his pre-birth existence. In the pre-earthly life the human soul is living among cosmic beings, is penetrated by them and follows them. This "habit" is taken through the gate of birth into early childhood and is seen in the forces of imitation. The child's imitation is a double process: He receives through the senses, and grasps and imitates with the will. Rudolf Steiner describes the development of the will in *The Education of the Child* in this way:

> *By a right application of the fundamental educational principles, during the first seven years of childhood, the foundation is laid for the development of a strong and healthy Will. For a strong and healthy will must have its support in the well-developed forms of the physical body.*[1]

We know that all the organs of the young child are relatively unshaped. They do not yet have the physical form which one sees in the organs of the adult, and the rhythm of each organ is not yet developed. We must ask ourselves, "How does the forming of the organs take place and how will they develop their rhythm? How will they work together rhythmically?" A seemingly different, but related, question is, "How will the will of the child become purposeful and orderly?" Both happen primarily through the influences from the world outside the child, especially through all the rhythmical events during the day or week.

Now let us look at the period of the first three years of life. There we can see that the child has many possibilities to use and exercise his will forces, though of course this happens unconsciously. What a great activity of will is involved when a young child comes slowly into the upright and acquires the ability to walk! Then he follows his mother or father through the house "working," doing some laundry, cleaning the floor, packing and unpacking the grocery basket. The more the parent works in good order and without being hectic, the more the child's will is guided into a strong direction. In this way, the child no longer moves chaotically with his hands and feet as he did as a newborn.

Everything the child does is done without reflection or consideration. He acts out of imitation and habit. The quality of example will determine how habits develop, and in the same way children will experience their limits. If the adult laughs only when a child, for example, dumps spinach from his plate onto the table, or pulls on the tablecloth or the cord of the iron, then the child learns bad habits and develops an unhealthy orientation for his will. Instead of laughing and running after the child, the adult should think ahead. The adult should use his imagination or fantasy to divert the child from those activities which are inappropriate. The adult should be consequent and follow through to establish limits. This means that the adult has to be a representative of everything for the child, so that the child has a clear orientation and a sense of reality. It is important that the child is always surrounded by meaningful will activities as long as he is unable to guide himself.

The first real crisis occurs when the child experiences his own will for the first time. Then he begins to use the word "I" for himself and the word "no" to others. At the same time he experiences a conflict between his growing will and the will of those around him. His own will can show itself only in relation to the will of the others in his environment. The child has to slowly learn to bring his will into a harmonious relationship with the wills of those around him. Here again we can see how wonderful and healthy are good habits and rhythms in the child's environment, especially during these years. They help to overcome many difficult situations.

During this first period of early childhood, the will of the child is engaged through a strong connection to the parent's activities; in the second period, between the third and fifth years of age, the will becomes more and more connected to the awakening imagination and begins to work within the child's fantasy. During this period, the child's fantasy needs the inspiration of objects in her environment. For example, the child sees a piece of bark and a few stones and takes it to be a boat with people. She sees a doll and starts to feed it. She sees a little bench and uses it as a mailbox. The will within the child's fantasy is able to transform things, and the child no longer needs only realistic objects in his play. But the object has to be simple enough to allow space for this creative activity. The objects in the child's environment spark her fantasy. The child feels great joy and freedom through creating new things which for her are real. An example of how children transform items from their environment into play materials is the following: The mother has prepared a large package, and she puts the leftover piece of string over the back of a chair. The child ties a wooden spoon to one end, pulls at the other end and plays crane.

Between three and five we can see that the child's fantasy and the child's faculty of memory appear at the same time. Only things or events can be remembered which have been seen before. How does a child remember? How does fantasy, the bringing together of a memory picture and an object, actually occur? And then, how does the child carry this fantasy into his creative play? The answer is through his will forces. Without the will forces nothing will happen. If the will forces are chaotic, nothing meaningful happens in the child's play. Thus we see how important it is to care for the right development of the will.

A healthy and harmonious child always has new ideas to bring to the same materials or the same play. She is always active, always busy with her will. For example, the little bench which was the mailbox now becomes the manger for the animals, a bed for the doll, a stove, or many other things.

We are all familiar with our difficult and inharmonious children who are not able to play but like to disturb the others. We also have those children who don't do anything, but just stand around looking at the others. They seem to be apathetic. These children have to experience, for a shorter or longer time, the meaningful work of an adult as well as the strong rhythm and the warm atmosphere of the kindergarten.

Around the fifth year, a second crisis is seen, mostly in the children who until now were always busy and knew just what to do. What is happening now? The fantasy apparently disappears; the will seems to be paralyzed. Children may say, "I don't know what to do today," or "I'm bored." A big inner change is taking place. At this time it is important that we not appeal to the fantasy forces for they now need a quiet time. We shouldn't say, "Yesterday you built up such a beautiful landscape, do it again." Instead, let them do real things, such as making and sewing a little book for their dolls with drawings, sewing a little book out of felt for needles, or sanding a letter opener which you have just carved.

It is important that all these activities have a strong connection to the adult's work. It is still the period of imitation, but we can more and more use words in guiding the child to an activity. We can ask them to come and help us in our work, but not with questions! If we want them to help in the kitchen with cooking and baking we should say, "Come, give me a hand," rather than "Will you give me a hand?" After a short time of such working, new impulses for the child's play will arise.

At this new stage of development, around the fifth year, there arises within the child a picture or mental image of what she wants to do. Now the will forces have to join or enter into the mental image. That needs much effort. The child is still in the kindergarten, and the play materials have not changed. When plans arise in the mental image such as the operation of a hairdresser's shop, an ambulance, a fishing boat, or restaurant, then the child needs a power for fantasy trained during the years before. And the child needs patience, enthusiasm and staying power. These are all faculties in which the will works strongly.

Before five the stimulus for play comes from the outside. A child sees a curved stick and says, "Now I am a chimney sweeper." After five the child says, "I would like to be a chimney sweeper, and I need a broom with a long handle." He looks for something similar, sees feathers, puts them together, attaches a long, curved ribbon and is happy. Before five, the will activity works with all that which stimulates the fantasy from the outside. After five the will forces have to make an inner effort. The will now joins together with the mental image and joins also together with the well-trained fantasy. Thus the child creates new objects which appear in his mental image without an outer stimulus.

At this point in the children's development we may think that they must do strong physical work such as sawing, nailing and hammering. They may do such work, but we shouldn't forget that the will forces have to be exercised not only within the muscles, but at this particular period of life, they also have to grow strong within the inner being of the child. They are needed within the mental image.

Here are two examples of play situations which show you how we can help children during their play, as of course children do need help sometimes.

> *Florian, aged six years, four months, plays that he is a circus director. He dresses many children as different animals with various cloths. He tells them what to do and where to stay. All of them are happy and follow his lead for a period of time. When he has no more ideas and some "animals" have already left, I tell him, "The circus is now finished and all the circus people must have a snack." Florian replies, "Yes, and then they will pack everything and go to another town. Oh, yes, this could be my circus-wagon. It always has a round roof, doesn't it?"*

> *The object he points to has previously been a "cage" and stood beneath the table where I was working. He builds up his "wagon," then looks out of his little window at me and says, "Oh, I am already close to the border! Now I am going to drive into another country and there will be a large amount of snow, and there one needs a snow plow."*

Then he fixes a little wooden dust pan to the front of his wagon as a snow plow. In the back he builds up something for spreading salt. He uses little benches with small holes on the top for carrying. He stacks them one on top of the other and through the holes he throws chestnuts with great joy.

The next day, Florian again builds up a wagon, but this time without snow plow or salt machine. When he is finished he says, "Now it is a locomotive." Then he builds up two more wagons behind. Other children want to play with him but do not really know what to do. I say, "One wagon could be for my luggage, and some porters could come to get my suitcases, for I have to travel. The other wagon can be the dining room, for I would like to eat something during my journey." A great "busyness" arises among the children. Some of them carry all my cases (big logs) to the train. Others set up the tables in the dining car. I am given a menu out of folded cloths and have to choose and to order. Then they bring wonderful dishes and set my table. I am totally integrated into the play of the children, although I am still sitting at my work table. They do not mind at all that I am not sitting with them in the dining car, as I do sometimes.

I think we are lucky to have some children every year who are able to play in such a fulfilled way. They stimulate the others. Another example is Simon, age six.

Simon has built a camping place underneath a table. After he is finished, nothing more happens. Then I say, "In a camping place, there is always a fireplace where people cook their meals." "Oh yes, may we get some sticks?" I reply, "Yes, take three." They attach the sticks together to make three legs. With red and yellow cloths, they make a fire underneath. A little basket is fixed in the middle of the sticks. It is the cooking pot. They ask for two more sticks, put them between two chairs, put big cloths over them and make tents. Within the tents they have woolen carpets and cushions. These activities last until cleanup time. Then the boys are a little disappointed because "they haven't played yet."

The question is: What can the adult do to help strengthen the will forces such as they appear in these play situations? If indeed, as Rudolf Steiner says, it is from the outside that the impressions on the organs come about, and also that well-formed organs are the best support for the will, then in the environment there must be order in manifold ways: rhythm, good habits, and love. To come to an appropriate order around the children, the adult has to think ahead. Then her gestures will become calm and purposeful and well thought through. She will not run about fetching things, because she has forgotten this or that. Also, to think ahead helps heal the bad manifestations of the will of the child. For example, if a child slams the door, we shouldn't say, "You shouldn't do that." Rather, with our full consciousness we should be with the child in the situation in a consequent way. Thus, when he is approaching the door, we follow his actions in our mind.

The adult also has to be well-engaged in his own work before the children arrive. The mother is already busy when the children awaken in the morning. When the children arrive in the kindergarten in the morning, the adults are already busy there. The will of the child nestles itself into the atmosphere of activity around him, which is created by the adult. The child is totally free to choose his own work. They may be involved in the work of the adults whenever possible.

Another prerequisite for the children's play is that the adult cares not only for a rhythmical arrangement of the day, but also for the rhythm of the year in his own working activities. Without being a pedant he can repeatedly do specific tasks at certain times. For example, in my kindergarten, in the autumn I am mainly making things for the Christmas Bazaar. After Christmas, there is a period when I do embroidery, and after Easter I do wood carving. I do these activities nearly every day for several weeks, and do not do a different activity every day. The one exception is painting day.

Each day during the free play time, I proceed with my work. I have not created "projects" for the children to do, but I do make certain that enough materials (mostly remnants from my own work) are there for the children to use. All my scraps from cutting fabric or paper, woodcarving, or sawing I put into the children's baskets. The children may freely take what they need from there. They create a variety of things. Some attempt to do what I have done, others have their own ideas. In November, for example, when I glue together the painted and oiled lanterns for the children and then make transparencies for the Christmas Bazaar, for at least two weeks every day (except painting day) the big table is set up with scissors and glue, and the children's baskets with colored paper. Gold paper pieces are also at hand. Some children make small lanterns and transparencies, others make crowns or other small toys for their dolls, which they then take home with them.

While some children come many days to work at the "glue table," others might not come at all at this time but will come later in the year when I have a time for sewing aprons for the kindergarten or embroidering table covers. Then in the children's baskets there are pretty colored threads for sewing. Fabric scraps left after cutting are also placed in the children's baskets for free use.

When I carve small bowls, spoons, candle holders, etc., there are always small pieces of wood left over, with which the children build or which they wax. Carving knives are naturally not put into the children's hands, but sometimes they take pointed sticks and "carve" with them outside on rotting stumps.

In this way the work of the adult is always purposeful and useful for the life of the kindergarten. The children take part in it in a variety of ways, or they play around the teacher who is at work. They are always aware of the work and take a warm and loving interest in it.

For all of this work the prerequisites are orderliness, rhythm, and good habits. These belong to the "right physical environment" in which the children may receive order and strength in their will forces because they are imitative beings. Imitating is will activity! You cannot teach imitation. It has to be done with one's own will. Will activity is very individual, and it is united with the ego.

We can observe this in the different ways children imitate. Everyone has the same example in front of them in the kindergarten, but their reactions are quite different. Some immediately start to imitate or to play nearby, taking in the atmosphere of the working activity, while others don't get the impulse at all. Within imitation there is great freedom. If we are willing to work on ourselves, then we need to also work on the prerequisites described above. Then every child will find for his will development what he himself needs and what he is unconsciously seeking.

To guide the children in their play we have to always think of the differentiated steps in their development. Now I would like to talk a little more about the last period between five and seven years of age. After age five, a transition takes place from what the child wants to do to what the child should do. This does not mean that we give the children orders or commands which just come to mind. Rather, out of the strong connection built up with the adult during the preceding years, the children now want to do what they should do. But even though we may use more words and appeal to the mental images of these older kindergarten children, even if we tell them what they can do and how they can do it, even if we inspire their forces of patience, even then: imitation is still the main thing!

Until now the children have unconsciously noticed that the adult has done what was needed in the kindergarten, what was needed in order to finish her daily work, to care for the environment, prepare for the festivals, etc. The children have noticed that the adult hasn't always done what she would like to do but rather what she needs to do. This attitude can also be imitated by the children after age five. How? The children observe, for example, that the adult takes a long time for her work. Either she makes many things of the same project such as for festivals or for the Bazaar, or she needs a long time to make only one thing such as with carving or embroidery. Children see the perseverance, the patience and care which the adult brings to her work. They are interested in the process from day to day. They see also that the adult does things which are uncomfortable for her to do, but that she tries to overcome this. For example it may not come naturally to her to sew with a thimble, but she always uses the thimble nevertheless.

Another aid to getting children to do what they should do or how they should do it is to talk about specific people, how they behave in their professions, or what they would do in a certain situation. Between the ages of five and seven, children do not have to have the physical presence of someone working in front of them; they can also build up a picture inwardly by hearing about the person. For example, I may talk about the master of embroidery who taught me to embroider, or about a tailor who would never sew without a thimble, or about the servant called Ludwig whom I got to know when I went to a conference one day (see "The Story of Ludwig" at the end of this essay).

During the second half of the school year before they go into first grade, we may request the eldest children to do a specific task. Then they have the possibility to strengthen their will forces by pursuing a certain goal. I always offer these eldest children the possibility of making their own very simple, knotted dolls. Rudolf Steiner says that a self-made "Bajazzo," knotted out of an old rag and with ink spots for eyes, is able to awaken the genius within the child.

We start by embroidering the doll's blanket after Christmas. Then we tease the wool by hand to form the doll's head and knot the hands, using a pink flannel cloth for the doll. The children make their own eye spots using a colored pencil. After that they start sewing the hair and some clothes for the doll. Some children have a great many dolls by the end of the year. Some only one! From the moment the doll is finished, it is integrated into the children's play. One often sees a difference here between boys and girls. The girls feed their dolls and play with them in a variety of ways, and sew them many, many clothes. The boys put them in the cars they build and take them for rides or use them for patients in their ambulances. Over the weekends the children take their dolls home, so that they can be cared for during the weekends as well.

Around age six, the children may also follow instructions. They are asked to do things and they like to do them. For example, a child can go as a messenger to another class, get the broom and dustpan, or may be asked to help dry the dishes. We should never ask for the child's help by questioning the child. Try to know what the specific child is able to do and what he would like to do, and sometimes what he needs to do! It may happen that a child rejects doing what he is asked to do, but some others then come and ask, "May I do it?"

Children of this age are able to understand our instructions. They can transform the mental images which arise through words into their own activity. In their earlier years we had to divert children from the things that they shouldn't do. Now they need clearly defined limits and clear directions such as "We don't shoot," or "I don't like this." It must be said in such a way that the children still feel the love of the adult and feel his conviction as a loving and loved authority.

Everything which I have tried to point out here has been said while bearing in mind the following:

> ...*before the second dentition [the child lived mainly] in the region of the will, which... was intimately connected with the child's imitating its surroundings. But what at that time entered the child's being quite physically also contained moral and spiritual forces that became firmly established in the child's organism.*[2]

This means that the will of the child can be developed and become strong through good habits, consequences, and limits set by the adult as his example.

When the child enters first grade, the will has to be trained more and more consciously. Now he must follow a task given by the teacher for a period of time such as watering the flowers, dusting the window sill, or cleaning the blackboard for a week. The child has to remember every day and has to do it, even if he doesn't want to. He has to overcome himself. During the kindergarten years it is too early to insist on repeated tasks for particular children. With the most sensitive feeling, we have to guide the children from the way of imitation to loving authority. This is a great art!

I hope I've helped to raise appreciation for how great the significance of example is for the child's imitation and for the development of the will. The question of whether there is a time of "kindergarten readiness" has become an urgent question in Europe only in the last few years. Not long ago, in our experience, a child rarely came into the kindergarten before the end of her fourth year. There was no room. With the decline of the birthrate, however, an increasing number of kindergarten spaces became available, and younger children entered to fill them. The kindergartens want to fill their places, and the mothers are glad to be able to bring their children into the kindergarten early. Thus, the age of the children who come into the kindergarten is now lowered to such a point that it is necessary to become clear about what constitutes kindergarten readiness in a child.

We want to disregard external necessities for bringing children into the kindergarten early—whether it be that the mother must go to work or that the atmosphere in the home is such that one would like to remove the child as soon as possible. The central question remains before us: How do I recognize whether a child is really ready for kindergarten?

In his speech, today's child often says "I" as early as two years old. In the etheric body, the child's head becomes independent around the age of two and a half, and he begins to think. But the I-experience still does not fully happen today until the child is three years old. Only after this step has been fully accomplished does the child slowly begin to make verbal contact with other children. This is achieved at about four years of age. At this age, the remaining speech development is often already complete, but not always. Children who cannot yet pronounce g–k–ch sounds have difficulties in their will development; while children who have difficulty pronouncing s–sh–st are behind in their intellectual development in certain cases.

When one considers the independence of the children, much depends upon the parents' home. Whether a child can dress himself, whether he is clean, whether he can use the toilet independently are, to be sure, essential for the kindergartner, but these factors alone do not determine if the child has reached kindergarten readiness.

One must pay attention to the mental and physical stamina of the child. Can a child last four hours (the duration of the normal kindergarten in Germany) without actually needing a nap? Is the child so susceptible that he would catch every sniffle in the kindergarten and become sick? Is the child already far enough along to handle the childhood diseases, or would it mean a premature exposure in certain cases? The child should already have developed a beginning sense of time. She must also have already overcome the first phase of defiance which still belongs to the I-discovery. And she must be able to tolerate other children—many other children.

The Story of Ludwig the Servant

Ludwig was a real servant in the home of an elderly lady. We stayed in her home during a weekend conference. At breakfast time when things ran out, Ludwig was there to bring more food, but he always waited at the threshold of the room, and the old woman brought it from there out to our table.

In the kindergarten I gave a nice verbal description of Ludwig to the children. After that I asked a six-year-old boy to bring the cups from the tray to everyone's place. He looked over all the cups, chose one out of the middle and put it at his own place, very satisfied for he thought that it was the fullest one. Then he looked at me, by chance, and I said, "Ludwig wouldn't have done that; he always serves the others and takes the last one himself."

"Really?" asked the boy.

"Really," I answered. Then he took the cup, put it at another place, served all the others, and took the last one for himself.

Notes

1   Steiner, *The Education of the Child* (Great Barrington: SteinerBooks 1996).
2   Steiner, *The Child's Changing Consciousness*, (Great Barrington: SteinerBooks 1996), p. 116.

Thinking and the Consciousness of the Young Child

Renate Long-Breipohl

From A Warm and Gentle Welcome (WECAN 2012)

The first three years

Recently while observing young children in a childcare situation, I watched one little boy around the age of two who was totally immersed in moving blocks into various positions. He stayed absorbed in his activity without looking up or saying a word. Does he think? Something is happening within this child that I want to understand in order to adjust the environment around him so that nothing disrupts his concentrated activity.

My own study of the subject of thinking set me on a journey: I re-read essential works on the first three years, looked at developmental research, and observed children whenever the opportunity arose. Here I would like to share some aspects of my work in progress that relate to coming to terms with thinking as an adult, the development of thinking as a process during the first three years, and events occurring in the third year of life.

To say it bluntly, thinking is not a favorite activity of our time. While we are surrounded by an endless variety of products based on sophisticated human thought and created by a fairly small group of highly trained engineers and designers, the actual process of thinking for oneself is experienced as stressful by many contemporaries. Students often find it strenuous to pursue a train of thought related to a question, and teachers find it difficult to engage students in processes that require concentrated thinking activity.

In adult learning, more and more visual aids are appearing, and the more they are used, the less we need to engage inwardly in a thinking process. This one can experience as an average computer user or by perusing a typical student textbook. It all comes down to information intake and information processing, following ready-made pathways or existing mental frameworks. Knowledge is broken up into small paragraphs, the main thoughts are boxed so that one can take them in at a glance and, overall, there is an abundance of accumulated information. Steiner predicted that human beings would gradually lose the ability to think, and yet he regarded the human faculty of thinking as the gateway to spiritual development.

What is the faculty of thinking in human beings?

It is important to have an understanding of what thinking is when we approach children. Thinking is an activity that takes place within the inner realm of the human being and, in its highest aspect, is wisdom in individualized form. One can describe thinking as a supersensible faculty, since it does not derive its essence from sense experience. Thinking cannot be perceived directly by others. Concepts are formed and woven together through the activity of thinking, and in everyday life these concepts assist us in ordering, structuring or giving meaning to experiences.[1]

Through thinking we are free to reach toward high spiritual ideals, but our thinking can also be reduced to rationalizing our wishes, desires and actions. Then it binds itself too deeply to the material aspect of existence and is in danger of hardening and losing its connection to truth. The destiny of thinking is a theme to which Steiner returned in his lectures again and again. In our time many people find it difficult to devote themselves to thinking as a spiritual activity, or to think freely. However, one needs to consider thinking as a spiritual activity if one wants to find the key to thinking in the young child, as I will further elaborate in this essay.

Child development and thinking

In his book *Spiritual Guidance of the Individual and Humanity*, Rudolf Steiner spoke about the first three years of life and the evolving human being.[2] He described how learning to walk, to speak and to think is a three-step process in which the growing, incarnating child adapts to earthly conditions, and in which essentially spiritual faculties take hold in the child under the guidance of higher spiritual beings. Through this process, faculties gained in the spiritual world are transformed and reappear as the human faculties of thinking, feeling, and willing. These faculties develop within the bodily processes of achieving an upright position, turning the speech organs into instruments for the expression of language, and molding the brain into an instrument for thinking. Finally, in the third year, an evolving ability to think connects the child to the world community of human beings.

Active within these processes is the "I," which through walking orients the body to three-dimensional space, and through speech attunes the child's soul to a specific human community according to the individual destiny of the child. This activity of the I can be described as the streaming in of spiritual forces from a spiritual aura around the child. It is a process of which the child has no conscious awareness.

From this picture of human development questions arise regarding thinking in the young child. Why is the development of thinking primarily identified as occurring in the third year of life? Is it not a continuous process? What is our understanding of recent neurodevelopmental research that interprets early responses of babies to stimulation as forms of intelligence and that points to the ability of very young children to communicate from day one? And if there were a major leap in the development of thinking in the third year, why, then, would one wait until the seventh year before addressing the child's thinking in education, as Steiner has suggested?

The first and second years in relation to thinking

It is generally acknowledged that thinking develops in the young child in accordance with the maturation and differentiation of the brain and nerve-sense system. It is interesting that Steiner spoke about thinking as a spiritual, as well as an earthly, faculty; he said that thinking originates in pre-earthly existence as a supersensible faculty of the human being, yet it is also active in and bound to earthly life through sense experience.

There are two aspects to thinking in the young child: The first relates to the supersensible nature of thinking, which is linked to the etheric body. In the very young child these etheric forces are still active from outside, sculpting and fine-tuning the head and bodily organs, without the child being conscious of it. "Connecting threads develop in the brain, and the forces which organize the connecting threads are seen by the clairvoyant during the first few weeks of the child's life as something that is forming extra sheaths for the brain."[3] The etheric body is still engaged in shaping the brain and radiating into the rest of the body.[4] This image often appears in children's drawings in which rays are depicted around the head of a human figure, connecting it to the world beyond.

I remember an eight-month-old child in a restaurant, sitting in a high chair, enthralled with a spoon he held in his hand; he moved it from one hand to the other. He licked it, turned it upside down and moved it faster and faster until the spoon fell to the ground. Does thinking play a part in such an activity?

Georg Kühlewind[5] points out that a young child absorbed in exploration lives naturally in a state of pure attentiveness, which may be achieved in adults only after intense practice in awareness. He describes pure attentiveness as an advanced stage of thinking activity, based on the ability to maintain the intentional quality of the will without pouring it into action. He calls it "soft will," that is, will purely within the activity of thinking. The child is able to be in this state of attentiveness naturally and is fully devoted to the object of his exploration.

This attitude of surrender is also found in the ability of the young child to imitate, an ability present from the very first stages of life. Steiner points to how thinking is dependent on imitation: "The child learns to think because it is an imitative being, wholly given up to its environment. It imitates what happens in the environment under the impulses of thoughts."[6] Sense experience and thinking are one. The child imitates and simultaneously is able to understand what is going on the moment the sense perception happens.[7]

Steiner speaks about the work of the "I" in the first three years as molding the brain. Two important influences are part of this process: Sense activity on the one side, leaving imprints of sensations in specific areas of the brain (as described by Eugen Kolisko in *The Bodily Foundation of Thinking*), and movement on the other. Steiner uses the term "bodily geometry" for the movement of the young child that allows her to find her place within spatial dimensions. Thinking is prepared through both activities.[8] Thinking and movement, originating from head and limbs, form a polarity that organizes development during the early childhood years. The head pole relates to the etheric forces working from the head downward, and the limb pole relates to the human soul-spirit or "I" working from the lower part of the body upwards. This is the organizing principle that underlies the process of coming into uprightness during the first year of life. The "I" activity of movement has an influence on the healthy development of thinking. Steiner's spiritual research into this process is now confirmed by developmental research and the therapeutic practice of stimulating thinking through movement.

As the child approaches the end of the first year of life, we may assume that the processes of intensive looking, touching, moving, and exploring have left within him many imprints, mental images which, however vague they may be at first, will eventually be met by concepts formed through the inner activity of the child.

A new quality is added to those early internal pictures flooding through the child once the child can anchor them in speech. Now words become the vehicle for the development of thinking. "Just as speech develops from walking and grasping, in short from movement, so thought develops from speech… and since the child is one great sense organ and in his inner physical functions also copies the spiritual, our own thinking must be clear if right thinking is to develop in the child from the forces of speech."[9]

Karl König has beautifully summarized the process of speech acquisition in *The First Three Years of the Child*, in which he describes how the child progresses from expressing physical well-being or physical needs to expressing his relationship to the outer world in words (naming) and, increasingly, in short sentences. Speech mirrors the child's being in relationship to objects and people. It links the child to the fine nuances of feeling expressed in language. How does thinking manifest at this stage of development?

Recent developmental research has described how adults can stimulate memory in children between the ages of one- and two-and-a-half years if in the presence of the child adults verbally recollect recent events of the child's life.[10] Russian educational psychologist Lev Vygotsky (1896-1934) suggested that intellectual development depends on the adult's verbal communications being slightly above the child's current level of communication.[11] His observations are interesting in that they point to the connection between speech and thinking. Could one say that the child, through the adult as model, is able to imitate memory activity?

Thinking in the child who is approaching age two can be observed in the child's solitary play. The child moves objects, covers them, puts them side-by-side or on top of each other. The purpose is solely to make contact with the world of objects and to change their positions. Steiner states that it is through this interplay with the environment that the child finds his way spontaneously into thinking. While observing a child engaged in such play, one can experience concentrated attention. If the child has sufficient opportunity to play without disturbances, this mood will be recreated in play for years to come.

Thinking in the third year of life

What is the gift of the third year of life? The soul-spiritual forces in the child now complete their work on the foundations of the child's faculty of thinking. The I of the child has penetrated the physical body, the limbs, the rhythmic system, and the head. At the same time some part of the etheric forces of the head are freed. "At the age of two and a half, the child's head organization is developed far enough for those forces of the ether body which have been working on it to become released... acting now as soul and spiritual forces [available for other developmental tasks]."[12]

What can be observed in the child of this age? A vivid memory, a more elaborate way of speaking, original word creations and thought connections. The child enjoys playing with words, turning them around, inventing new ones — and he can surprise us with his own original ways of arranging syntax or linking sense impressions. Speech develops in leaps and bounds. This stage of development shows new achievements of thinking in everyday life. It becomes easier to follow routines, because the child can understand more of the meaning of what is done. Therefore it becomes easier to guide the child. In talking with the child, she seems more able to take in what is said. It is fascinating to observe in children of this age that they not only are creative in inventing their own words, but also in producing their own logic. Interestingly, the very individual and unusual thought connections of a three-year-old do not arrive out of a conscious thought process, but seem to emerge often unexpectedly, as if from somewhere else.

It is tempting for the educator who witnesses these new faculties as they arise during the third year to approach the child's thinking capacity with formal instruction. The ability of the child to process instructions addressing the intellect at age two has been documented in developmental research and has been utilized in program development for early childhood education. The third year is when many early learning programs begin.

One can understand the motivation for using learning materials such as picture and word cards to support concept building, verbalization or memory, since the thinking potential is there in the child and can be called up. But the constant involvement of an adult is needed to keep this process going. What is learned at this age is not retained unless it is continually repeated. Steiner has warned of the consequences of adult intervention and demands on thinking and memory before the age of three: "What then will happen, if we make too great a demand on the intellect, urging the child to think, into thinking as such? Certain organic forces that tend inwardly to harden the body are brought into play.

These forces are responsible for the salty deposits in the body and for the formation of bone, cartilage and sinew — in all those parts of the body, in short, that have a tendency to become rigid. This normal rigidity is over-developed, if intellectual thinking is forced."[13] It is of great importance that those who live with young children understand the spiritual background of the capacity to think. Steiner affirmed that we are to become, and need to become, free-thinking beings in order to develop our humanness.

"When the child learns to think — well, in thinking we do not remain in the realm of the individual at all. In New Zealand, for example, people think in exactly the same way we do here today. It is the entire earth realm to which we adapt ourselves, when as children we develop thinking out of speech... In thinking, we enter the realm of humanity as a whole."[14]

In each child this possibility is established and in that respect the third year can be regarded as a culmination point of early development, representing in seed form the essence of the human being. This needs to be acknowledged in everyday life, so that one does not merely familiarize the child with thought processes related only to the immediate material environment and mundane situations. Often adults take pride when the child can already express himself intellectually in a way similar to older children or even adults. Yet too much praise and encouragement of the child's intellect can cause the child's thinking to become fettered to fixed thought-forms and prevent the child's thinking from flowing creatively and freely between the two worlds of thought: the spiritual and the earthly.

Only the emergence of consciousness of self around or shortly after age three will bring the child's thinking closer to the earthly realm and change the sense of "It thinks" into "I think." This step indicates that the child has become more conscious of himself as different from others and from the surrounding world. He has to leave the experience of oneness behind; it is the price for becoming an individual. From this time on, the child will feel himself as the originator of his thoughts.

It is important to notice that I-consciousness is achieved only after the I has been active in the process of brain development and, thus, in establishing the possibility of thought as a universal human activity. Steiner has stated that even though the child might use the word "I" correctly already at around the age of two-and-a-half, the appearance of I-consciousness happens after the age of three. In developmental psychology, the same phenomenon is called "the emergence of the psychological self" at around age three.[15] Professor of child psychology Laura Berk, a researcher and author on child development, also describes phenomena of "metacognition" in the child, such as the use of the words "think," "remember," and "pretend," and the child's realization that thinking is going on inside his head.[16]

There is a deep wisdom in the sequence of development as I have outlined above. Thinking is not a personal achievement in the first place, but is established within us under the guidance of higher beings. Thinking becomes personal through consciousness of self, but always encompasses the possibility of expanding beyond the individual into the universal realm of thought. Stimulating self consciousness at an early stage poses the danger of closing the door to the universally human realm.

However tender and immature this consciousness of self may be, there is a general eagerness in educators to use this emerging consciousness of the child for reflecting and reviewing processes, such as making choices and decisions. These may relate to the child's actions, social situations, daily routines, food and clothing. But consciousness of self is a double-edged sword. It requires maturity to handle it, more maturity than can be expected of a three-year-old. In becoming conscious of their wishes and choices, some three-year-olds are overwhelmed by their own desires and become demanding. They also may change their minds quickly and can appear swayed by emotions. In such cases, parents often complain about their child's self-centeredness. Some children, when made conscious of their actions, become overwhelmed and react with insecurity, lack of confidence in their abilities, and fear of failure. It happens as early as three years of age that children say, "I don't like my drawing," or "I can't do that." Steiner speaks about this early appearance of consciousness of the I as a great mystery and, in a certain sense, as being premature.

Some educational conclusions

Modern education has regarded and used the child's ability to think as an opportunity to introduce early instruction. Undoubtedly there will be more research identifying the potential of the child to think at an ever earlier age. Programs have been designed for stimulating aspects of the young child's thinking, such as memory, color and form discrimination, and concept building. With this the child's thinking becomes tuned to the particular mode of abstract intellectuality prevalent in our time.

Steiner recommended strongly that we leave alone the child's capacity for thinking at this stage, avoiding outer intervention. He was not concerned about intellectual progress, but, rather, about morality. In 1906 he wrote, "[Young] children do not learn by instruction or admonition, but through imitation. The physical organs shape themselves through the influence of the physical environment. Good sight will be developed in children if their environment has the proper conditions of light and color, while in the brain and blood circulation the physical foundations will be laid for a healthy moral sense if children see moral actions in their environment. If before their seventh year children see only foolish actions in their surroundings, the brain will assume the forms that adapt it to foolishness in later life."[17] Steiner points to the link between thinking and morality, on which depends the future of humanity. He is concerned with how the quality of adult thought influences the child. Therefore he emphasizes the self-education of the adult. "The education during these first two-and-a-half years should be confined to the self-education of the adult in charge who should think, feel and act in a manner which, when perceived by the child, will cause no harm."[18] And again, "Why have so many people 'nerves' today? Simply because in childhood there was no clarity and precision of thought around them during the time when they were learning to think after having learnt to speak... The organs and vessels develop after the models of love, truth and clarity."[19]

How might this understanding change our approach to young children in our care? We may find ourselves paying more attention to our own thinking and how that might relate to the child's thinking. There is already among Waldorf educators an awareness regarding the importance of self-education and self-development, as well as a recognition of how speech relates to thinking. But as yet not enough attention is paid to the detail of the child's play in the third year of life. As Waldorf early childhood educators, we should make ourselves heard in the general field of education, where the child's intellectual development is so heavily emphasized. If we are clear in our own understanding of the child's development of thinking, then other educators will be open to what we have to offer, and more children will therefore benefit from educational and childcare practices that truly support them.

Let us return to the example of the child playing at the beginning of this essay. This play expresses the child's activity of thinking before the emergence of a consciousness of the I. This play of the young child marks a specific stage in development and should not be seen merely as a precursor to the "real" play of four- and five-year-olds.

Sometimes one will find that among Waldorf early childhood educators there is too little differentiation in how they approach the play of the child under the age of three versus that of the child over three. Steiner describes the very young child at play as a "hermit," totally immersed in his own world. This play needs to be nurtured by providing a quiet space and adjusting the daily rhythm to allow for the unfolding of undisturbed individual play. Through this play, the child weaves his connection to universal human thought before being drawn into an awareness of himself.

Often the rhythm of the kindergarten day is used as a model for the rhythm of the day in play groups and childcare settings intended for younger children. But is it appropriate for children under three to be interrupted in play in order to make space for group activities such as the morning circle? What is the right daily structure for this age group? How can one create a balance between togetherness and the child's natural desire to follow his own inner impulse? One can find answers to these questions by observing young children and by becoming more and more attuned to the wonderful processes of thinking in the young child.

Notes

1. Michaela Glöckler, *Gehen, Sprechen, Denken* (*Walking, Talking, Thinking*; not translated) (Stuttgart: Internationale Vereinigung der Waldorfkindergärten, 1997), p. 40.
2. Rudolf Steiner, *The Spiritual Guidance of the Individual and Humanity* (Great Barrington: SteinerBooks, 1992), pp. 3-24.
3. Rudolf Steiner, *Understanding Young Children: Excerpts from Lectures by Rudolf Steiner* (Silver Spring, MD: Waldorf Kindergarten Association, 1994), p. 55.
4. Rudolf Steiner, "The Child Before the Seventh Year" in *Soul Economy and Waldorf Education* (Hudson, NY: Anthroposophic Press, 1986), p. 112.
5. Georg Kühlewind, "Learning from the Child to be Human." *Kindergarten Newsletter UK* (Issue 36, 1999), p. 5.
6. Rudolf Steiner, *Education and Modern Spiritual Life* (Great Barrington: SteinerBooks, 1989), p. 77.
7. Michaela Glöckler, "The Birth of the Etheric" in *A Deeper Understanding of the Waldorf Kindergarten* (Waldorf Kindergarten Association of North America, 1993), p. 45.
8. Rudolf Steiner, *The Child's Changing Consciousness and Waldorf Education* (Hudson, NY: Anthroposophic Press, 1988), p. 19.
9. Rudolf Steiner, *Education and Modern Spiritual Life*, p. 112.
10. Laura E. Berk, *A Study Guide for Child Development* (Massachusetts: Viacom, 1997), p. 277.
11. Vygotsky's ideas are outlined in Berk, pp. 247-250.
12. Steiner, *Soul Economy and Waldorf Education*, p. 117.
13. Steiner, *Education and Modern Spiritual Life*, p. 122.
14. Steiner, *The Child's Changing Consciousness and Waldorf Education*, p. 55.
15. Berk, p. 279.
16. Berk, p. 281.
17. Rudolf Steiner, *The Education of the Child* (Hudson, NY: Anthroposophic Press, 1996), p. 19.
18. Steiner, *Soul Economy and Waldorf Education*, p. 115.
19. Steiner, *Education and Modern Spiritual Life*, p. 112.

The Development of Memory and the Transformation of Play

Louise deForest

From First Grade Readiness *(WECAN 2009)*

It is increasingly apparent to those of us working in the educational realm that the age at which a child enters first grade can be very significant in terms of academic and social success throughout the entirety of the educational process and beyond. A child who is too young for first grade, although many first grade readiness signs are already apparent, may spend his or her grade school years working very hard to keep up, never feeling that he or she fits into the social or academic world of his or her classmates. For some, this feeling of having to pedal very fast to stay on a par with others continues into adulthood, where they always have the sense that they don't quite "get it." Others may feel that there is still something unfinished in their growing up years. Early in my teaching career, I had the great good fortune to work with a very experienced and inspiring early childhood teacher. When I asked her what in her life had led her to teaching kindergarten, she answered in all seriousness, "I went to first grade when I was five."

For those children who enter first grade older than the optimal age there are also dangers and long-term repercussions; as we know, our curriculum is based on Rudolf Steiner's understanding of human development and the content of the main lessons of each grade is geared to meet the needs of that particular stage of development. A child who is too old has the disadvantage of passing through thresholds of development without the accompaniment of his classmates or of the curriculum, leaving that child feeling isolated and different. Many of these children, not being met by the curriculum and not feeling integrated into the social world of the class, quickly lose interest in school and studies and can become under-achievers and never quite shake the feeling of being different.

In many of our schools, however, there is no educational "readiness" consultant and the teachers often do not have the experience, knowledge or confidence to evaluate readiness. Signs of readiness are often confusing and contradictory; is it the losing of the teeth or the growth of the molars that is one signal of possible readiness? To make it even more complicated, each child develops according to his or her own individual timetable; one might be showing all the signs of physical readiness while still being socially immature, while another may be "awake" enough for first grade but still need more physical development. Too often we rely only on the birth date to move a child forward into the grades.

But children are always revealing to us their needs, gifts and challenges, if only we know how to read the signs. Everything they do, be it walking, playing, eating, even how they get sick, reveals something unique about them and their stages of development. They want to be seen by us, and it is up to us to develop the capacity to observe them objectively, with no preconceived ideas or judgments, and to put our observations into the context of human development. In this training—for that's what it is—I have found Rudolf Steiner's lecture "Practical Training in Thought"[1] very helpful, for it gives very specific exercises to develop both our thinking and our capacity to observe.

In his book *The First Three Years of the Child*,[2] building on Rudolf Steiner's insights, Karl König speaks about the three phases of memory development over the first seven years. Every human being experiences these three types of memory (indeed, all humanity has passed through this evolution of memory), and if we're observant we can actually see the transformation from one to the next. The first and earliest type of memory, which began in Atlantean development, is called Localized or Spatial Memory and is often confused with the more mature Time Memory. This Localized Memory, however, is completely dependent on outer stimulation, and a memory only comes to mind because something in the environment of the child has reminded that child of something. A child can be going for a drive with her parents, for example, and suddenly begin to describe Grandma's house, complete with all the details. Parents often remark on what a developed and precocious memory their children have but what has really happened is that the child saw something—a tree, flowers, a house of the same color—and through that object, "memories" of grandma's house streamed forth. The same child would not be able to describe what Grandma's house looks like if asked under circumstances that did not spark the memory, so to speak. Once sparked, the memory floods through with all the details. This stage lasts up to the second to third year of life.

In the play of toddlers, we can also observe that the inner activity of imagination and creativity do not play a big role; instead, it is curiosity, the instinctive drive for varied physical movements, and the need to understand the world that propel the child through his or her day. The favorite play of the very young child, as we parents all know, is banging pots and pans, climbing onto and into every available spot, pouring, fitting one thing into another, etc. A walk is often an excruciating experience for the adult who is trying to get somewhere, as the toddler needs to touch, taste, observe and interact with everything that crosses his path. I remember with some shame and regret how exasperated I would get from the near constant dropping of objects—food, spoons, cups—from the tray of my children's high chair, and I couldn't help but think they were doing it out of mischief and joy in seeing their mother so frustrated. But if we truly observe what they are doing, we will come to understand that they are really trying to discover the laws of nature, things we as adults feel are self-evident. The material world is very new to our young ones and they spend their first years discovering how it works: gravity will pull an object, any object, down, no matter how many times you drop it; what goes up does come down, and so on.

I remember one of my children sitting in the bathtub as the water ran from the faucet; for weeks he would repeatedly and with intense concentration try to grab the water coming from the tap. Finally he repeated it enough times to learn an essential lesson about the fluid nature of water and happily went back to splashing and pouring.

Somewhere between two and three, we begin to notice a change in both how memory works and in the play of the child. Steiner talks about this time as the birth of the I, when a child recognizes that he or she is a separate, independent being. My youngest son, Ry, then two-and-a-half, woke up one morning and, as if drunk, ran around the house saying/singing, "I am Ry. Ry am I. I, Ry." This rapture lasted the whole day and, while he continued to be the ever-active, rambunctious boy he has always been, he was also different from that day onward. In play, too, we begin to see that "pretend" has entered. Now the children cook, take care of babies, go off to work (if they have Waldorf teachers as parents, they go to meetings), and are Mommies, Daddies, and babies. At first they pursue house-related play, imitating what they see in their own homes. They are not so much playing together as they are playing the same kind of play, side by side. Slowly, over the next few years, the pretending becomes more elaborate and veers from the home-centered play to imitating and playing the activities in the world around them. Suddenly we have carpenters, doctors, snow-shovelers, and teachers and, instead of the side-by-side play, children are playing together. Play is enormously creative and imaginative at this time, between three and five-and-a-half, and is constantly in the process of becoming; a truck becomes a spaceship which becomes a restaurant which becomes.... It's a bit like the water streaming from the faucet that my son tried so hard to hold—totally fluid and unpredictable and in constant movement. As Rudolf Steiner puts it, "Imagination in children represents the very forces [etheric] that have just liberated themselves from performing similar creative work within the physical formation of the brain." [3]

A healthy child will completely invest him- or herself in the role that he or she is playing and the objects become what the imagination makes of them. Children are often indignant when we adults call this "pretending." We can learn much about children, watching them play at this time in their lives when we can see how creativity feeds creativity and play is a form of nourishment. In the lecture titled "Self Education in the Light of Spiritual Science" (GA61), Rudolf Steiner says, "Where do we find what works on the child as a higher Self, and which belongs to the child, but doesn't enter his consciousness? Astonishing but true: it is children's play, the meaningful, well-carried-out play of all children, that the higher Self works on." And later, "...a child educates himself for life, simply through play." [4]

Memory also changes; what was once sparked by an outer object has now moved more inward, relying on rhythm to put an event into the stream of time and space. König calls it "Rhythmic Memory" (as did Steiner) and the basis of this kind of memory is repetition. We Early Childhood teachers experience this type of memory after two or three weeks of school when our new nursery or kindergarten children, seeing the big bowl on the table and the grinders standing ready, know it is Bread Day—*localized memory*—which means that tomorrow is (for example) Painting Day—*rhythmic memory*. As parents, we see this in the daily rhythms we have put into place around our children; when it is bedtime, for example, once the regular routine is started, the rhythmic memory leads the child from bath to pajamas to brushing teeth to story to bed and good night.

And so we draw near to the six-year change, that developmental threshold when the etheric forces are freed from their formative work on the physical body and released into the capacity for thinking and independent picture-making ability, essential skills for the academic work that lies ahead. Almost overnight the child now can, at will, recall experiences or people she knows and create clear inner pictures of real or imagined things. A friend of mine in Finland described a conversation she had with a six-year-old in her class: they were harvesting autumn fruits and vegetables when this child asked her where the watermelon tree was so he could pick watermelons. She answered that watermelons were too heavy to grow on trees and that they grew on long vines on the good earth. The child looked very puzzled and finally said, "But how can that be, when I can see a watermelon tree so clearly in my head?" Dr. Claudia McKeen, an anthroposophic doctor in Germany and a leading researcher on the question of first grade readiness, tells of a child who went on vacation in the Swiss Alps one summer; months later, having breakfast with his mother, he looked dreamily out the window for several minutes and then said, "I am walking up the path and I can turn around and see the village below. Now I am at the foot of the mountain and I can see the path we will climb." Several minutes later he said, "And now I am at the top of the mountain and everything below looks so small. Mom, can you see things in your head, too?" Konig calls this type of memory Time Memory, when we can produce an inner picture out of our own forces and the released forces of the ether body can begin to work in the soul realm of mental images.

In children's play, too, we see a change. On the one hand, the wellspring of creativity seems to have dried up and we hear, "I'm bored!" or "There's never anything to do!"—quite a change from the ever-active and ever-inventive child of only a few months ago.

They mope around the classroom or the house, they are out of sorts most of the time, and the rest of the time, little rebels. They no longer give themselves over to the artistic activity, be it drawing, painting or beeswax, but seem to struggle with technique and achieving the look they want, which often results in frustration and discontentment. But once they become engaged in play, one immediately notices a different quality to their play. Now the child enters the classroom with a fixed and clear idea of what he is going to play that day and spends the rest of his time gathering the materials he will need to realize the idea he has. As I mentioned above, frustration comes easily, because it is now important that the outer object (a painting or a drawing, the rocket ship or boat) match the inner picture. No longer do the materials in the classroom determine the play; instead, they serve to enable the child to recreate his or her inner picture. One can notice that the child has left behind the physical active soul–fantasy forces and true inner imagination begin to develop.

There is also a new social quality to the play. in the past, the role of each child evolved as the play progressed, gender appropriateness was basically irrelevant (boys could be mothers, girls could be big brothers), and it seemed that the children were carried by the play. Now, with older kindergarteners, the children carry the play and individual roles are assigned right from the beginning. There are rules now, more prescribed ways of playing the roles, and there is a strong impulse towards community building. Very often the play of the older child tends to encompass most, if not all, the class. Postman, Santa Claus, and restaurant are a few of the many plays that tend towards inclusiveness, almost always carried by the older children. Six-year-olds are social geniuses!

It is vitally important for the child's future health that she be allowed to build this healthy foundation for thinking with no interference from well-meaning adults. "Accomplishments that come with forces that are available later on should never be forced into an earlier stage, unless we are prepared to ruin the physical organism."[5] While we adults often think that fantasy denies reality and that we have an obligation to bring children into the real world, "fantasy is the continuous joy that the child experiences on his waking to the earthly world."[6] As teachers, it is our obligation and responsibility to safeguard this sacred time.

Notes

1. Rudolf Steiner, "Practical Training in Thought" in Rudolf Steiner, *Anthroposophy in Everyday Life* (Great Barrington: SteinerBooks 1995).
2. Karl König, *The First Three Years of the Child* (Spring Valley, NY: Anthroposophic Press, 1984), chapter 3.
3. Rudolf Steiner, *Soul Economy* (Great Barrington: SteinerBooks 2003), p. 114.
4. Steiner, *Self-Education in the Light of Spiritual Science* (Spring Valley, NY: Mercury Press, 1995) p. 10-11.
5. Steiner, *Soul Economy*, p. 116.
6. König, *The First Three Years of the Child*, p. 64.

School Readiness and the Transition from Kindergarten to School

Claudia McKeen

From *School Readiness Today* (WECAN 2014)

Why is so much emphasis placed on school readiness in Waldorf education? Why is it so essential that children start school at the right time, that is to say, at the moment when they are ready to move on from "implicit" learning, that is, learning unconsciously through imitation, experience and repetition, to "explicit" learning, that is, the targeted absorbing of information which can later be deliberately recalled or remembered?

There is no scientific study which proves that an earlier school entry would support or enhance successful learning in children. On the contrary, for approximately seven years now, children in Germany have been starting school earlier. Quite recently the German newspaper *Tagesspiegel* reported that in Berlin, where in 2006 the school entry cut-off date was brought forward by six months to December 31, or at the age of 5.6 years, ten times more children than before have stayed a year longer in the school entry phase (first two years of school). It is also known that early school starters often have to repeat a year in the course of their schooling, or leave school at an earlier stage than children who were older when they first entered school. These children are given the feeling that they are not good enough and they tend to feel overchallenged as a result. Their motivation for learning is compromised in a way that jeopardizes their future relationship to learning and their whole educational biography.

These facts alone would suggest that a later school start is the better option. They don't even consider the effect that earlier school entry has on a child's health in later life as a result of premature intellectual demands and the cutting short of the time spent in kindergarten. Early school starters have less time to play freely, to take hold of and work through their growing bodies, and to mature. The forces needed for implicit learning, which are naturally active in children during the first seven years of life, are inhibited prematurely as implicit learning is replaced by explicit, intellectual learning. Younger children do not yet have the necessary forces for this approach, nor are they sufficiently mature physically. The age of school entry is not just a question of greater or lesser learning success; it affects whether or children can develop into healthy, creative and autonomous adults. Pedagogical knowledge and experience and economic-political interests are fighting a hard battle over this question.

In an address Rudolf Steiner gave on the evening before he started his lectures on *The Foundations of Human Experience*,[1] he spoke of this cultural battle: "The Waldorf

School will be living proof of the effectiveness of the anthroposophical orientation toward life. It will be a unified school in the sense that it only considers how to teach in the way demanded by the human being, by the totality of the human essence. We must put everything at the service of achieving this goal." He then spoke of the flexibility and willingness to compromise needed to "conform to what will be far removed from our ideals." He added, "We have a difficult struggle ahead of us, but nevertheless, we must do this cultural deed."[2]

The question we need to ask today is: How far can we go in making compromises and when have we reached the point where what we offer is no longer Waldorf education? The question of school readiness is one we must not compromise on! How do we find the arguments that help us to raise our voices in this cultural battle for the child, for the future of the emerging adult? Are we spiritual revolutionaries?

The metamorphosis of forces of growth into forces of thinking

What is the nature of the forces that, at the time of implicit learning, shape the child's body and organs, and later form the foundation for conscious memory? What is the ether body? What does it mean that the ether forces metamorphose? How can we understand the process in which forces that were used to form the body and the organs are transformed into the forces needed for conscious learning and remembering?

The child's individuality arrives from the spiritual world and incarnates out of lightness and spacelessness into the earth's gravity and materiality, connecting with the earthly substances that make up the body. This process does not happen all by itself. The spirit-soul needs a mediator, and it finds this mediator in the etheric forces. The etheric forces are the link between the spirit-soul and earthly materiality. They can take hold of matter so that it ceases to follow its own physical laws and begins to obey a higher order: the laws of life. The etheric forces build up a material earthly body for the spirit-soul to reside in. Once the etheric forces have formed the organs and built up the physical body, the part of them that is not needed for the preservation of life and organ activity will become available to the life of spirit and soul.

In the 1924 book *Extending Practical Medicine* Rudolf Steiner described to physicians how the ether and growth forces relate to the ordinary forces needed for thinking and mental representation:

> *At the beginning of a human life on earth—most clearly so during the embryonic period—the forces of the etheric body act as powers of configuration and growth. As life progresses, a part of these forces becomes emancipated from activity in configuration and growth and is transformed into powers of thought, the very powers that create the shadowy thought world we have in ordinary consciousness. It is of the greatest importance to know that ordinary human powers of thought are refined forces of configuration and growth.*[3]

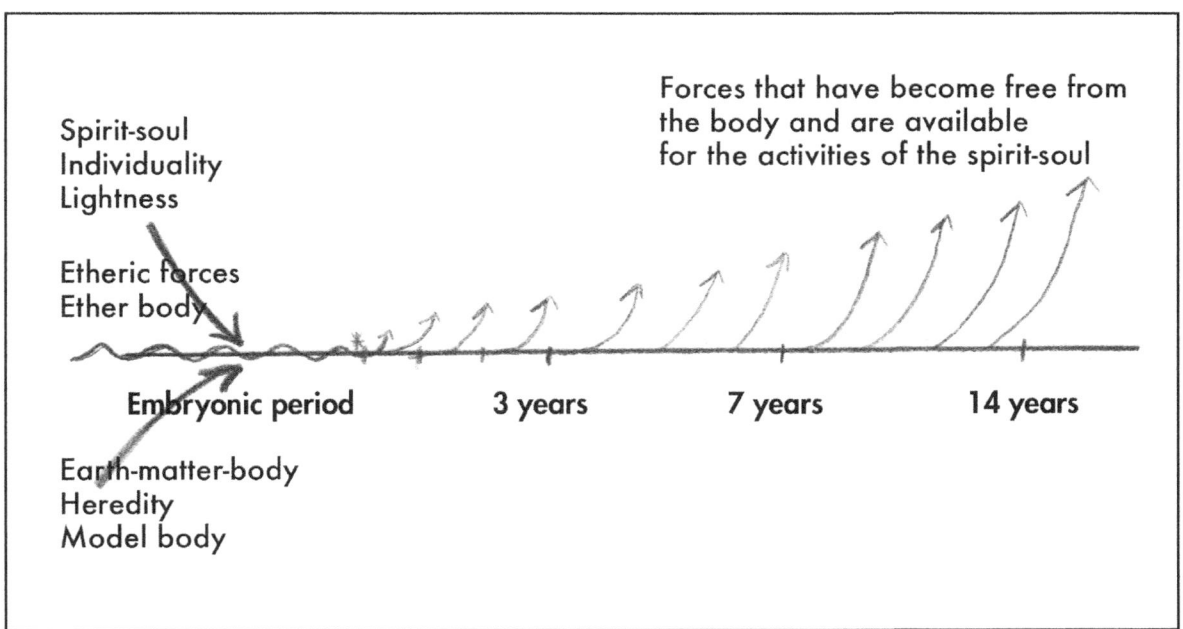

Figure 1 The etheric forces' gradual emancipation from the body and increasing support of the activities of soul and spirit during child development

These formative, sculptural forces, which build up the organs, become available for the activities of soul and spirit inasmuch as they are released from the physical body (see Figure 1). They return to the body if they are needed as healing forces in case of illness in order to support regeneration and the building-up of organs. When we are sick we lie down in bed and notice how our awareness, our perception and soul life are weakened until the ether forces become fully available again, often in a new form, once we have recovered. Equally, these forces are active in us when we are engaged in artistic or creative work and they help us to attain higher knowledge.

There are always two sides we can look at in child development: there is the body that grows, ripens and evolves, on the one hand, while, on the other hand, a relationship evolves with the surroundings through perception and conscious awareness that comes to expression in the life of spirit and soul. At every step of physical development we can look at the spirit-soul and ask, "What is new now?" and vice-versa.

There is a tremendous scope of opportunity for research in developmental physiology, a field that needs the cooperation of teachers and physicians. What soul faculties emerge when the lungs or the liver have finished growing? What about when the child's physical form changes in the seventh year? Once we understand this, we will be able to recognize abnormal developments at an early stage and prevent them. Children's drawings, and the way children play, reflect this inner development.

With the change of teeth around the age of seven, the formation and building up of the dental enamel, the body's hardest substance, comes to an end. Behind the twenty milk teeth, thirty-two permanent teeth lie hidden in the jawbones, ready to be forced out gradually (see Figure 2). We notice how the forces that were previously active in building up the teeth are released and appear in the child's spirit-soul as powers that preserve and maintain form; as the ability to accurately mirror thoughts, experiences and learning contents; and to consciously remember them.

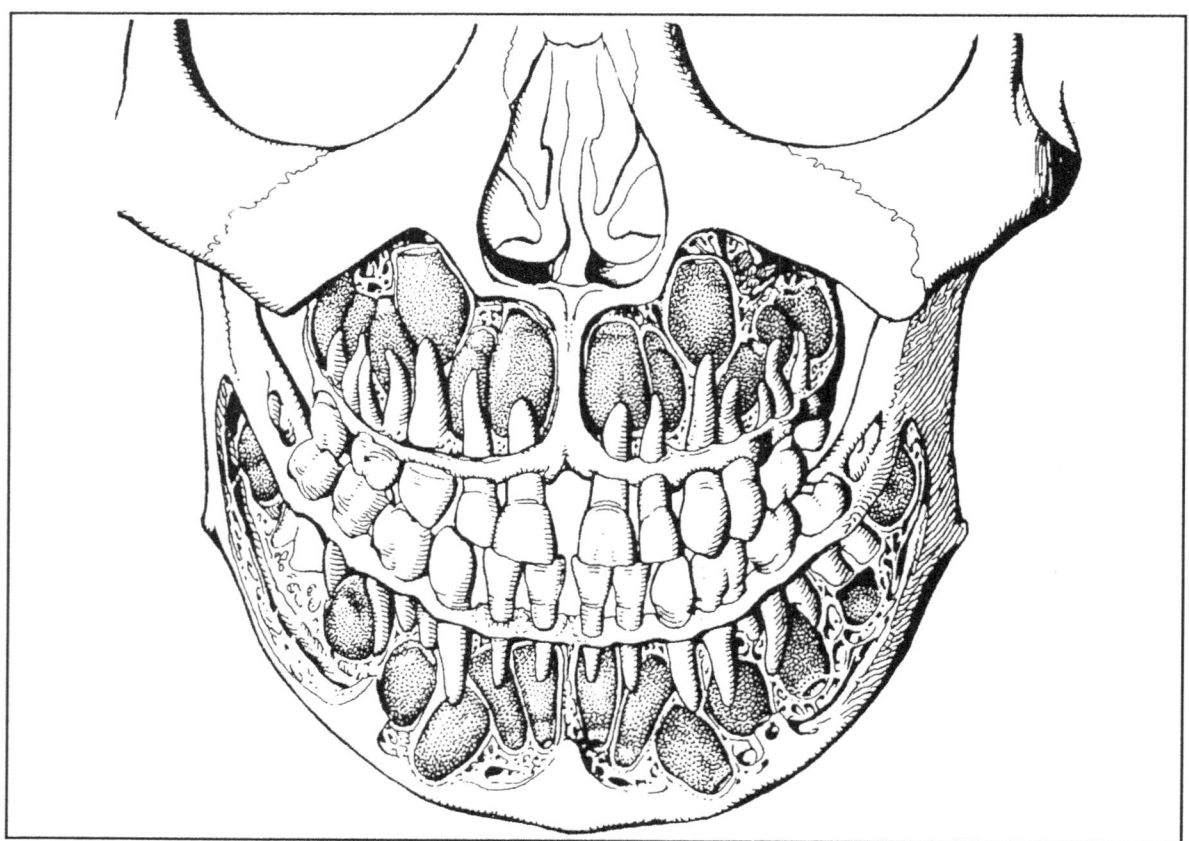

Figure 2 Teeth in the jawbone of a six-year-old child. Next to the milk teeth we see all 32 permanent teeth, fully developed.

From the age of seven, around the time of school readiness, children are able to follow a longer story because they are now able to relate the end of the story to its beginning. If we look at the development and bone structure of the limbs at this age, we see how the individual bones become more and more connected due to the progressing calcification. If we compare this stage with that of a one-year-old, whose ossification centers still appear like isolated islands floating in the fatty tissue, we get a sense of how the etheric forces, which are at work in the calcification and ossification processes, provide the possibility for coherent thinking in the spirit-soul once they have become free. The image of the one-year-old reflects the evanescent impressions of the young child whose perceptions are separate and unrelated (see Figure 3).

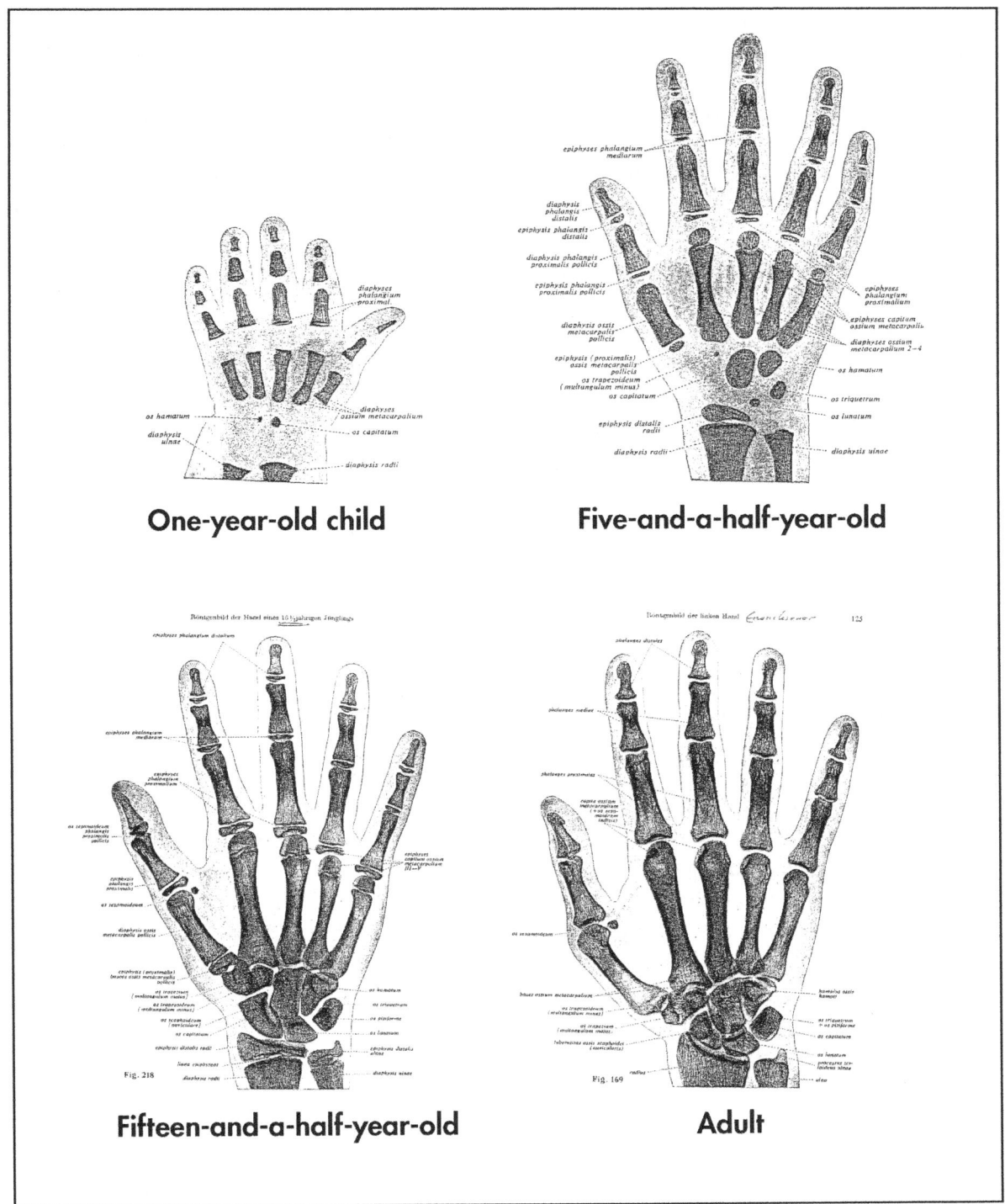

Figure 3 X-ray images of the hand at various ages, showing the progressing ossification.

II. The Developing Child

There is another aspect to how the ether forces affect the child's body in the first seven-year period. Rudolf Steiner spoke of it on March 1, 1924, in his Karma Lectures. "...or in effect, when he is at the change of teeth, man not only exchanges the teeth he first received, for others, but this is also the moment in life when the entire human being—as organisation—is for the first time renewed... Man, we must say, when he is born, receives something like a model of his human form. He gets this model from his forefathers; they give him the model to take with him into life. Then, working on the model, he himself develops what he afterwards becomes. What he develops, however, is the outcome of what he himself brings with him from the spiritual world." Rudolf Steiner then asked, "Why do human beings need such a model at all?... Originally... man was pre-destined to come to the earth in such a way that he could form his own physical body from the substances of the earth, just as he gathers to himself his ether-body from the cosmic ether-substance."[4]

If that were still the case, we would form a physical body that would "fit" our spirit-soul perfectly. Our body would always be in perfect harmony with what we are in spirit and soul. We lost this faculty due to the luciferic and ahrimanic influences and we therefore need to take on a hereditary body. As a consequence of the Fall of Man we need a hereditary body that serves us as a model for seven years. We then build up our own body that is more or less individualized depending on how strong or weak our "I" is. The success of this transformation and adaptation of our body determines the extent to which we are able to know and put into practice our spiritual impulses in a given incarnation. In the same lecture Rudolf Steiner said, "If it is a true school, [a school] should bring to unfoldment in the human being what he has brought with him from spiritual worlds into this physical life on earth."[5]

The consequences of premature school entry

In observing the metamorphosis of the growth forces, we discover the laws of the ether forces, which build up the body and the organs, and which also work freely in thinking and mental activity. Observation of the transformation of the model body shows us furthermore how the inherited body needs to be individualized. This is what children do during the first seven years of life. In rebuilding the model body they inherited, children need to wholly take hold of it so that their spirit can imprint itself into the new form. For this to happen, the body needs to be supple and malleable. Only then can it be a suitable vehicle for the child's individuality and destiny.

A number of factors can hinder this process of individualization. Vitamin D and fluoride, for instance, harden the body too early. Vaccinations, antipyretics, and antibiotics prevent the inflammatory, warm diseases that help children to re-melt their model body. The same happens when children are addressed intellectually too early, when they start school before they are ready, and when the transition from implicit to explicit learning is induced prematurely. Instead of being given time to work on the body, the organ-forming forces are drawn upon for learning, abstract thinking and conscious memorizing. The child's reshaping of his or her model body is interrupted or cut short.

It makes a difference whether or not we give a child time and support for working on his or her inherited model body at all levels in order to individualize this body. This work, which proceeds in stages, needs time. In the first two or three years, mainly the head and neurosensory system mature. The process of gaining awareness, of learning to stand up and master the body, starts with the head and the senses. It involves forces that are activated in the body through imitation and that, as sensorimotor intelligence, enhance the child's mobility. Between the ages of three and five, the child's respiration and heart rhythm are established. The rhythmic system is taken hold of and individualized. The forces which gradually rise up from this sphere to the child's consciousness are the ones that enable children to unfold their magical imaginations. In the last third of the first seven-year period, children take hold of the system governing metabolism and the limbs. They develop secure motor skills, their movements become more differentiated, and with the change of their outer form the transformation of the model body comes to a conclusion. The growth forces are now set free to appear as forces of memory and imagination in the conscious awareness of the child who has attained school readiness.

If we draw the growth forces away from the neurosensory system prematurely and direct them to the child's consciousness, if we use them too early for thinking and mental image forming, they will be missing from the process of growth and maturation that is still going on in other parts of the body. What we increasingly see as a result of this is the dissociation, the drifting apart, of the cognitive faculties, which appear isolated and excessively pronounced; and the stunting of the child's social and motor skills, which cannot come to maturation due to insufficient development of the rhythmic system and the system of metabolism and limbs.

It was not until 1924 that Rudolf Steiner spoke of the model body and its transformation during the first seven years of childhood. He did this in the Karma lecture of March 1, 1924,[6] in the lecture of June 25, 1924 of "Education for Special Needs,"[7] and in lecture 4 of the "Pastoral-Medical Course," given on September 11, 1924.[8]

In the latter lecture, Steiner looked beyond the healthy transformation of the physical model body in the first seven-year period to the developments in the second and third seven-year periods. He explained that the quality of this transformation process would affect whether or not a person could "be given full responsibility" in later life because the connection between their "I" and physical body had come to be too loose or too tight.

There is a second set of questions connected with the remolding of the model body that concerns early childhood educators and lower and upper school teachers alike:

What indications are there in kindergarten as to whether children transform and individualize their inherited model bodies in a healthy and appropriate way? What indications are there for class teachers and upper school teachers as to whether the transformation of the model body proceeded harmoniously or whether the development was in parts too fast, too slow, or incomplete? What can be done during the school years to help the body catch up with what has been neglected in maturation so that the children can find the impulses they brought with them in their biographies?

The healthy metamorphosis of the growth forces is hindered today not only by premature school entry but by many other factors such as vaccinations, by giving children fluoride and vitamin D, and through premature intellectualization, all of which tend to harden the body too early and bring about the withdrawal of forces that are then missing at other levels of the human organization.

Notes

1. Rudolf Steiner, *The Foundations of Human Experience* (Great Barrington: SteinerBooks 1996).
2. Ibid., pp. 29-30.
3. Rudolf Steiner and Ita Wegman, *Extending Practical Medicine* (London: Rudolf Steiner Press 1996), p. 6.
4. Rudolf Steiner, *Karmic Relationships: Volume 2* (London: Anthroposophical Publishing Co. 1955), pp. 78-80.
5. Ibid., pp. 80-81.
6. Ibid.
7. Rudolf Steiner, *Education for Special Needs* (London: Rudolf Steiner Press 2005), Lecture 1.
8. Rudolf Steiner, *Broken Vessels: The Spiritual Structure of Human Frailty* (Great Barrington: SteinerBooks 2002).

III. The Rhythm of the Day

Rudolf Steiner did not prescribe a particular curriculum for the Waldorf kindergartens. He guided teachers to protect the senses of the child, teach through imitation, and, above all, for the teacher to have gratitude, love and devotion for his or her students.

Indeed, he said that, especially for the young child, a curriculum is not important. What is important is for teachers to work in the way that he has indicated: "If you make a surly face so that the child gets the impression that you are a grumpy person, this harms him for the rest of his life. That is why it is so important, especially for little children, that as a teacher one should enter very thoroughly into the observation of a human being and human life. What kind of a school plan you make is neither here nor there; what matters is what sort of person you are. In our day it is easy enough to think out a curriculum, because everyone in our age is so clever. I am not saying this ironically; in our day people really are clever. Whenever a few people get together and decide that this or that must be done in education, something clever always comes out of it. I question having a program of this kind. What matters is that we should have people in the school who can work in the way I have indicated. We must develop this way of thinking, for an immense amount depends upon it, especially for that age or life epoch of the child in which he is really entirely sense-organ" (see Note).

Although Steiner did not indicate a set curriculum for a Waldorf kindergarten, teachers have long applied Steiner's teachings on human development to their own classroom observations and worked together to describe a comprehensive Waldorf early childhood curriculum. In the essays below, teachers share rhythms and activities that have worked for them in their classrooms.

Ingeborg Schottner describes a home-like, rhythmical day filled with creative play, artistic work that is freely taken up, a snack, outdoor play, and a story time.

Freya Jaffke describes working with a mixed-age kindergarten group and creating a rhythm that includes activities connected with real life, rather than abstract or disconnected from life's rhythms. Kindergarten activities she suggests include housework, toy making and toy care, garden work, and experiences on walks. She also notes that it is "not necessary to have extensively prepared activities in which the children are restrained and told, now and not later, this and not that, this long and not longer or shorter, together with these children and not alone in that corner." These words speak to the rhythmical, creative, and imitative nature of education in the kindergarten.

Barbara Klocek describes various activities including play, story, circle, and weekly tasks. Tim Bennett exhorts teachers to "keep things simple, slow down, and be present for each family and child and don't forget to have fun and smile." His kindergarten rhythm includes daily nature walks in the parks near his school and flexible outdoor games. In her essay, In the next essay, Rune Bratlann presents another daily rhythm practiced at the early childhood center Nøkken in Copenhagen, Denmark, and asks kindergarten teachers to be clear and present in their work with young children.

In the final essay of this section, "Finding your Rhythm," the authors outline possibilities for a rhythmical parent-child group.

Note
See Rudolf Steiner, *The Kingdom of Childhood* (Great Barrington: SteinerBooks 1995).

A Day in the Life of the Kindergarten

Ingeborg Schöttner

From *An Overview of the Waldorf Kindergarten* (WECAN 1993)

"What we wish to achieve," said Rudolf Steiner in his Study of Man, "will only be fully attained when someday mankind is so far advanced that even parents will understand that the first years of education pose a special task for mankind today. To perceive this special task is our aim" (see Note).

Let us look at the course of the normal day in the kindergarten as it divides up, between 8 a.m. and noon, into free play, rhythmical activity, snack, walk or outdoor play, and story time.

In the course of this day, the kindergarten teacher works as the center. What she thinks, feels, and wills streams out to her children as they approach her. They will with all their wills! The "center," the teacher, gives form to this will activity, not by her demands but by her very being. What takes place in her being streams out of her actions; the child sees her and wants to do that too. And therein lies the foundation of the education in the first seven years: example and imitation. What the kindergarten teacher does and how she does it work decisively in the development of the child.

The kindergarten is a big household. At home, mother or father cooks, bakes, washes, irons and mends, sweeps and cleans; and the same things happen in the classroom. Singing belongs with work. Watercolors and wax crayons are ready for painting or coloring. Sewing baskets are in demand. For diligent craftsmen there is a workbench. Brightly colored cotton beckons to be finger-crocheted, knotted, and plaited. The little weaving frames are gladly brought out. Pictures are laid out with brightly colored wool. Rakes and little hoes stand in the garden. And before festivals there is the joyous preparation of the room.

The day begins with free play. How is this free play time given shape and form? During this time, the teacher, for example, works deliberately and consciously so as to leave the children free. She works and she carries out the work carefully. Let us suppose, for example, that she sews. Children come into the room. They are attracted by the activity. They watch a moment. Some immediately get needle and thread. One child runs out to a play corner, gets a cloth and sews with his finger. Another irons a cloth with a stick of wood, folds it in a special way, and lo, it is sewn!

Other children have taken up extensive play of some kind. Some bounce around. One sits, finger in mouth, and seems to dream away. One of the bouncers, when asked, brings the teacher a cloth that was lying on the floor. Suddenly he takes an interest in the sewing, sits down, and goes to work. The others that were "playing" with him follow him. With no great fuss, the group gets into purposeful occupation. The finger sucker may find it hard to play even at home. It is often a long time before he can get into any activity; the patience of the teacher can help him.

During free play time all is in motion and an air of "you may" pervades the room. The healthy child naturally perceives the objects in the room as his property; they are tools for creation. A piece of wood becomes a doll, a disc cut from a tree limb becomes bread, a piece of wood carved to suggest a house also serves well as a chimney, with wool as smoke.

Cleaning up ends the free play time. It is important that the children and teacher clean up together. And cleaning up can also be play. A storekeeper sells cloth for cleaning; the trash collectors gather up what is lying around; mother and father put their house in order.

Some children are already sitting in a corner beginning to talk together. Gradually one can come to washing hands and combing hair.

Then a particular song and a rhyme lead over into the rhythmical part of the day. Now the teacher, for example, works consciously on forming the movements. Contraction, expansion, and again contraction—therein lies the rhythmic. As with everything in the kindergarten, this part of the day is in tune with the season.

It is very valuable if the rhythmic part of the day can be built up in blocks lasting three or four weeks. Little plays based on fairy stories can, to the joy of the children, be carried through two or three months. Rhythmic repetition sets the tone for this part of the day. Conscious movements and careful articulation invigorate both speech and play.

A rhyme announces snack time. If the snack can be prepared in the kindergarten, the process will enrich the whole morning's activity. If that is not possible, then the teacher is grateful if the snack bag of a child contains nothing special: a roll and an apple are sufficient.

After the snack, it is time to play in the yard or to go for a short walk. A stone along the way, a stick, the sand, a tree, a waving leaf, a blade of grass, a beetle, a snail, some insects, the blue heaven, the clouds, the wind, the murmuring brook, or a bird—all these are experienced by the child in the way that their central example, the teacher, perceives and experiences them.

Back in the room, the story concludes the morning. The pictorial speech of the fairy stories is language education in the highest sense. The Word, used like gesture in an image created by speech, loosens up a one-sided way of forming concepts and enriches the fantasy. The folk tales are treasures of wisdom. The child can still directly experience the image of the tale, and its figures take on life before him.

If we look back on the course of the day in the kindergarten, we can say that the seed planted by the teacher can bear fruit only with the cooperation of parents. So visits with the parents also belong to the day of the kindergarten teacher, as do meditation and reflection on the children as they were during the day—the fore-work and after-work for her time with the children—and some artistic or cultural activity, work with herself and on herself.

To find the special task of teaching children in the first years of life requires, above all, a conscious and loving devotion to the child.

Note

See Rudolf Steiner, *The Foundations of Human Experience* (Great Barrington: SteinerBooks 1996).

Kindergarten Education with Mixed-Age Groups

Freya Jaffke

From *A Deeper Understanding of the Waldorf Kindergarten* (WECAN 1993)

In this essay will be given an example for how the type of preschool education for which we aim is feasible, particularly when the children's group is composed not only of one age group (ages five and six), but rather of three to four age groups (ages three to six). To what extent the adult masters the necessary differentiations of the various age levels and satisfies the different needs of the children depends largely, to be sure, upon her imagination and inner versatility.

In such a mixed-age group, the children live together as in a large family. They learn from one another and help one another in a way that is rarely necessary or done among those of the same age. It is even quite realistic for the three-year-olds to experience that the six-year-olds may be allowed to do things that they are not yet allowed to do; and, conversely, the three-year-olds are excused from many things that the six-year-olds would not be.

If one wishes to lay a foundation for later ability in life during the preschool years, one cannot do better than to have children learn about the diversity of life. It is the adult's task to choose from the world's fullness what is particularly beneficial for the children's different developmental levels. She will not attempt to introduce too early certain activities (especially in the intellectual domain), so that the development does not proceed in a one-sided manner.

The way a child learns from life reveals itself in her urge to participate in all activities or events in his environment, joining in immediately or carrying them out by imitating them in play. This is, however, only possible when these activities can be looked at and experienced in connection with real life. Therefore, it is the educator's duty to include in the kindergarten plan whenever possible the necessary work of daily life. Some examples:

- Housework—cooking, baking, washing, ironing, sweeping, dusting, and flower care;
- Toymaking and toy care—to this belong, among other things, sawing, rasping, cutting, gluing, repairs of all kinds, sewing, and mending;
- Garden work—digging, sowing, planting, watering, weeding, mowing, and harvesting.

- Experiences—on walks, for example, encountering rubbish trucks, street workers, woodcutters, chimney-sweeps, the ironing woman, the workers in the adjacent nursery.

Nevertheless, the quantity of experiences is not of primary concern, but rather that the children can experience the work as well as the attitude of the people doing the work—how they perform the various jobs one after the other and how they work hand in hand helping one another. All this will be taken in by the child, not with the intellect in a critical or reflective way, but with his entire being which is so capable of surrendering itself to experiences. In this way impulses for his own activity and practice are awakened, and, simultaneously, the forces that build up and form the body are stimulated in various ways.

From these developments arise the guiding principles for the educator's methodology in the preschool years. She herself will work together with the children in significant, necessary ways so that they can take up the work directly and be imitative in their activity. She will not, however, teach this information about life in a scholarly fashion. The aimed-for method is comprised of a well thought out and richly endowed education of opportunities that, however, leaves quite open:

- what the respective child grasps for imitating;
- how the child imitates the activity, according to age (from three to six years old);
- which results will arise from the imitation in the developmental progress of the individual child.

It is not necessary to have extensively prepared activity times in which the children are restrained and told now and not later, this and not that, for this long and not longer or shorter, together with these children and not alone in that corner. The imitative ability and differentiation in this respect depend upon quite definite suppositions:

- about the way the adults shape the world to be imitated;
- about the age of the child within the first seven years; and
- about the individuality of each child.

In the following example of different work situations (in a group of twenty-three children from three to six years old), the explanations should become clear. Such work happens during the children's free play time and consequently becomes an organic part of the daily and weekly rhythm of the kindergarten.

The gardener gives us a freshly cut birch tree, from which we want to saw new pieces of wood for building. The five- and six-year-old boys immediately take the meter-long pieces of trunk, lay cloths underneath and push the wood like a train over the floor and under tables draped with cloths (tunnels). Other six-year-olds are again nearby, helping and competing with one another for who can work up the most sweat. After a while, Jan and Markus, both six years old, begin to build a railroad through the whole room with tables placed one behind the other. The three- and four-year-olds, as patient passengers, get on and off the train at the conductor's order. Suddenly, the big children notice that the saw's noise fits well with their railroad, and so we agree to be attentive to one another. First we go slowly, then faster, then slowly again, then a pause. With great enthusiasm the engineers look out of their window to the carpenter's bench and follow with close attention how quickly the saw goes through the wood. Shortly before the block of wood falls off, it seems that they hold their breath and in the next moment breathe out again forcefully, shouting out the station's name with joy. The conductor urges the passengers to hurry, for he notices that the pauses made by the saw do not last very long.

Under the carpenter's bench, eager hands are gathering the sawdust and pieces of bark. Markus, four years old, takes it as feed for his horse; Gernot, four, lets it snow in the room; Tanja, five, bakes a birthday cake out of it and decorates it with fruit pits from the store. Next to the pieces of wood which are yet to be sawed, Mathias, Aurelia and Susanne, all four years old, are standing and saying, "Here you can make a bridge out of it," "That would be a good coffee can," "Look, if you saw off some here, it will be a little house with a chimney," and, "That looks like a dog." They use some longer branches as a flute, violin and cello and move through the room playing music with them. Shortly afterwards, they carry the branches on their shoulders by twos and offer "apple juice" for sale from the buckets hanging in the middle. But the variety of possible uses for their branches is still not exhausted. They also serve as walking sticks, ski poles, and finally—furnished with a crocheted band—as bow and arrows.

Georgia, three years old, is standing next to the carpenter's bench with a doll under her arm. Delighted, she waits for each piece of wood that is sawed off to fall down or to be ably snapped up by an older child. In between she brings single blocks to Helge, six, and Michael, six, who are building in the corner with bark and big pieces of wood. After the sawing work is done, the remaining branches will be dragged outside, the carpenter's bench pushed against the wall, the work things cleaned up, and the sawdust swept into a pile.

It is now time for the breakfast preparation. There is muesli, and the apples for it must be peeled. Stephen, three, stands next to me and enjoys the long peels which may be eaten. He then goes into the playhouse and tells the other children, "We have already peeled the apples." Cornelia and Aurelia, both four years old, would also like to peel

III. The Rhythm of the Day

such a long peel but barely succeed in going once around the apple. Eventually, they have finished peeling an apple all the way. Their great satisfaction lasts for several weeks. They like to imitate this activity in imaginative play, for example, by wrapping a crocheted band around a block of wood for the apple peel and letting a piece of bark be the knife. The "work" is quickly finished in this way, and the imagination has the possibility of using the same items in another way by letting the band be the shores of a lake and the bark a little ship; or the band is wrapped around a big piece of bark to become a stringed instrument—a kantalina. Jan, Michael and Antje, all six years old, notice that I peel the apple in a spiral and that in this way the peel becomes very long. They are unable to do it the same way and do not stop until all the apples are peeled.

During this whole time, Ulrike, six, was busy sewing. She has put a pin cushion, scissors, thimble and material scraps into the little basket and taken it into her "house." She has knotted herself a little doll and, in addition, has sewn two pillows. She has allowed nothing to disturb her, not even Dietmar, five, who has requested several times that she try on a pair of fur shoes in his shoemaker's workshop.

This small glimpse into a play and work situation of a mixed-age children's group already shows how differently the individual children participate in adult work, how they act according to their age, and how many possibilities for differentiation can arise. Thereby, three very different developmental stages can be recognized, the knowledge of which is a necessary presupposition for the stimulation of the children. For playing and being purposefully active need to be relearned today by many children, especially when they come into the kindergarten for the first time at age five and have not had opportunities beforehand to play imaginatively.

In the first developmental stage, which is just ending for many children as they begin their kindergarten time, a large change in activity can be observed. They watch, help out, in some cases let themselves be included in a game by the older children, and for moments become absorbed in play to the extent that they forget everything around them. The activity of the four-year-olds is also defined by a large change, but now it is through their developing and often exuberant imagination. A prerequisite for this is a toy selection kept simple enough to stimulate the imagination as well as allow for transformation of the toys themselves. After the fifth year, when the child has more and more capacity for imagination and memory at his disposal, spontaneous play activity is organized gradually into purposeful activity. When several children of this older group are together, the play is mostly a question of a project that will be logically accomplished. This does not preclude spontaneous ideas arising and totally changing the play situation again and again. However, the play of these older kindergarten children is usually goal-oriented and resolute.

Difficult situations can also be overcome if, as an educator, one bears in mind how the children's behavior is based on age, which is only briefly sketched here. This should become clear in the following description of cleanup after free play time.

During cleanup time the three- and four-year-olds are either busy beside the adults or "thoughtlessly" busy, for they do not yet quite understand the correlation and purpose of this activity. In certain cases, with the best of intentions, they move things which have just been put away in the correct place to another place.

The four- and five-year-olds eagerly help out, but often make a game out of cleaning up and need much encouragement. When we can manage it, it suits the child well if we build a picture for him, for example: "You can now be the farm boy who is bringing all the animals back to their stalls form the pasture," instead of the abstract order, "Now put the animals back on the shelf." When four- and five-year-olds, for example, pick up building blocks, fold cloths or bring chairs to their places, it often happens that they do it in very creative ways stimulated by their rich imaginations. The cloths are slowly pulled over the edges of the tables or "ironed" with a small, turned-over stool as mother does it at home with the iron. The chairs will perhaps be carried on their shoulders, because they are just being brought in from the "carpenter's," or they are pushed in a row in front of the children as a train. The building blocks will be laid, for example, on a slope to a basket after being hoisted up, because the cleaners have just become dump truck or ship loaders.

The five- and six-year-old children can already distance themselves from the play and accomplish independently a task requested of them. They either choose for themselves an area that they want to clean up alone or they ask the adults for a job. In general, they pay very close attention to how the adult does his work and try to do it as carefully and as well. For example, they fold cloths very neatly or arrange the baskets in the building or shopping corner. They have an overview of the work sequence and its logic that they acquire through the repetition of doing it again and again during the year, and they can give a hand independent of the adults. Thus, they already fetch the broom and dustpan for sweeping when the building corner is barely finished being picked up.

Such differentiations in the various age levels are represented in all activities that take place in the daily life of the children's group. Each child can normally fulfill the developmental stages appropriate for him or her in such a group situation. The modeling effect of the children on each other in the mixed-age group is also invaluable. The concern that perhaps the five- and six-year-old children would not come into their own in a mixed-age group—that they would be hindered in their continued development—is only justified when the actual group includes more than twenty to twenty-three children, and when, because of space limitations, play which requires a lot of room is not possible. After these outer considerations, however, all else depends on the inner activity with which the adult carries out her work. For this is also perceptible to the children and, therefore, is imitable and helps the children learn to evolve their own initiatives.

In the later life of the child, much will depend upon what type of experiences they encountered in the first six or seven years. For what is germinated in these early developmental stages must appear one way or another in a later stage. Thus, abilities and deficiencies can occur in many areas. For example, a child who has been allowed, by imitating, to absorb purposeful and understandable work from his environment will, as an adult, have a command over such abilities on an intellectual level; as an adult, he will have at his disposal logic in his thinking. All that which a child perceives in the working adult and can practice by imitating—like consciousness, attention, order, purposeful results of work—is accompanied by intensive experience. With this, the experiences go into deeper levels which later can be stirred from the consciousness and can assist in an independent, goal-directed shaping of one's life. A child will be able to follow the teacher's words with greater alertness and concentration if he has had the possibility in every respect, especially in his limbs, to attain numerous skills. In this way, the child will be able to control his movements. He can then achieve an outer calm and increase more and more of his inner activity. Of course, in addition to the capabilities, which, as indicated, are transformed, there are also some which intensify in a linear manner.

The work of the adult and the transformation of the work throughout the children's play have been depicted here. The artistic activities (eurythmy, painting, modeling, music-making), the storytelling and the outdoor play are, of course, equally important components in the total educational work. In each of these activities there could also be shown both the specific formative value of the activity and the differentiations according to age levels.

Creating a Flow in Time: Breathing through the Day with a Mixed-age Kindergarten

Barbara Klocek

From *You're Not the Boss of Me!* (WECAN 2007)
See Note about the author's sources

There are many possibilities in shaping our time with the children in a mixed-age kindergarten. We all know that Waldorf education stresses the fundamental value of rhythm in organizing our time with the children. A health-giving foundation is laid as we breathe in and out of our activities during the day. It has been wonderful to be a part of the working group on the older child in the kindergarten and to experience the various ways that each of us have met this challenge. We thought it would be helpful to share these various ways with you to encourage you to find one that fits you, your children and your situation. Over the years I have experimented with different rhythms and have found this to work best for me at this time.

Our day with the children begins at eight a.m. as they and their parents begin to arrive. For the next twenty minutes the yard fills and there is the hum of voices as the children greet each other and the parents visit. We have designated this time as a "walking time," instead of running, out of respect for the many toddling brothers and sisters. At eight-twenty the bell is rung and the children come slowly into our entrance space with cubbies and change into their slippers. We gather on the red rug and play finger games and quiet games until all of the children have finished getting on their slippers. We sing our opening songs and verses (see below) and then joyfully dance together through circle. There is a mood of satisfaction as we finish this breathing together. We then breathe out into free play. The children eagerly flow into play, often taking up images from the circle. An activity such as bread- or soup-making, sewing, felting, finger knitting, or woodworking is begun by the teachers. Often children are invited to join these activities before going into free play, especially if they were restless during circle. On Monday, all of the older children are asked to help fold napkins, small towels, or painting cloths. This allows the younger children to find their way into the space and begin their play while the older children are helping. Often the older children can dominate the play and it is good to give the younger children an opportunity to initiate their own play first sometimes. What a nice mood it creates at the beginning of the week.

III. The Rhythm of the Day

During this wonderful out-breathing of free play, the room is transformed into boats, houses, bridges, etc. A happy hum fills the room. Sometimes I hum or sing softly some of the songs from circle if the noise level is getting too loud. As we are nearing the end of free play, we sing, "six-year-olds may come" to help set the table for snack by carrying pitchers of water, bowls and cups. This supports the six-year-olds to have special jobs to do as well as to help them come out of play. When all that preparation is finished, the teachers sit on two little chairs on the red rug (our open space) and sing,

> *With a voice so tiny, and with eyes so shiny,*
> *Our house elf says, let's clean our room. Can I help?*

All the children gather, and our two little house elves—small dolls about four inches tall with gnome-like hats—often comment on what happens when all the children have gone home or make up a little movement game with the children. Then the children hear their task for the day. We keep the same task for three weeks, the same rhythm as our story. We use this time to have two or three children work together who might benefit from being together, to develop a friendship or to help learn how to do the task, often having the younger and older children work together. This conscious transition from free play to bringing order to the room has made cleanup time so much more pleasant. It creates an opportunity to let go of the imaginations from free play, and, with a fresh breath, we can then move into another activity and imagination. I find there is much less chaos. When their task is done we ask the children to come to us to ask, "what can I do now," so they can help with another task or wash their hands. It is wonderful to see how the tasks become easier over the three weeks and what joy the children have in completing them with a friend.

We then have a short in-breath. After the children wash their hands, they lie down to rest on the red rug. This brings the children into stillness as I am sitting on a chair on the rug singing,

> *I'm looking to see who is quiet as can be.*

When I see a child is quiet, I call them to me and each day a few children can sit on my lap and play the kinderharp. The older children often still want to be active and are given the opportunity to tidy the corners, to wash some of the surfaces and floors or to be "scouts" to see if anything is out of place. They love this because it's almost as if they get to stay up later while the little children have gone to rest. After all are resting, there is a short lullaby sung and a few minutes of quiet. We all relax into this silence after play and cleanup.

We then go on to our snack time. After snack, the children wash their dishes, and then some are excused to go outside. Some children are chosen to wash the tables, others set out chairs, and two older children wash the dishes again with the teacher. Again, these tasks provide time for certain children to be working together and have the added advantage of promoting smoother social interactions. One year we had an older girl who frequently excluded the same girl. We gave them the task of washing the dishes together for three weeks, and sure enough, they became friends. If we are setting up a puppet show or play many of the older children will ask to stay in and help. Usually two or three are chosen and they eagerly help, and nearly set it all up if it is the second or third time for the puppet show or play. As the year progresses sometimes the younger children also ask to help and enjoy participating "backstage."

As we go outside, often the older children will help the younger children with tying shoes or putting on rain gear. We have a large yard with a digging hole or hill (depending on the time of year), garden, sandbox, climbing structure and wagons. We have horse reins, which are a favorite activity, as well as ropes for jumping, tying, and all sorts of creative uses. All the older children learn to jump rope as the teacher turns it. Sometimes the younger ones surprise us with their ability to jump as well.

After an hour-long outside playtime we come in for story on Monday, Tuesday and Friday. On Wednesday we go for a long walk and on Thursday we paint. Our story rhythm usually runs in a three-week cycle. The first week is for telling, followed on one occasion by beeswax modeling. The second week is for puppet shows, first done by the teacher, then by a few older children and then often done as a puppet show in the round where everyone participates as we pass the puppets on their journey around the red rug. The third week the story is done three times as a play. These plays are usually done in the round with simple capes and caps or crowns. Mostly everyone participates, with some children being trees in the forest, or a well or a basket—whatever images are part of the story.

The parts are planned in advance and I try to choose the children for the first play who can carry it the most deeply. Often, in the following plays for pedagogical reasons, children are chosen who could benefit from the role. The plays offer a wonderful opportunity for the older children to learn to carry larger parts. Children who are self-conscious or silly early in the year learn to live into the imaginations deeply and, with practice, develop poise. These plays continue the dream-like consciousness of the kindergarten, with the teacher walking beside the different children and speaking the parts, guiding the children throughout. So the children are not usually speaking or even acting out but rather dreaming through the story.

We have a short goodbye song (from *Let Us Form a Ring*):

Oh lovely sun, oh lovely earth, good friends all gathered here.
Let's all join hands so there may flow, a stream of warmth and golden glow.
Goodbye.

III. The Rhythm of the Day

We then all sit and have lunch, which has been brought from home, together. We used to end the day at 12:00, but found that many children were very hungry and were having meltdowns or eating in the car on the way home. When we first started having lunch at school, the children would love to sit and talk rather than eat. But when it was time to pack up they complained they had not yet eaten. We now light a quiet candle for the first fifteen minutes of lunch with the song,

See the little candle, shining, shining bright.
Quietly we eat as we watch your light.

After we see that many of the children have eaten most of their lunch we sing, "Thank you little candle for your golden light." When it is blown out, it is a sign that we can now talk quietly. This has led to a very peaceful lunchtime. There are always children who take more time to eat, so we often have the ones that have finished come and sit on our laps as we sing a song to them. It is a nice way to have music surrounding the children in an informal way.

Our day ends at 12:30 as the children put on their shoes to go outside and meet their parents. In our kindergarten yard there are two kindergarten classes present at going-home time. We struggled with having so many people on the yard for several years because the children wanted to play with their friends and the parents wanted to visit; it was chaotic with so many people, large and small. Now after five to ten minutes we ring a large cowbell and everyone knows it is time to leave. Then the children staying on for nap have a peaceful yard in which to play. What a "wonder-full" day it has been.

Here are some of the songs and verses that surround our morning circle:

Circle beginning

Gentle fairies, wise elf men, come join us please do.
We bring golden light from our garden to you.
Our angels they guard us by day and by night,
From the sun and the moon and the stars shining bright,
Light fairies come to us, bring to us your golden light.
When everything is so quiet...
The light fairies come, bringing light from stars and sun.

(to light the morning circle candle)

Down is the earth, up is the sky,
There are my friends and here am I.
Good morning dear Earth,
Good morning dear Sun,
Good morning dear stones and the flowers every one.
Good morning dear creatures and the birds in the trees.
Good morning to you and good morning to me.

(sung once in standing and again holding hands and moving around circle)

For we are guarded from harm, cared for by angels,
Here we stand, loving and strong, truthful and good.

Circle ending

I dance with the flowers, I sing with the sun.
My warmth I give to everyone.

Here is a spark of Father Sun's light,
To keep in our hearts so warm and bright.

(to put out morning circle candle)

Note

All examples of verses are taken from *Let Us Form a Ring: An Acorn Hill Anthology*, edited by Nancy Foster (Silver Spring: Acorn Hill Waldorf Kindergarten and Nursery 1989).

Sailing Our Ship in Fair or Stormy Weather

Tim Bennett

From *You're Not the Boss of Me!* (WECAN 2007)

As the teacher of the Rosemary Kindergarten in Seattle, I am the captain of my ship, as well as the navigator of its daily journeys into charted and uncharted waters. Inwardly the captain's heart holds two questions: Who are these children? What are their needs? Because of my responsibility for these children from the moment they pass through the gate until the moment when they return into their parents' arms, there are a few important rules I follow when on board this ship: keep things simple, slow down, be present for each family and child, and don't forget to have fun and smile.

The parents are asked to drop off their children between eight-thirty and nine a.m. I use this time of arrival to tidy up outside, do garden tasks, talk to parents and so on. It is the transition time from home to school and an opportunity to play outside in our schoolyard. We have swings, a slide, balance boards, stilts (for the six-year-olds), and shovels in our sandbox ready to dig for pleasure or for treasure. I also have parents turning a jump rope. And of course there are the chickens: Honey, Ruby and Blackie. We check for eggs and say good morning to our beloved chickens. Sometimes our chickens also have unusual adventures—like the day when one of the older children took Ruby from the chicken house and held her while skipping rope.

Ahoy mateys! At nine a.m., I gather the families together and we begin to form a circle. As a community of people, we greet each other and greet the day. I always have a little song or verse for the season. If it's raining, as is sometimes the case in our fair city, I sing, adapting a poem by A. A. Milne :

> *John has a great big pair of waterproof boots on.*
> *Splish splash, splish splash, splish splash splish!*
> *And John has a great big waterproof mackintosh*
> *and John has a great big waterproof hat!*
> *And that, says John, is that, and that, says John, is that!*

Then we become a bit more reverent for a moment and we say our morning verse:

Our hearts open wide, light streams deep inside.
Stars, moon and sun shine down on everyone.
On earth now we stand, giving all our hands.
Good morning, dear friends.

Then I sing what will happen today: "Ring a ring a Rosemary day, welcome, welcome, nature walk day and painting day." After this opening to the day, I begin to feel that we are a group and that we have built up some substance through our interest in each other and our movement together as we have our daily greeting.

It is time for our ship to set sail! We head for the school gate, where we find walking partners and say goodbye to the parents and little brothers and sisters. The captain is at the helm, the crew is ready and we set out to seek an adventure in the great wide world, waving to the parents as we go. As the captain, I carry a sturdy backpack, filled with a long rope, snacks, water, a first aid kit and a cell phone. My faithful first mate (also known as the kindergarten assistant) has a red flag that we take with us to help us get across the five-way intersection on our way to the park. My rule for crossing the street is that the red flag must be in the middle of the street before any child takes a step off the curb. My intrepid assistant goes out onto the road, makes sure the coast is clear, and then we can all safely cross the street. Upon reaching the other side, the children know that they are free to run, skip, and cavort. Our nature walk has truly begun.

We have set sail and are now out on the open seas, surveying the landscape far and wide! Nature adventures are rich and nourishing for the children in so many ways. The most obvious healing aspect is simply being in nature, in the outdoors in all kinds of weather during the four seasons of the year. In the Pacific Northwest, this is possible because of the mild temperatures in both winter and summer. The children really have a daily dose of what it means to be on the earth, surrounded by nature and the ever-changing weather. We always "dress" for the weather. For most of the fall and winter, we wear raingear and a warm hat. Being in nature also brings the possibility for a strong connection with the fairy world and the materials of the earth: sticks, stones, leaves, moss and so on. The senses are enlivened when out in nature and the children more easily fall into play in a lively and healthy manner. Dirt, mud, dust, rivulets of water, autumn leaves, bugs, squirrels, spring blossoms, still air, and whipping winds all build their feeling for beauty, goodness and truth. These experiences provide a foundation in the child's will and feeling life to support the science lessons that will have deeper impact in future years. Experiencing the gifts of the earth in these early years will plant the seed for caring about the future of our planet in later years.

I started the daily nature walks because more children were coming to me who were weak in their physical and etheric bodies. There were also other children who were overly physical in their limbs and could not find any rest or peace. Both of these kinds of children found a healing in the movement possibilities of the nature walks. The weaker children found strength and eventually a great joy in movement. The overly physical ones could freely move and gradually come into a rhythm through the regularity of our walks. Being among the trees and under the great sky gives the children a picture and a feeling that they are a part of the kingdoms of nature. In sharing the space with the elements of the earth and the kingdoms of nature, they can find their place in the world. Of course, this happens for them in an unconscious and powerful way.

As the navigator of the journey, I choose to go to different parks during the week; we have three parks within walking distance. We go to a large woodsy park twice a week. This place is full of maple, fir, and cedar trees. There are lots of hills and valleys to explore. Here the children can really get a taste for adventure, sliding down muddy hills, climbing up a fallen tree, jumping off small rocks and cliffs, and building fairy houses or shelters in the woods for those cold winter days. Sometimes I throw a rope over a tree branch and make a rope swing for the children. The older children love this. Usually we walk for a while and then stop to play in whatever secret garden we have found. This is when some of their deepest play happens. They build houses out of sticks and branches, play knights in the forest, build fairy houses or gather treasures: a bottle cap, a special key, a magic stick or stone. The children often name these beloved spots on our walk. We play at the "Rolling Hills," where there are many dirt bike hills just perfect for running up and down. Then there is "Bunny Hill," a place where a huge pile of rocks provides a home to ongoing generations of wild rabbits and former "pet" bunnies. Naming a spot makes it our own and places it on the children's growing map of their expanding world.

At this point, the crew often becomes a bit tired and hungry, so we take a short rest and serve up some grub: salt fish, biscuits and rum. Well, we've run out of fish, biscuits and rum, so it will have to be trail mix, rice crackers and water for the captain and crew today. After snack, we start back to school. On our way back, I usually play a short game to re-enliven and focus the children, helping them come along home together as a group. I like to play "Sheep and Wolves." Half the children are sheep or shepherds (the shy ones who only want to watch the game) and the other half are the wolves. I say, "Run, sheep run!" and the sheep run out from their house (near a tree where they have previously gathered). Then I say, "Run wolves run!" and the wolves run and try to catch the sheep before they can get back "home." If a sheep is caught, it can become a wolf if the child wants to. I keep the game fun with a lot of running about and I always play with them. I am usually a sheep and the children love to catch me. Other games we play are seasonal games that work well outside: "What Time Is It, Mr. Fox?" or a simple version of "Red Light, Green Light." I play any simple game that has to do with running, chasing, and stopping.

I also take a jump rope along with us. We can tie one end to a tree and do all sorts of jump rope games. The games can help to build up different rhythmic movements, as well as build self-confidence in one's growing physical abilities. After games, we continue on our way back to school, stopping at different points along the way to wait for the slower ones and slow down the faster ones.

During the entire walk, I watch the children form their social connections for the day. There is something about the nature walks that helps the children breathe out into the world of the "other," not just into the world of nature. I always get the sense that the children come from all over the city and need to shed the morning car ride and whatever dramas might have been going on at home. Our adventures help the children to come into social harmony. The walks allow them to shed the past, live in the present, and move, literally, into their future. This is the magic of the act of walking into nature. The children are drawn to the world around them and then are drawn to the friends who share this world. Again and again I see the forest being the mediator in helping these friendships to blossom. For example, children who like to go "hunting" for imaginary raccoons or coyotes join together in close camaraderie. Other children who like to collect treasures gather together in search of special leaves, sticks or rocks. Our ship glides into port at the schoolyard gate between ten-thirty and eleven a.m. We all disembark for circle or story time. We have circle on Monday and Tuesday. We have story time on Wednesday and Thursday. On Friday, we have circle games. I also like to incorporate folk songs, simple folk dances, and some basic circus skills. All the children love to stand on my shoulders and become a giant! At story time, I usually tell the story. After the class knows the story, we can act it out. The six-year-olds always lead the acting out, showing the little ones what they know. I also do puppet shows in a similar fashion, first doing it myself and later having the six-year-olds move the puppets that have a minor role in the show. This is a place where the six-year-olds can really let their new capacities shine out for the whole class to see.

Next, we move on to our snack time, seated at three small tables. I strive to make this a time to be nourished by the food while we are in the presence of each other. I use snack time as a breathing-in during the flow of the day. So we have a quiet snack with "no talking." I find that if I say, "No talking," this is clear for the six-year-olds, and the little ones will follow along. The children take this time to rest and enjoy the quiet and peace around us. Also, at snack time, I always choose two six-year-olds to be the "waiters," pouring tea and water for the others. The younger children love to be served by their older friends.

Next is our free play time. In fall and winter, we play indoors, but in spring we play outside when the weather allows. Besides the free play, in the winter we have opportunities for the six-year-olds to be involved with some projects. They make felted hats and mittens that can keep both their heads and hands cozy. I have also found that the six-year-olds like to build elaborate structures, so I make sure that there are a lot of ropes, pulleys, large pieces of driftwood and sawn wood, metal clips, and wooden clips. These materials encourage the older ones to use their growing physical strength and newly acquired ability to carry out plans to their hearts' content. It is during this free play time that we also do our artistic activities: painting, coloring, beeswax modeling, baking, and cleaning.

At 12:20 p.m. we have cleanup time. First everyone leaves the room to wash their hands and get their lunches from their cubbies. When they come back into the room, they put their lunches at their places at the table and then begin to tidy away. There always seems to be a bit of magic at tidy-away time, as we set our house in order and anticipate eating our good food.

At 12:40 p.m. we have lunch. Again we begin lunch with our quiet voices. Once everybody is settled down and eating, I tell a story from my life or stories that have been passed down to me by some colorful characters. The children love these stories and sometimes share them at their dinner tables at home! They then get ready to leave school. I often put up a balance beam on two chairs and have the children "walk over the bridge" to say goodbye to me after they have packed up their lunches. Having sailed over waters both calm and stormy, the children then find their parents, who are waiting outside on the porch to sweep them up and take them home. The old captain and his faithful first mate swab the decks, secure the rigging and make everything ship-shape for the next day's journey.

Working with the Will

Rune Bratlann

From Nøkken (WECAN 2015)

In Nøkken, we work with children as beings of will. Manual work, singing, unspoiled experience of the change in the seasons, tired feet and ravenous appetite, the smell of good food, are all elements that make a direct appeal to the will-power of the little child, which here is allowed to develop freely and in safe and recognizable surroundings. Although every day is different from the others, the rhythmical repetition and the organization of the day is the spine of the whole kindergarten.

The staff meets about one hour before the kindergarten opens, around seven-thirty. After that, the food is prepared and set to cook; the tables are set, the fairy tale room is prepared; the strollers are made ready and packed with blankets, water bottles, diapers, toilet paper; the pail with butter-knives, which the smallest children use to "whittle" with, plus all the different things we use in the preparation of our annual celebrations.

The little red cabin is the home of the youngest group of children, from one to three years of age. Here the cribs are made ready in the very best way, and the oven, which is in use from early fall to mid-spring, is lighted, with the smell of authentic comfort as a result. This is where we begin our indispensable morning reading at eight sharp, even though everybody is not in the circle, because this way no one slows the morning down for everyone else, if he or she is not able to let go of a task. We start out by reading a selected text by Rudolf Steiner for about fifteen minutes, and within this period everybody in the circle is reading aloud from the text. Then follows the current verse from Rudolf Steiner's soul calendar, which helps us to weave ourselves into the day in the best possible way. After this, we go over the coming day in its more technical/practical aspects: who is sick, who needs extra care, who of the staff does what, and so on. Finally, we wish each other a fine day in the circle. Everybody knows what to do. The time is eight-thirty, and the first children and their parents are already waiting outside the gate.

Every day, the children and their parents are met with a warm handshake, after which the parents, quickly and without too much talking, disappear. The children then occupy the large and magnificent playground. They share it with the white Angora rabbit—which is often used as a transition from mother or father to a new day in the kindergarten for the youngest children. There are also our chickens, who, besides giving us their eggs, also work as a guarantee for all of our leftovers to be used, which is totally in agreement with the ecological spirit of the location, where nothing, even the dishwater, should be wasted. Instead, it must be integrated in a healthy, continuous consciousness of how everything is connected, lived out in a warm loving practice.

The children and adults gather in a circle at nine o'clock, and with a song, we welcome each other. We then walk for about twenty minutes, by routes we know like the backs of our own hands. We stop for just over one hour at our usual playground—a big field with old trees and many excellent hideaways. There, the children can play by themselves in the beautiful surroundings while the adults work to prepare the next annual celebration, collect garbage from the area, build small twig-houses for the hedgehogs or whittle small wood figures.

When we come back home, we are all hungry. After we have taken off our outdoor clothes, changed from outdoor shoes to slippers, been to the toilet and washed our hands, the good food, which is always prepared in the most simple way and out of the finest biodynamic raw materials, is consumed with great appetite. We sing before and after the meal, and when we are finished, we all help each other to clean up the table, so the whole kindergarten can sit there and paint, while the adults and a couple of helpers do the dishes and sweep the floors.

After some time, the fairy tale is ready, and the children can now enter the little and very cozy fairy tale room. After taking a deep breath, we are all looking forward to come out into the garden, where the children can play by themselves until one-thirty, when fruit and water is served at the tables in the garden. After that, the adults begin to clean up the garden, normally assisted by some small helpers, the parents start to show up, and then the kindergarten closes for the day.

All day long there are things to be done—necessary and meaningful work that must be done in order to make life fit together. The children experience the working process from start to finish and can easily relate to what is going on, without words and admonitory speech, but rather full of joy in life itself.

The more conscious we adults become, the better we can ask ourselves this question over and over again: Why do I do what I do the way I do it? Thus it will become easier to enter the absolutely intimate, close, and practical reality that surrounds the children and defines their beings. Here it is of great importance that we endeavor to be present. Even in the smallest of our movements, we must fill out our body with consciousness in such a way that we—in the most literal understanding of the word—learn to stand up for what we are. To attain this goal, I cannot think of any better way than to be with young children. Nothing else can motivate that sacrifice it some times can be to get rid of all our little uglinesses, to grow out over the borders of our own (imaginary) limits, and to strive to become that truly happy and healthy human, worthy of imitation as an ideal, that the children need so deeply.

Rhythm and Time in the Child's Daily Routine

Eldbjørg Gjessing Paulsen

From *Trust and Wonder* (WECAN 2011)

Rhythm (from Greek rhythmos, any regular recurring motion, symmetry) is a "movement marked by the regulated succession of strong and weak elements, or of opposite or different conditions."[1]

Rhythm is an important aid to the upbringing of the growing child, and indeed is a necessity for our lives as human beings. It is given to us by nature; we find it everywhere where there is life and growth. Rhythm is about cadence and tempo, regularity and measure. We experience it whenever there is alternation between two polarities. These alternations can be fluid and mobile at the same time that they follow a definite sequence and order, which is continually repeated. For example, think of water drops falling from the roof or a water tap dripping.

In our daily lives, rhythm is largely about expansion and contraction. We experience how day expands our vision and our activity, and night brings us back home to rest. In the change of seasons we can see the alternating expansion and contraction of the earth, its breathing in in winter and out in summer.

We can compare rhythm in nature with the rhythm in our physical body. We can look at a brook where the water is in movement. The water itself has no inherent rhythm, but as it trickles and flows downwards it creates one. The water's movement depends on what it meets on its journey: stones, twigs, and other objects contribute to the way the water will flow, but the flow pattern that we see is repeated again and again and never ends. If we put a stone in the brook or a large branch, the water will still continue flowing, but will find new ways to do so.

In us, rhythmic movement is experienced in our breathing and blood circulation. The same rhythm is maintained as long as there is no interference from outside. However, as soon as something happens to us, whether to body, soul, or spirit, our breathing and blood circulation is affected. Just as the movement of the brook is influenced by outer conditions, so is the child affected by outside happenings.

The earthly rhythms of living beings are interwoven with universal cosmic rhythms. The moon and sun have their own rhythm connected to week, month and year. Our planet needs twenty-four hours to turn on its own axis, which creates the alternation of day and night that affects every living being on earth. At the same time each individual has its own unique rhythm. Human beings have not only physical rhythms, but also soul and spiritual rhythms that are at work throughout our lives. Understanding the importance of rhythm helps us grasp the significance of bringing it into the child's life.

The Significance of Rhythm in the Child's Development

We no longer live according to nature's rhythms as our ancestors did. Science and technology have revolutionized our everyday lives and transformed the way we live. In place of the experience of natural dark and light, we press a button and there is light, even if it is in the middle of the night. We use artificial light and warmth to grow flowers and plants. We also interfere in people's lives by using chemical medicines that affect blood circulation and breathing.

Nevertheless, we must not forget that we still are subject to nature's rhythm. We cannot get the sun to rise in the evening or prevent plants from turning toward the light; it is the law of nature that the sun will rise in the morning and that plants will reach out toward the sun. The rhythm in nature still affects us and our development. We must take this into account in the upbringing of our children, keeping it in mind as we shape our daily routine.

Everything that happens in and around a child affects the body's rhythm. Regularity in everyday life helps strengthen the child's growth and progress. An everyday life that changes from day to day is disturbing to the child. Predictability, on the other hand, gives a sense of safety.

We should be aware that the rhythm in children's everyday lives has changed radically in the last fifty years, generally becoming less regular and predictable. For example, rather than staying in one place, the child of today has often moved or been abroad several times before starting school.

The child comes into the world from a protected time in the womb where she has shared the mother's rhythm during pregnancy. From birth, the infant starts to experience living at her own pace. She takes her first breath, breathing in, breathing out. Initially the breath is uneven, but after a while, it acquires its own individual rhythm. Influences from outside, whether they are movements in the room, sounds, or feelings of hunger, discomfort, or happiness, will all have an effect on the child's breathing. Each time the child is fed, wakes up, or goes to sleep, it leaves an imprint on the daily rhythm.

In the beginning after birth, the mother's rhythm is still a strong influence. Later on, the child finds her own tempo. This is affected by cultural practices. In Africa, where it's common to carry the infant on the back, the child experiences the mother's rhythm as she moves and works. Children who are rocked in a cradle have another experience of rhythm. Many parents tell us that those children who have been rocked as infants become calmer and more amicable.

Little children need a more rhythmic, regulated day than adults do. It is easier for them to orientate themselves when they know what is going to happen. In contrast to us adults, children experience just as much excitement with the familiar as they do with the unknown.

To create a good rhythm for a child takes a great deal of time and patience. It is only possible if we repeat the same thing over and over again, every day, for a long period of time. Only then will it be regular enough to influence the child positively.

In earlier times, children experienced rhythm more strongly through the manual work of those around them. Mothers did laundry by rubbing clothes on the washboard, or kneaded bread by hand. Cutting grain with a sickle was another activity with recurring movements. Today there are not many children who experience these rhythmical movements, especially in the Western world. We really do not wish to go back to the times without mechanical aids; however, we can see the importance of learning how people performed these tasks. Children do not have the possibility to observe the working process when it is done by machines. If we believe that the power of imitation is the child's tool for learning, it is important that the child have something to imitate. It's much easier to imitate an adult washing up than a dishwasher that does the same job!

All regular processes affect the child. Breathing, nerves, and blood circulation are affected, and the consequence is either calming or disturbing. Children are happy and content if their world is calm and mostly regular. This can have a calming effect on restless or nervous youngsters. It creates a safe and predictable environment.

In the Waldorf kindergarten, we alternate between ordered activities on the one hand and free play on the other. This gives the child the possibility of a rhythmic "breathing" during the kindergarten day. When the child has to concentrate, that is an "in" breath. Activities prepared and structured by adults demand concentration within given limits. When a child plays by himself, there is also deep concentration—but the child sets the limits, and because it is not directed from outside, it is an "out" breath. The alternation between directed and free activities gives the child space for rhythmic "in-breathing" and "out-breathing." We clearly see this when we tell a fairy tale or a little story. Children absorb the words with full concentration; it almost seems as if they are holding their breath. When the story is finished, we see how they expel the breath.

A child's daily routine needs to contain both breathing polarities in alternation, organized rhythmically by the adult caregivers. The child has more than enough to handle in performing his daily tasks, and at the same time exploring his own dexterity, without uncertainty being added to the mix.

The rhythm in everyday life is important, but it is also important to make room for the spontaneous. We can allow ourselves that, once we have created a solid everyday routine. It is not little exceptions that disturb the routine, but continuous changes. A few exceptions spice up the day, while the routine gives stability and safety. When we are on holiday or have a day off, we break the normal routine. We enjoy lazy mornings without an alarm clock telling us to get up. Sometimes we turn the day upside down. This can be exciting for a while, but eventually most of us long for the known routine. We like to have some order in our lives. For the little child this is of paramount importance. Children can behave spontaneously, but are happiest in a routine provided by adults.

Taking Time for Children

Children spell love: T-I-M-E—Dr Anthony P. Witham

We all have our mechanical helpers, which should give us more time because they handle many of our daily chores. However, we still run out of time and do not get everything done. We often feel that "if I could only get this thing done, everything would be so much better." Nevertheless, as soon as we complete one task, another appears.

We can take control of our time again by having a greater awareness of what we actually want and need to do. We can choose to have less activity during the day and make room for quietness, which is something we all need. All of us, children and adults, need enough time and space for ourselves.

The age of each particular child, his stage of development, and his personality give us a hint as to what he needs, especially during the first three years. That is the period when children acquire many skills in a short span of time. During these years, they not only learn skills, but also need to practice what they have learned. They need repetition and time to practice. We tend to forget that when a child has learned something new, he needs time to learn, adapt, and repeat that skill before hurriedly moving on to the next item.

Our children are our teachers when it comes to upbringing. Rudolf Steiner maintains by reading the child's nature, you will know what he needs. In his book *The Education of the Child* he speaks of educators of the future who will observe children deeply: "They will invent no programs, but read from them (the children) what is already there. What they read becomes in a certain sense the program itself, for it bears within it the essence of development. For this very reason a spiritual-scientific insight into the being of humankind must provide the most fruitful and most practical means for the solution of the questions of modern life."[2] That means that we, as educators, must learn to listen to and observe each child during each phase. This will give us the knowledge we need to help the child in his development. For the little ones it is obvious what they want and need: constant repetition of actions and words. Everyone who works with children of this age hears constantly, "Do that one more time," and "Tell us again."

Young children want to spend time with adults on a daily basis, and participate in various daily chores. They do not look for "entertainment" or wish to be kept busy with all sorts of activities. It is for our own convenience that we put a child in front of the television while we are cooking supper. I believe that if children could choose, they would choose the company of an adult unless they have acquired other habits.

We also need to give children enough time to adapt to all the new impressions that bombard them. The experiences that a child is exposed to during a normal day trigger different images in the brain and contribute to the foundation for future thoughts. The more logical actions that happen in the day, the more logical the thoughts will be that are formed later. In addition, the more children perceive and understand through their own actions, the easier it will become to understand cause and effect when they are older. Children need to feel, observe, and do things themselves. We need to give them space, peace, and enough time to do just that. All healthy progress, growth, and maturation needs time.

Emmi Pikler writes in her book *Lass Mir Zeit*[3] ("Give Me Time") how important it is that we observe the child and create the right conditions for independent movements and actions from birth. Having studied young children over many years, she describes the skills they have for movement, the progression during the first years, and how those skills are used. The book's title says it all! With toddlers, especially, we have to have enough time for what we want to do and be present in what we do. In that way the child has the opportunity to be deeply focused in the activity, and this will later give a further understanding of what is happening. Today, when most things happen at the speed of lightning, it is very important that we give children—and ourselves—time.

The consciousness of time is closely connected to the maturation of the brain, which continues through life. At birth the brain surface begins to mature, so that the brain cells can start functioning. This happens as sense impressions from outside are absorbed and adapted by the child. At the beginning, babies have no conception of time. They live in the present, and time is connected to specific events. Only later will time be something the child understands as a concept. A first experience of time comes about when something is repeated and is connected to a sense experience of touch, sound, smell, and taste. An infant cries because she is hungry. When the mother puts the child to her breast and the baby feels the mother's skin, the cries change to "happy" sounds because she knows that milk is coming soon. This is the beginning of understanding the concept of time.

In general, timing is the key to healthy eating habits. When a youngster is hungry and wants food we do not wait hours or days before giving him the food she needs. We know that if we waited too long, the child would develop problems with the digestive system and might get stomach cramps. Digestion is connected to the type of nutrition the child receives and to regular feeding intervals. In the Waldorf kindergarten we place an enormous amount of importance on healthy and nutritious food, mainly biodynamic and natural unprocessed foodstuffs, and meals are at set times.

The importance of time is not so obvious when it comes to soul nourishment. Most children let us know when they need our attention, be it with words, body language, or behavior. We do not always have time there and then, and we may ask the child to wait a little while. Sometimes a long time passes before we attend to the child, or we forget that she has tried to make contact. We do not always recognize the problems or consequences that can follow when the spirit does not receive the nourishment it needs at the right moment. The implications of that could show up later in adult life.

Anna Tardos, the daughter of Emmi Pikler, gave a lecture about children at an International Kindergarten Meeting in Belgium in 2000. She made a strong impression on the audience when she spoke about and demonstrated the phenomenon of time. When she sat, she sat. When she stood up, she stood up. She took a lot of time performing these actions and every movement was slow and obvious. We experienced this as a movie in slow motion. Her point was that we have to learn to use more time in everything we do, and do one thing at a time. At home, this is not always possible, but as educators and workers in a kindergarten, we have the opportunity and obligation to give the time the child needs, and create space so that it can be possible. We need to learn the value of slowness and presence, especially for children. In today's society in the Western world, time may be the most valuable commodity we can give children.

How to Create a Good Daily Routine

Parents often feel they do not have enough time for their children. We also experience this in the kindergarten even though our objective is to have enough time. Much has to be done to cover basic needs. The daily routine must be planned based on individual needs and the amount of time considered necessary.

During the first seven-year period, we work with imitation. That means we have to look at ourselves as role models and ask ourselves how we work with rhythm in our own lives. Do we have enough time for an out-breath and rest? Do we exhaust ourselves or burn out coping with daily chores? If that is the case, we should make room for "little pockets" of time, whether for art, meditation, or just a quiet moment. It creates a counterbalance that helps us, and in turn affects the child.

In the kindergarten in the infant/toddler group, we put an emphasis on a good daily routine with meal times, care, sleep, and play. In addition to that, we wash clothes, iron, dust, water plants and do other tasks when we have time. The children need good activities to copy and enough time to absorb them. That is why we choose few activities and allow ourselves plenty of time to do them.

Meals are prepared with the help of the children. Sometimes they are actively involved, while at other times they sit and watch. We make a point of working slowly enough for them to follow the process. They see how the apple is peeled and cut into pieces, or how we mix flour, yeast, and water when baking. They have the opportunity to follow our movements in everything we do. The slower our movements are, the easier they are for them to understand.

Through repeating various chores each day, we create good habits and a safe setting for the children. The way in which each child perceives what is happening and the way in which he will emulate the adult is an individual act. It all depends on the children's own innate abilities and personality and what opportunities they have. With children under three, it is not important to fill the day with too many different activities. At this age they have enough to do with exploring their own abilities and surroundings. They need adults who look after them, giving help where it is needed, while busy doing useful household work. Through this, the child experiences safety and predictability. Unforeseen occurrences do happen in this group, and this is something we need to take into account. Diapers need changing, a nose needs wiping, somebody fell, or someone is crying. Conflict happens, and time is needed for comfort and coaxing before we can resume normal activities.

The rhythm in this group must be primarily to accommodate the children, but it must also be good for the adults. If the children are happy, the adults are content. If the adults are happy, the children flourish. To create a happy day, the prerequisite is that we have enough time. That is reflected in everything we do.

A good daily routine is of paramount importance, especially in autumn when children enter the kindergarten for the first time. There are lots of things for the children to get used to and many new experiences during the course of a day. The proceedings are, for the most part, the same things that happen at home within the family: play, meals, singing, and movement.

A Day in the Kindergarten

Here is an example of a day in the kindergarten, one way of doing it. The model is the toddler group in our kindergarten in Norway, with ten children ages one to three.

7:30 The children arrive and play freely while breakfast is being prepared

8:00 Breakfast

8:30 Free play

10:15 We wash our hands, and have singing and movement in a "ring"

10:30 Lunch

11:00–2:00 Care (changing diapers, preparing for sleep), followed by nap

On waking, small fruit meal and drink, time depending when children wake up, followed by care

1:30–3:00 Free play, outside or inside, depending on season and weather. Some children go home between 2:00 and 3:00.

2:30 Meal for afternoon children

3:30 Free play, or a quiet time, e.g. "reading" a book

4:15 Kindergarten closes

To provide one example from our kindergarten, we will follow two-year-old Pia during a regular day. Pia is the second of three siblings. An older sister is in another section of the kindergarten and the youngest brother is still at home.

It is eight o'clock and Pia arrives with her sister and mother.

A joyful Pia comes through the door and runs straight away to her place in the locker room, sits down and starts taking off her shoes. She wants to put on her slippers by herself and she tries, but needs a little help from her mother before they are on comfortably. Now Pia is ready to go in. The educator carefully opens the door to the main room where breakfast is being served. Mum stands in the doorway and says goodbye. Pia first looks into the room before she turns around to her mother and says "cuddle." Mum gets a cuddle and Pia runs to the table.

At mealtimes, the children have their fixed places. They sit in high chairs around the table. The ones who are able to climb up have permission to do so.

Pia climbs up by herself, but needs a little help to get into the chair.

Once most of the children are in place, we light the candle and everybody sings: "The soil nurtures the little seed; the sun ripens the grain to bread. Dear sun and dear earth, thank you for the gifts on our table. Bless the food." We all hold hands (this is voluntary) and then we start eating.

Pia wants crispbread, and with a little help from the adult, she gets butter and cheese on her piece and starts eating. Pia can manage two slices of crispbread or a slice of regular bread for breakfast. Pia enjoys her food, frequently puts a hand on her neighbour, and often has lots to say.

After breakfast, while we tidy up, is the time for free play.

Pia climbs down from the chair, but needs a little help to get right down onto the floor. She runs to the adult and asks for a dishcloth; she wants to help clean the table. This takes a while and the dishcloth lands on the floor. Then she is in the corner with the dolls, where she has found a knotted doll that she carries around with her. She spots Jacob who has a little cat. Suddenly she really wants that cat. She lets go of the doll and takes the cat from Jacob. This results in screaming and objections. Pia looks impervious and holds on tight. The adults want to help. They find another cat, give it to Pia and together they return the cat to Jacob. It is not quite what Pia wanted, as she'd rather have the cat that Jacob had, so after a bit of coaxing Jacob accepts the new cat and Pia gets to keep the one she wanted. Big smile, and a few seconds pass before Pia returns the cat to Jacob. Now he has two cats and Pia has already moved on to something else.

Free play among the little ones is constantly changing; sometimes it's not possible to follow all the details.

When playtime is over, the adults tidy up before opening the door to the bathroom where everyone has to wash hands.

Pia has found a bag that she has filled with blocks. She is sitting on the floor engrossed in emptying the bag. Then she realizes that the door is open. She leaves the bag and runs into the bathroom to wash her hands. Someone is already standing at the basin. She wants to push him away, but is stopped by the adult. She protests a bit, but accepts having to wait for her turn. At the basin, she lets the water run across her hands and wants to linger there, but there are others waiting behind her. She gets help with drying her hands, then runs into the room again and sits down on the carpet.

One educator helps with the washing of hands and another sits down on the floor to gather the children for song and play, while the third makes sure we have all we need for the meal.

Pia wants to sit close to one of the adults. If someone is already sitting there, she tries to sneak in between so that she is sitting alongside an adult or on the lap. Sometimes this works, but at other times she has to find another place. Most of the time Pia participates in singing, rhymes, and jingles, but at other times it is more fun to hide under the table or run around a bit.

Depending on the child and the situation, we bring the children back to the group, or we let them be and they come back when are they ready. Most of them participate in all the songs and enjoy the repetition. Often we sing the same songs throughout the year. The latest one is "We are traveling to Eating land" and all the children are mentioned by name in the song.

Pia is one of the first to run to the table and sit down. She would prefer to climb up by herself, but needs a little helping hand.

When everyone is in place, an adult walks around and puts a drop of oil (lemon or lavender oil) in the children's hands, while we recite a verse. We massage the oil into the hands; feeling the warmth and smelling the wonderful fragrance and sometimes touching each other's hands.

Pia sits and waits for the oil; she loves the fragrance and warm hands of the adult. She would really like to massage the hands of Preben sitting next to her, but he will not allow it.

The children are wearing large bibs. The candle on the table is lit. We sing the same song we sang at breakfast, "The soil nurtures the little seed." Each child receives a plate of food according to the daily menu and we start eating. We try to keep a peaceful mood at the table, so the adults do not talk more than necessary. There is generally a little prattle going on, as someone is usually repeating and practicing new words just learned.

Pia loves to natter, even though she does not have all the words to express her meaning. However, through her body language and mimicry she succeeds in expressing most things.

Not everyone finishes eating at the same time, but we close off the meal with a verse that expresses, "Thank you for the food, it was very good and we are all satisfied." The children who want to will hold hands. After the meal, they are all cared for before having a nap. This is the time of day where each child gets his or her own time with the adult. One by one, they are taken into the baby care room for a diaper change before a nap. The parents decide whether the child should sleep outside in a pram or inside in a bed.

We try to use as much time as we can for this part of the day. Rhymes, jingles, and songs are used when removing the socks and finding all the toes, or getting the arms through the pullover. If there is time, we use a little oil for massaging legs or arms, which helps foster a sense of well-being and calm before falling asleep.

Pia sleeps inside and she happily follows the adult to the care room to get a clean diaper before lying down. Again, she wants to climb onto the washbasin by herself, which she manages most of the time. With a little help, she gets ready and finds a clean diaper on the shelf. The diaper is changed, but before the long pants are put on, we play a little game with her toes, saying Tip, Tip, Tip every time we touch one of them. We could repeat that over and over again and she would never get tired of it, but now she must sleep.

Each child has a favorite song, which we will sing at this time. Some want the same song twice; others want two different songs or maybe even three different ones. A children's harp tuned to the pentatonic scale D–E–G–A–B–D–E will calm the children and help them sleep. The soft and tender tones of the harp are soporific. Some enjoy being tucked in, while others are happy with a touch on the cheek; others again need a bear hug before settling down. The needs of the individual children vary and as we get to know each and every one, we come to understand them. It is very important that the children bring their own familiar bedding from home, or at least a scarf from Mum or a T-shirt from Dad, especially in the beginning. The smell of home can create a feeling of safety and help to make sleep easier.

Pia has two songs that she wants to hear before going to sleep, "Hum to me, Mummy" and "My guardian angel." Both songs are repeated a couple of times before she gets a cuddle and is then tucked in. She falls asleep easily. Sometimes we need to play on the harp a little, but as a rule, she falls asleep quickly.

Waking up is just as important as falling asleep. Again, we need time for each of the children, in order that they enter peacefully into our world again. They meet us in individual ways when they wake up. Some children are wide-awake straight away and stand up shouting; others stay under the covers and need a long time to waken. The way that we interact with them at this point will often determine the rest of the day. As adults, we feel very privileged to be part of this segment of the child's life, when they come from a deep sleep to an awakened state. Sometimes it is necessary to have children on our laps for a while, to give them enough time to wake up. A touch on the cheek or stroking the back makes it easier for them. One way of "waking" the child is through songs or fingerplays that are connected to rhymes and jingles.

Pia normally sleeps one to two hours every day and she wakes up as peacefully as she falls asleep. Happy as a little bird, she often stands up in the bed waiting to be picked up. She does not need much time before she is ready to be dressed.

Most of the children need help to get dressed. As they grow, they become more independent and want to do it themselves. This can take time, but that is something we can provide. It does not matter if it takes a long time to put on a sock or trousers. Usually when given enough time the child will succeed, but we adults have the tendency to do it for them in order to speed up the process and, therefore we rob them of the chance to do it themselves. Later on, they might not want to dress themselves, although by then we expect them to, and they might need the help they did not want when they were younger.

Pia is a girl who wants to dress herself, but does not always get it right. With a little help from the adult, she has the impression that she has managed by herself and is beaming with satisfaction when all the clothes are on and she can join the other children.

The children also get a piece of fruit and something to drink at this time, before they go out to the others. The time outside depends on how long the child has been sleeping, but everybody gets some time outside before they are either picked up or return inside for the afternoon meal. Weather permitting, they are allowed outside again after the meal and do not return inside until the end of the day.

Pia loves being outside and the first thing she does is to look for her sister. Normally there is mutual joy when they see each other unless big sister Linda is busy with something special. Pia thrives outside in the sand pit, which is the most popular place. An adult is always present. She spends much time digging or filling the bucket with sand. In between, she walks around, but mostly with an adult or big sister. Pia is one of the children who stay until the very end of the day. If she has had a good sleep during the day, she is in a good humor throughout, but if she has had too little sleep, we notice that she is very weary in the afternoon. She is extremely happy when Mum or Dad comes to fetch her and her big sister. She waves goodbye to the educators smiling and happy, and sometimes she gives a hug to those close by.

Weekly and Yearly Rhythms in the Kindergarten

Even though we don't have many different activities for each weekday, every day has its distinctive stamp. In the group for the youngest children the daily routine is made up of cooking and domestic chores and the menu is the distinguishing feature of each day. Cooking is our main activity and we have a bread day, a porridge day, a rice/pasta day, a soup day, and a baking day.

Monday is the walking tour day for the bigger children. The little ones don't participate, but still are very aware that today is excursion day. They watch through the window when the others set off with the adults. Sometimes we hear singing as they pass the window and many of the small children run to the window to have a look. The walking tour day also influences the atmosphere in the building. It is quieter with fewer children in the house. It is also noticeable when we go outside to play. We are on our own.

On the outing day, the little ones have Bread Day. On the menu we have bread and butter and delicious herbal tea.

On Tuesdays we have rice or pasta. Wednesdays is porridge day and also bread baking for the breakfasts. Each day is characterised by cooking that brings warmth and aroma to the room. There are always some children joining the adults at the pots, hence the need for lots of chairs around the place of activity. The adults work peacefully at the table or stove, while the children smell the food cooking and may even get to have a taste.

Thursday is our soup day. We prepare this in conjunction with the older groups. Vegetables are peeled and cut into small pieces with the little ones, while the soup is cooked outside on a fire in an iron pot. The bigger children are outside all the time, helping. As the little children get bigger, they are allowed to be outside while the cooking takes place.

Friday is baking day in all sections of the kindergarten. Every child who wants to can knead, taste, and smell the dough that finally becomes the best bread rolls. With butter they taste scrumptious.

The daily routines are more or less kept throughout the year, but when Christmas is approaching and the routine has been established, we have an "open day" on Fridays. Then all the children are allowed to visit each other across the sections. Most of the time it's the bigger children who come to visit the smaller ones. Only in spring we do see some of the little ones who are going on three venturing across. We take this as a sign that they might be mature enough to be moved up to the kindergarten itself.

The yearly routine is related to what is happening in nature and the cycle of festivals we celebrate. For festivals with the little ones, it's enough to make small changes, such as a flower on the table, a special tablecloth, or a new candle. We may dress up for a party. Perhaps we might have apple juice instead of tea or frozen strawberries in the drinking water, or a soft bun instead of bread. It doesn't take much. We simply mark the occasion by having something we don't normally have and something that is connected to the season. The adults' ceremonious and festive mood is enough for the children. We prefer to wait, and not force experiences on the children that will happen when they are mature enough to move to an older section. The atmosphere is felt by the little children, even though they don't participate. In some of the festivals it is possible for the youngest to be included in age-appropriate ways. For instance, the Thanksgiving meal in autumn is shared by all. At other times we just peep into the big section to see what's going on, and that in itself is rather exciting!

Notes
1   Oxford University Press, *The Compact Edition of the Oxford English Dictionary II* (1971), p. 2537.
2   Steiner, *The Education of the Child* (Great Barrington: SteinerBooks 1996). p. 4.
3   Emmi Pikler and Anna Tardos, *Lass Mir Zeit* (Munich: Pflaum Verlag 2001).

Finding Your Rhythm

Nancy Macalaster, **Susan Weber**, and **Kimberly Lewis**

From Creating Connections (WECAN 2014)

A central element in a relaxed, welcoming parent-child group is its rhythm. Naturally, each teacher will find his or her own rhythm through consideration of her guiding ideas, the setting and its potentials, and experience over time. Most important is that the rhythm meet the children's developmental phase. Clearly, the rhythm of a nursery or kindergarten group is not the rhythm for infants or toddlers! Their shorter "breathing," their need for food at shorter intervals, all need consideration. Additionally, a group leader wants to consider carefully what rhythm and elements within it will provide a truly relaxed experience for today's parents. Again, this is dependent upon the age of the children.

Here follow two rhythms that have been developed over many years of experience in two different settings. We hope they will provide inspiration for other class leaders to develop their own.

A Parent-and-Infant and Parent-and-Toddler class rhythm from Sophia's Hearth Family Center

Here is the rhythm that we have come to over many years that begins with the youngest infants (four weeks) and grows with the children as they grow, adding additional elements and duration. The full group time is one-and-a-half hours. Infant groups meet in the afternoon, children with two naps meet in the afternoon, and once children have moved to one nap, their groups meet in the morning. Flexibility for the youngest children and their evolving sleep patterns is important in offering support for parents.

Arrival and checking in: Time for parents and facilitator to greet one another and for the facilitator to take the pulse of each family. Important aspects include freely initiated play for the children in the intentionally created environment as they are comfortable leaving their parents' sides; time for adult exploration of topics, questions, challenges; time for children to orient themselves to the space and to the others that fill the space for this day.

Lullabies, touching games, gesture games (see Note), *lap games and songs*: This is a progression of offerings designed to meet the infants and toddlers at their developmental stages and is designed to support the the attachment relationship between parent and child and opportunities for imitation by both parent and child. Also included in the intention is support for language development and experience of tone.

Snack: For children 14 months and older, a carefully designed simple ritual offering caregiving through washing each child's hands, slices of fruit to eat (we offer a pear), and water to drink; the snack experience is enriched with more detail as the children grow older.

Observation time: Time to bring adult voices into quiet, creating the space for infants' self-initiated exploration of their own bodies and movements, progressing developmentally as the children grow in mobility. Play then moves more deeply into exploration of the objects around them. This time continues into the toddler months as physical exploration of space and large motor capacities expand, and the children find more engagement in their social relationships with peers.

Sharing: The observation time is brought to a close by the adults' sharing of their observations, their own inner experiences, and perhaps insights into the expressions of individuality of their own children. The observation time diminishes and is eliminated altogether as the children's consciousness grows and adult sharing is no longer appropriate within the context of the parent-and-child group.

Closing: A song or group musical-language activity, possibly a small puppetry offering as the children reach two years of age.

Clean up: Together the parents—with children's engagement as they find interest—return the room to its original arrangement.

Dressing for leaving together: Cleaning up as well as dressing for outdoors provide opportunities for learning by both parent and child, as the facilitating teacher models putting play materials away and caregiving in helping children to dress for outdoors.

Outside play and social connecting between parents in the outdoor play space for walking children.

The sequencing of elements in the rhythm is central; the time for each element can adapt to the group's needs over time.

A Parent-and-Child Class Rhythm from Tucson Waldorf School

Greeting and settling in: Families of such young children arrive when they can. Each is greeted individually, and there is a brief check-in, making sure they are comfortable and that the adults know the others in the room. There is some introduction to the day (the theme, any seasonal craft possibility). The adults find a place to settle while the children either stay near or freely explore the carefully created environment (it's a little different every day based on developmental needs of the children and creative inspiration). The teacher can take time to answer questions that have come up during the week, or to discuss a handout or chosen topic coming from their questions or her own. When the group is new, adult observation of the child for five to ten minutes can be introduced; with more established groups, twenty minutes of observation is encouraged. The teacher handles all conflict during quiet observation. This is the longest part of the morning.

Songs, games, verses: Interactive touching games, riding games, finger plays, seasonal songs/verses or even simple movement and circle games are introduced primarily to the adults. The children are free to enter and exit the activity as desired. The ages and interests of the children are gauged and adjustments made.

Basic Tidying: Almost everything is put away in preparation for a snack, with parents' help. Since children are free to continue to play, a few items are often left out.

Snack: Snack in the parent-and-child class is an opportunity to share, for adult imitation, an example of exquisite care of the child. It's the teacher's opportunity to demonstrate being with each child one hundred percent, one-on-one; to wash their hands with their permission (usually permission is given non-verbally); to offer care without asking questions; to pay attention to each child's uniqueness and preferences; to really be with the children with interest and enthusiasm for who they are. Demonstrate freedom of movement during eating: the table and stools are designed so the children can come and go. Demonstrate boundaries: the food is not to be taken away from the table and children are requested to sit to eat. Demonstrate active participation in their own care: the children soon want to carry their own stools, wash their own hands and face, clean their spot on the table, pour their own water, and put their dishes away at the end. The snack is simple and prepared in advance so it's ready when we sit down.

Tidy-up snack table and transition to outdoors: Children and parents help move from snack to outdoors.

Garden, chickens and good-bye: We are fortunate to have an area on campus for our garden and chickens. We walk out together. The outdoor environment is wholly different from indoors. Except for the infant group, all the classes are invited outdoors. During this time, the teacher tries to do an individual check-in with each parent; it's valuable one-on-one time with them. The parents are most free at this time to visit with each other. The class ends with a good-bye ritual and song.

Note

The gesture games of Wilma Ellersiek form an invaluable tool for the early childhood educator. Four volumes have been translated into English (and one into Spanish) and are available from WECAN.

IV. Activities

As Stephen Spitalny quotes Rudolf Steiner, "The task of the kindergarten teacher is to adjust the work taken from daily life so that it becomes suitable for the children's play activities. The whole point... is to give young children the opportunity to imitate to imitate life in a simple and wholesome way" (see Note).

There are many real life examples of possible activities for a kindergarten class, including practical activities, painting, music, circle songs, circle journeys, games, and of course, creative play. The following essays illuminate aspects of these activities. Of course these are possibilities and not prescriptions, and each teacher and class must find their own rhythms and activities.

Dora Dolder describes handwork in the kindergarten as being one aspect of creative play arising from a child exploring the natural world — for example, the making of "little trees" from pinecones and adorning them with things found in nature, or the fastening of little leaves into a basket or crown. She writes of handwork that arises out of a child's play in nature.

Dolder also writes "the secret of leading a kindergarten class lies in letting the children imitate as many life circumstances as possible. Just as through imitation they learn how to walk, talk and think, so in the kindergarten age the form of life around them should inspire and shape the child's development. Everything that is artificial, devised, or systematically divided into learning steps can only produce something wretched which will later become a weakness in the life forces."

Stephen Spitalny writes about the importance of meaningful domestic work and the warm and purposeful attitude of the caregiver in relation to this work of mending, ironing, cleaning, fixing, washing, cooking, and so forth. Freye Jaffke gives advice about painting with young children, leading them via imitation. She also writes about how the experience of painting with watercolors metamorphoses in the child later in life. Margaret Constantini and Nancy Foster explore music in the kindergarten and the mood of the fifth. Foster also offers advice for creating and maintaining healthy circle activities in the kindergarten.

In the final two essays of this section, Joan Almon writes about profound importance of healthy, creative play. Childhood play has been deeply eroded by media consumption, aggressive scheduling of extra-curricular activities, and early childhood academics. Almon writes about this tragedy and also gives tips for creating the conditions for creative play.

Each of these essays help to give a picture of some of the possibilities for activities that are available for the kindergarten teacher and the children in his or her care.

Note
Rudolf Steiner, *The Child's Changing Consciousness* (Great Barrington: SteinerBooks 1996).

Handwork in the Kindergarten

Dora Dolder

From *An Overview of the Waldorf Kindergarten* (WECAN 1993).
The first known publication of this beloved essay was in *Die Menschenschule* in May, 1971.

Introducing unspoiled children of preschool age to their first primitive handwork is not difficult when one appeals to their imitative capacities and their love of movement. For the will to express itself in practical activities is a fundamental element of their lives. These first, initial works with their hands are different from the handwork lessons of the school in a basic way. In the school, there is a step-by-step building up of practice, learning, and work. In the kindergarten there is a wondrous experimentation, imitation, and new creativity—everything is still play. Activity and fantasy flare forth simultaneously.

The handwork in our kindergarten begins outdoors with the actual experiencing of nature. The garden offers an abundance of possibilities for activity, which appears in the life and play of the children throughout the whole year. The children are always there, wanting to form something with their hands out of blossoms and leaves, with pine needles and grasses, with bits of wood, fruit peels and seeds, with sand, stones, and earth. Yes, even in winter they can model wonderfully with the snow. Just a few of these activities are briefly mentioned here. Through all their senses, the children grasp these seasonal activities from the world around them.

In spring, when the trees begin to bloom and the fir in the middle of the garden throws down its cones, there arises a game which speaks to all of the children, from the wildest to the most placid. We call it "decorating little trees." We search for a handful of fallen blossoms, flowers, grasses, pebbles. It is easy to place these ornaments in the somewhat opened fir cones, and even the little hands which are impatient and unskilled can do it. Around these newly blooming trees, worlds arise. With further natural materials from the garden, pretty little things are tied together, wrapped round, placed within, braided and built. Thanks to the power of their fantasies, everything comes to life, going far beyond what is physically apparent to them through their senses.

An "art" which is especially appealing to the girls is the fastening together of leaves. For this the leaves may not be too delicate, nor the needles of thin twigs too coarse. This work requires care and a fine sense in the fingertips. The joy is then great when the crown, the little hat, or the little basket holds together! And if it tears, one must just quickly gather anew and begin again. This belongs to the experiences of the five- and six-year-olds. One can recognize something of their temperament through this activity. Overall, one must stand by helpfully. One must be attentive and yet enter in as little as possible in order not to interrupt the stream of activity, thus helping along all the broommakers, switchmakers, grassbraiders, chivebundlers, wreathbraiders, and so forth.

In the fall, the colorful environment inspires further lovely things to do. Here are just two examples of occupations of this season which awaken enthusiastic activity: When "grinding flour," the dry, crackling leaves are rubbed in the little fists and are added to water, bringing forth color as if through magic. Are there children who will not, with great enthusiasm, try to find out which colors can be produced by mixing water with leaves, blossoms, nutshells, or wild cherries? They will mix them in water, stir it well, and strain it out. They may laugh and dance with joy if they are allowed to dip snow-white cloths of cotton into these colored waters. Even if their colors are pale, only a shade of brown, a tender green, or a hint of yellow or red, this can be just the right thing, for later one can make little dolls of the cloths and their faces will come alive.

These diverse, loving occupations with objects from nature stimulate the preschool child's imagination and delight in creating. The child perceives, through a still-dreamy empathy, a multitude of forms, colors, and movements that are full of life. One should not overlook the nourishment that comes through the flow of reverence (and which is such a contrast to the stereotyped and unyielding play with interlocking plastic bricks of fixed size and shape). These first experiences of basic human occupations such as searching, picking, wrapping, tying, knotting, sewing, dyeing, and also sowing, harvesting, grinding, and baking, come about through the child's own doing of them. He grows into life through these first combinations of play and work. These occupations grow into real abilities in grade school where the children master the technique of knitting mittens or crocheting. Then a real knowledge can shine forth.

A pure and beautiful material which brings us to ever new uses is plant-dyed sheep's wool. One can play and model with it in a beautiful way that is quite different from working with sand, clay, or beeswax. A basket of colorful wool calls every child's little hand to reach into it and to stay for a while, playing with these fine, gauzy, transparent tufts.

An especially beloved beginning is the making of airy balls. Each child may take one tuft from the basket of colored wool. These can grow, when little fingers carefully pluck the wool, into big, round, transparent clouds, swaying from one hand to the next. After this "snowy evening" or "thunder cloud" play is thoroughly enjoyed, we take the cloud between both hands and begin to round it, to turn it, to form it all around. Everybody will feel the warmth in the palms as slowly the cloud becomes smaller, and it can be made firmer until it becomes a little ball. In the hands it can be rolled and turned, going from one child to another, giving and taking, going back and forth.

This charming, never-tiresome play, accompanied by songs and verses, will capture the youngest children, whereas the more skilled ones will invent more dramatic games. For instance, from the flat hand the little ball is blown off and immediately caught by another child! If one puts the featherlight, round thing in the cup of the hand, with fingers well bent and blows—then brrh!—it cannot get away anymore. It rolls and rolls, turns itself as long as the wind blows, rests for a moment and soon tries to run again. With joyful practice each child finds out that the little ball, breath, and hand obey each other! It is easy to transform these little "turnovers." With the awakened formative force on the inside of the hand, the round thing can be formed into an egg shape. Through the slightest changes, the gesture changes. Small children are especially gifted at this.

If one now picks at the "small end" and twists the wool between the thumb and forefinger into a beak, a little bird will perch on the hand as in a nest. Although it is unfinished, or perhaps because of that, every child will be delighted and begin to converse with it. From fabric or tissue paper we can cut wings and sew them on the back with a few stitches. Finally the whole thing can be strung on a piece of yarn and tied to a twig so that it can be guided like a marionette from above. The child will run and jump with the bird. A rich play will develop from this simple bit of wool, formed by able hands. Many more things can be created out of this little ball by modeling it further, sewing a few stitches to fix the form, wrapping it with spun wool or sewing on some fabric.

It is always interesting to see how well-rounded lambs will roll from one child's hand, while long, prowling foxes will come from another, and plump rabbits or lean dwarves from another. In the moment of creation each little being comes alive, and with the joy of playing they will be placed in further scenes: the lambs belong with a shepherd, a dog, and a pasture; the foxes will need their caves; the rabbits their hollow; and the dwarves their realm with Snow White.

Children who are getting ready for first grade will develop a beginning story and will weave further with objects at hand: colored cloths, rocks, roots, or stumps will be brought together, and a little stage will be built on a table or in a corner. These little figures, which come forth in the spur of the moment, become part of an everyday scene or fantasy-filled picture and bring about the very best of play. Frequently the younger ones are the grateful spectators. Open-mouthed, they live into what is in front of them, moving, speaking, and revealing.

It can happen that the performers (the six- and seven-year-olds) are not satisfied anymore with using sheep's wool tufts for shepherds or kings. Special figures in their proper clothes are devised. This calls for making small dolls. Some new skills are experienced, with which the children help each other. A wool ball as round as the full moon is placed on a rectangular cloth, certainly a self-dyed one. Skillfully it should be put over the round head held in the small fist while a neighbor ties it together with thread. From the cloth that hangs down arms and legs can be knotted.

Children who have been busy all summer with silky, velvety, rough leaves and flowers will now touch and examine the fabrics and make their choices; a shepherd needs a cloak different from a king's, and different not only in color. One cuts an approximate rectangle for these "doll clothes" and makes little folds around the neck; again, a neighbor helps with tying a ribbon around it. A bunch of silk threads or sheep's wool is attached for hair with a few stitches and a knot, then eyes and mouth are drawn on—and there stands a little doll! These simplest little dolls, which only suggest the human shape, are usually loved wholeheartedly, because such a doll can do more things than the most beautiful and expensive dolls that one can buy. It laughs, cries, sleeps, leaps about, becomes ill, practically dies and then returns to school, and so forth. Why can it do all of this in flowing transitions? Because it is not perfect, only suggestive. The possibilities are open. Yes, something is created that must be continuously completed through the child's soul activities, which invent this or that and have to do it because no stiff, finished, forceful appearance of the doll immediately puts a lock on the activity of the child. These dolls have to get yet more outfits with crown and sword; shepherd's purse, hat and crook; apron, broom, umbrella; even a bed and house, etc. During all of this activity one should never get into creating the naturalistic or slipping into criticism.

It is important that one uses beautiful, pure material to awaken the artistic senses and sensibilities. Moreover, it is important that an active adult inspire the creative forces of the children. Yet in the kindergarten, one should not work out of adult perfectionism. To do so will hinder a child who, out of sympathy and vigor, will imitate and be clumsy. Only out of his own experience will the child acquire the right way of doing things. How ingenious and meaningful they often are!

Arising from life and from stories, many toys are made over the year, gifts of primitive workmanship which show the hands of their creators. Even without being very skillful, each child of this age is gifted to do everything in gestures and movements.

The task of the kindergarten today is to prevent the drying out of this seedlike lightness and smoothness in the limbs through too early an experience in useful, "unpoetical" handwork. The educational principles of example and imitation serve as key and path to an appropriate kindergarten education. The secret of leading a kindergarten class lies in letting the children imitate as many life circumstances as possible. Just as through imitation they learn how to walk, talk, and think, so in the kindergarten age the form of life around them should inspire and shape the child's development. Everything that is artificial, devised, or systematically divided into learning steps can only produce something wretched which will later become a weakness in the life forces.

Practical Activities with the Young Child

Stephen Spitalny

From *Gateways* Newsletter Issue 62 (WECAN 2012)
This essay was adapted from Stephen's self-published book, *Connecting with Young Children*.

> *The task of the kindergarten teacher is to adjust the work taken from daily life so that it becomes suitable for the children's play activities. The whole point... is to give young children the opportunity to imitate life in a simple and wholesome way.*
> —Rudolf Steiner, April 1923[1]

Imitation is the natural learning mode for the young child. Rudolf Steiner described it as a sort of bodily religion arising from a sense of joy and wonder with all experiences and sensations. The young child, so recently arrived into a physical body from the spiritual world, loves all he meets in the world. The adult, whether caregiver, kindergarten teacher, or parent, has therefore a huge responsibility since the child is molding himself out of his experiences, out of what and who is imitated. Therefore it is incumbent on the adults to create an environment of objects, people and activities that we would be happy to have taken up in imitation by the child. An environment that nurtures the child includes crucial elements that create form and order in the developing child: rhythm in daily life activities, safe and healthy boundaries, and adults' consistency in maintaining the boundaries and rhythm.

Young children naturally are most active in the doing, the willing realm of soul life. They are drawn to adults' work activity, especially when the adult is truly engaged in meaningful working. I experience that when a chair breaks, or we are making lunch—meaningful work that needs to be done—then the older children in kindergarten are attracted to participating and helping, while the younger ones exactly imitate the activities in their play. Young children are drawn to the activities of real workers and craftspeople like the blacksmith, carpenter, spinner, plumber, and so on. The experiencing of these activities is body-building for the child, as well as an example of focused adult will for the child's will forces. A young child who experiences, and even does, various types of real work is given a blessing of many images to incorporate into his or her development. As Joop van Dam writes, "her body becomes an instrument with all kinds of tones and colors. This is a body the individuality can enter and live in for a lifetime."[2]

When the adult fully engages in her own work, her will is engaged and it is a sort of invitation to the imitative will of the young child. There are certain qualities of this "real" work for the adult to develop. It is meaningful if you do the work whether or not the children participate. If you are simply doing something so that the children will join in, and then when they don't you put away materials and tools, then clearly it not something important that needs to be done. It is also an important quality to model that you are planted in one location while focused on the work, rather than a little work, a little roaming the room, a little more work and a little more roaming. This calls for being prepared when you set to the work—all needed tools and materials are at hand, as well as tools and materials for the children who choose to imitate your activity.

There is so much to do to care for a kindergarten home: washing, cooking, sewing, ironing, planting, weeding, pruning, repairing chairs, tables, dolls and other toys, making toys for the kindergarten, and more—not as activities that are done to give the children projects, but work related to the care and improvement of our kindergarten home.

All learning involves an engagement of the will. Learning requires effort. With young children, the will is directly connected to sensory activity, without the mediation of thinking or understanding—this is the process of imitation. It is a special art to engage the child's interest and attention, an art that adults must learn. When the adult takes up the tasks that need to be done with joy and with enthusiasm, with his or her own engaged will, then the child's attention is more likely to be present in the task as well. Tasks attended to with care and love engage the child's interest much more than tasks done in a disinterested or resentful way.

One's inner attitude to the work at hand is so important. Do domestic activities conjure thoughts and feelings of drudgery, of chores? If the adult is begrudgingly doing the task, the attitude that the task is unpleasant is passed on to the child. Also, if the adult's heart is not in it, the adult's will is not truly engaged. So the children experience an adult who doesn't want to do a task, but is doing it with just a part of herself involved. Even the name "chore" has a connotation of something one doesn't want to, but has to do. So consider the language used. "Task" or "job" seem to have a nicer ring to them.

We are working with the reality of educating the will of the young child. It is will education to make a toy while the child is watching. Will education is making a wooden crate for kindergarten while the children are watching, and perhaps some are even helping. The child learns that first of all, it can be done. Human beings can make things, and the children can even make things. We are continuing the work of the creator beings in ways that are easily experienced. "Oh, we make stuff if we need it."

And the adult taking raw materials and making something from them is an example for the child's imagination. This type of activity stimulates the child's imagination into creative mobility. The imagination resonates with the activity of making when encountering it. This resonance works deeply into the child's soul and physical body. It stimulates the formative forces working in the brain and works deeply into the developing breathing and circulatory systems. The activities of making nourish and energize the young child's will forces.

When an adult makes a toy in front of the child, a doll or wooden animal for example, the child's will is stimulated by the creating power of the will of the adult. Making is will activity, and is a dwindling art. We all can be makers! Through making we immerse the young child in our engaged will.

One role of the adult is to welcome the child into the community of human work by doing work as example and with the young children. The adult's work is the tasks that need attention; the children's work is their play. In kindergarten one day I was ironing and folding the napkins and placemats. "Steve, will you be a dog with us?" "I'll be a dog, but I'll be a dog right here doing the ironing." "Okay." The adult can be present, near the child's play, and engaged in adult activities. This example of working can be a stimulus for the child's play. The adult may of course initiate play, but needs to be aware of his or her role and the effect on the children, and know when to leave the children to play on their own terms. Children should not depend on adults to participate in their games, nor on adult attitudes. Free play will come from the children's own imagination, inspired by adults' working, songs, and stories, as well as everyday events.

If the adults are engaged in calm, purposeful activity, the children are likely to imitate it in their play, or even want to participate in the activity. Mending, sewing, washing, sweeping, and repairing toys are among the activities for the teacher to be involved in while the children explore the room, play, draw, and so on. When conversation is kept to a minimum—both with adults and with the children—the children can be more deeply engaged with their play. The atmosphere created by adults engaged in such purposeful activity creates a protective and nurturing environment for the child in which he can either help with the chores, or explore the world through play.

Janet Kellman once spoke about the myth of quality time. What is "quality time?" Many adults think "special" time going to "special" places is more valuable than other activities; it has more connecting going on. Quality time really is measured by how truly present one is with the children while one is supporting their developmental needs, the needs of the developing soul, etheric body, and will of the young child. Connecting with the children while immersing them in life activities, activities that nurture and sustain life, is a powerful support for the child's etheric and will development.

If one of our wooden chairs in kindergarten breaks, we fix it. We mend what needs repair, from chairs to dolls to children's pants and aprons. Whatever needs fixing, I always attempt to fix it myself before I call in a "paid expert." Perhaps if I don't have the tools or skills, I ask a parent to help, and have it done when the children are present.

IV. Activities

When something breaks, usually the children first try to fix it themselves. There always are one or two repair specialists who actually have the skills for many types of repairs. If those children can't do the repair, they bring it to me. We have created a culture of fixing and mending. One aspect of that is to acknowledge the situation right away, saying "We will mend this," even if it will be a while, or even another day, before repairs can begin. I always make sure to get to the repair project when the children are present, and not let it slide and end up forgotten.

Steiner said that it is important to bring life activities into the kindergarten, to surround the young children with real life. These life activities, life-giving and life-sustaining activities such as cooking, cleaning, gardening, and "housework," are nurturing the developing etheric body, the life body, of the child which will not, in a sense, be born until age six or seven. Life activities support the development of the life senses, the foundation for truly social life.

The whole point of a preschool or kindergarten is to give young children the opportunity to imitate life in a simple and wholesome way. This task of adjusting life as one carries it out in the presence of the child in a meaningful, purposeful way, according to the needs of each child, is in accordance with the child's natural and inborn need for activity and is an enormously significant educational task.

What are real life activities? They are real and they are life-based, need-based activities. At home or in the kindergarten, there are always domestic chores to be done: washing placemats and napkins; hanging them to dry; ironing, preparing and cooking meals, cleaning up after meals, weeding, pruning, raking leaves, and on and on. Both indoors and outdoors, there is plenty of work necessary for the maintenance of home and garden life. When we engage our adult will forces on this meaningful work, both the developing will and the developing etheric body of the children are strengthened. The children benefit from being surrounded by loving adults engaged in meaningful work such as housekeeping activities. The taking up of household tasks gives the children a sense of calm purpose and meaningful work. These activities help to create a sheath of warmth and protection around the children in our presence. And when the adult is meaningfully and joyfully engaged in work, the children play more peacefully, creatively and cooperatively.

Adults engaged in the domestic arts (cooking, cleaning, building) provide real work examples that stream into the play of children and are very much in need because of the children's widespread lack of experiences of housework done in the home. Kindergarten has to take on some aspects of what the home once stood for; the home is no longer the heart center of the family, but has become a resting place in between errands, activities and appointments, to which parents and children are often on their way. Waldorf early childhood centers more and more have become a replacement for certain aspects of the traditional home. They provide a place where there is enough time for housework to be lovingly taken up and accomplished with participation from children. Providing a home-like environment for children gives them the opportunity to do things out of their own initiative. And the children need time, enough time. We need to create the feeling of

"There is no rush. There is time to play."

Domestic activities, housework, taking care of the surroundings: all of these take us out of the personal and into the social realm. Caring for one's surroundings is a social gesture. We work together and for each other! The basis of our community life is the home, and social responsibility starts there.

Linda Thomas, whose cleaning company cares for the Goetheanum in Dornach, Switzerland writes:

> *There exists a great difference between cleaning and caring. When we clean, we remove dirt, and the result of cleaning sometimes does not even last five minutes. At the Goetheanum, you have barely cleaned the hallway, and already someone walks over it, leaving footprints everywhere. The same goes for parents with young children. For this very reason, many people consider cleaning a frustrating and unrewarding activity, a troublesome necessity.*
>
> *Yet, we should try to do this task with our full awareness, with all our love. Once we learn to consciously penetrate each little corner with our fingertips, then cleaning takes on a nurturing aspect and becomes caring. What is so wonderful about it is that the result of caring lasts considerably longer than the result of removing dirt! When we have taken special care of a room, the little bit of fresh dirt that is brought in is barely disturbing—one can live with it. The glow is totally different from areas where layers of dirt and grime have built up. Lately, a new cleaning culture, which we should really try to prevent, is trying to establish itself. There is supposedly a spray for everything—you spray and you wipe away—not much water is needed! One does indeed remove a small quantity of dirt, but instead of caring for a surface, you leave a chemical layer behind, containing quantities of dissolved dirt.*
>
> *While caring for a room, we do not only come into contact with the physical world. The whole atmosphere changes, the room is filled with light. Children react especially strongly to this transformation, and they also seem to perceive the change directly.*[3]

How can we redeem housework, the image of housework as drudgery, so we provide a positive example for the children? We can find joy in the work and express it in our movement and our gestures. We can bring order and planning to our work and finish it. Some projects take more than one time to complete, but persistence over time is important for the child to observe. All of these, though, are self-discipline on the part of the adult, and hard work at first.

We can cultivate an attitude of looking for work that needs doing. That is a real gift to the children. Rather than, "What should I do with the children today?" we can say, "What needs to be done, and how do I do it?"

Taking care of our bodies and our surroundings are most important. For me, craft projects are not as high a priority, though a craft project as a part of the preparation for a festival becomes a meaningful element in the life of home or kindergarten—for example, the making of a card for a birthday, or gifts for Mother's Day. But a project "to give the children something to do" is not so meaningful. Crafts and projects with the children can support creativity and motor skill development, but they don't exercise the will unless they come from the child's initiative. If the adult has a sewing project that needs doing—perhaps a cloth has torn—then of course you will have extra materials available as the children will also want to sew. And you can help them along as needed. Five- and six-year-olds will sometimes want to make something to bring into their imaginative play, perhaps a doll or puppet. But then it comes out of the child engaging herself, out of her own initiative, and based on imitation, the will is exercised and strengthened.

Domestic activities anchor the child in the world, both the physical world and the social world in which we live. Our housework provides a healthy example for imitation. We are helping to make the children truly capable and helping them toward their future with strong will forces.

It happens from time to time that a child is out of sorts and is not able to play constructively, either by herself or in the social setting. A magical cure for that child is helping out with some real work that needs doing. Folding the laundry or cutting the vegetables is an opportunity for the child to get grounded into the work, and the obstacle to relaxed and peaceful play they may have been experiencing dissolves. A few minutes later one hears, "I want to go play now." The adult can feel that the child is really ready to play. Her fantasy or imagination has woken up again from a small dosage of meaningful work.

Notes

1   Rudolf Steiner, *The Child's Changing Consciousness* (Great Barrington: SteinerBooks 1996).

2   Joop van Dam, "Understanding Imitation Through a Deeper Look at Human Development" in *The Developing Child: The First Seven Years*, Susan Howard, ed. (WECAN 2004), p. 105.

3   Linda Thomas, "Chaos in Everyday Life: About Cleaning and Caring," *Gateways* Newsletter, Issue 45 (WECAN 2003).

About Painting and Human Development through Art

Freya Jaffke

From *An Overview of the Waldorf Kindergarten* (WECAN 1993)

Human speech surrounds the newborn child from its first day. It creates an atmosphere permeated with spirit into which the child "breathes himself." The child imitates, listens, absorbs, and at the same time forms himself. Only through this can he become human and express his personal self through the word. Similarly, and in an equally important way, art—the highest expression of the soul-spirit forces of mankind—works on the developing child. In order for the child to develop his human capacities, an "artistic environment" is needed from the very earliest days of his life. First, the child takes in his environment; then he works upon it himself. Here it is especially important that the meeting with art is not only a gift offered by the educator, but also, at the same time, a calling forth of activity from the child. The cultivation of art awakens the hidden, creative, building activities and the soul-forces of the child. In this way each artistic activity calls forth a different perception through the senses.

In working with children of preschool age, it is necessary to create from the beginning an environment that takes into account the child's sensitivity to good artistic quality (colors, forms, wall decorations, sounds, toys, etc.). In this way a deeper effect is achieved with this age group than will be achieved through "art education" offered in a few spare hours.

It is clear that at this age the practical activities need some specific methods. Even the small child can find his way into a variety of artistic realms and work with them, but not with the purpose of getting specialized training. Certainly one does not want to begin preparing the child for a later profession such as musician, painter, or sculptor. The possibilities for artistic activities for children include modeling with beeswax or clay, painting, movement games which carry a strong musical-rhythmic quality, and playing on simple string instruments such as children's harp or kanteles.

But the most important point to consider in these efforts is the following: at this early stage the child takes in everything with his total being (as an entire body, soul and spirit).

What appears here in its embryonic form must appear at a later stage of development one way or another. Along with this, one must realize that in the thinking or social realms, for example, there will appear capabilities but also deficiencies, and their connection with the early artistic activities is not easily seen. There exists in human life, in addition to the abilities that develop in a linear, step-by-step progression, those abilities which appear in various developmental stages in a whole new way through metamorphosis.

In the following paragraphs, the example of painting is presented. For the reasons given above, this is an experience which should not be viewed as leading to a finished form, but rather it should be assessed as an experience which leads to abilities which can be transformed throughout the child's life.

Water Color Painting

Materials

- wooden boards, 50:35 cm (about 20"x14")
- painting paper
- flat brushes about 24 mm (1") wide
- artists' water color paints
- small jars for diluted colors
- water jars
- sponges
- small jars for stirring the paints

The children particularly love to help prepare the painting table. They are always interested in observing every job of the grown-ups and like to be active by helping with such activities. Now the tables must be covered with an oil cloth. The water jars must be filled and distributed. Next to every jar a sponge is laid, on which the wet brushes can be dabbed. The colors will be diluted in small jars and smoothly stirred, then poured into the color jars, and these are then placed on the table. The painting paper (absorbent paper, not too thin) is dipped in a water tub and carefully smoothed (well-fastened) onto a previously moistened paint board. Now the painting can begin.

Understandably such a joint preparation with the children is only possible when the group has no more than twenty to twenty-five children. (In Waldorf kindergartens this is generally the rule.) It is especially helpful if one has not separated the children by age, but has rather combined them in mixed-age groups (from three to six years). Then the different abilities of the children can be well-satisfied by the different activities of the watercolor process. While the three- and four-year-olds are fully satisfied when they can stir the colors and pour them into the glasses, the five- and six-year-olds take on more tasks (for example, gathering together all the supplies which are needed for the preparation, cleaning the painting table, washing out and drying the glasses, and cleaning up). The children notice the repeated sequence of events each time the group paints.

The Painting Experience

Without a previous call to order on the part of the grown-ups, which results in a consciousness of the activity, and without a presentation to the children or the introduction of a theme, the children dip their brushes in the color and its flowing trace is followed along the paper. The limits of the three primary colors, red, yellow, and blue, open to the children a color scale filled with nuances of unbelievable riches which they themselves can discover. Particularly for the four- and five-year-olds there is a joy of discovery connected with this process. For when the single colors flow together in various places and mix, there appear the "between colors" such as green, violet, or brown.

Alongside the color play on the paper, which the children frequently experience with words of wonder and joy, there is also the changing color of the water, in which the brush is well-washed, which plays a great part in the painting. When the whole paper is painted and the colors glow and shine through the watery element, there enters into the child a moment of great satisfaction, which often flows over to the free play following the painting. The picture itself is no longer important to the child when it has been put on he rack to dry.

The five-and-a-half- and six-year-old children come to the experience differently. Already before they dip the brush into the first color, they often have an image of a definite color they wish to use or of objects such as trees, castles, or rainbows which they would like to paint. The combination of liquid color and damp paper does not allow one to paint solid outlines, which is all to the good for further development of the fantasy forces. It often occurs that the children add a new color to the already started form, calling forth a new sense-association in their fantasy. While they are painting or when they are finished, these children will gladly tell the grown-ups or another child something about their picture—which color they especially like or what content they discover in the painted picture.

Even for the three-year-olds painting in this manner is a joyful experience. It is most important that one does not expect them to master the individual techniques such as, for example, washing the brush before they place it in a new color. It is also not possible for them to guide the brush in a directed manner. Often they move their brushes enthusiastically or timidly back and forth on the paper, and one perceives that for them the movement and the trace of color is the most important aspect of painting. Mostly the three-year-olds are satisfied with one color such as red, and they are only finished with painting when the glass of color is empty. When they get another color as well they do not add it by placing it next to the first color on the paper, but rather they paint over the first color. It is the same with a third color. The result is then a dark, undifferentiated surface, and the three glasses of color can no longer be distinguished one from the other regarding the color of their contents. If one begins with a single color and gradually increases the number of colors, then these children learn after a short time to paint laying one color next to another rather than painting over the colors.

The three-year-old children are mostly very still while painting and they are busily engaged with it, especially when each has his own paint jars to use. The four- and five-year-old children happily share with one another, in a more or less impulsive way, when something special develops on their paper. Among the five- and six-year-old children, the quiet, industrious mood again prevails in a thoughtful, careful manner. Occasionally while they are painting they will have exchanges with other children of their age regarding the colors or content of their paintings.

Learning to Paint through Imitation

The pre-school child best learns to paint as he learns every other skill—through imitation of the adult. Therefore it is most advantageous for the child to watch the mother, kindergarten teacher, or older sibling paint. He grasps it in the way described as appropriate for his age if no instruction is connected with it. Either he wants to paint right away while the adult is painting (the three-year-old) or he wants to paint by himself at another time (the five- and six-year-old). All of the technical tasks closely associated with painting, such as setting up and cleaning up the materials, will also become familiar through imitation of the adult. All the reservations about the amount of work involved are dissolved through the helpful activity of the children.

If the adult is careful that each time he dips into a new color, he first washes the brush in the water jar and wipes it on the sponge, then the child will follow this sequence more and more in the same way. For every healthy child has a strong inclination to go along with or imitate in fantasy play every deed or movement he sees in his environment. Therefore certain deeds of the adults work themselves much deeper into the young child than do words of explanation calling for the child's understanding.

With the beginning of the school years, this free fantasy-filled approach to color is replaced by a more directed experience of painting led by the teacher's words. This implies that the assignment of the teacher is presented with fantasy-filled word and usually in connection with what is occurring in the lessons of that time. The development of painting will progress through definite steps, and everyone will view the results.

Metamorphosis in Later Stages of Life

When an adult in a conversation brings forth his arguments, experiencing the different responses of his partner and at the same time allowing herself to be influenced by these responses, then she owes this capacity in part to her experiences as a young child with color and brush, which were her unconscious teachers.

What the adult knows as logic is always the inner result of a purposeful sequence of steps which the small child was able to take in from her environment through imitation. The inner order in the sequence of steps of painting insures a "useful" result. In adult thinking, the careful connection of individual steps leads to a sure conclusion.

One who at an early age has learned to pay attention to the strength or delicacy of color and to gradations in applying it will later find it easier to apply the same soul capacities in social institutions, for example in self-assertion and in acquiescence.

Painting includes processes such as being careful, paying attention, waiting, following the course of the work, experiencing the laws of color mixing, and applying color in varying strengths. All of these activities give ever-renewed stimulus to the gradually awakening soul of the child, helping him to grasp his physical body and make his sense organization and his limbs ever more responsive.

Naturally, the child is not conscious of this. He does not reflect on what he is doing, but lives intensively in the activities. In this way he has experiences at deep levels which can wait there to be grasped consciously in later stages of life and to find expression in an ability to lead his own life. These effects reveal the true human justification for artistic endeavors in the pre-school. Art is not an aesthetic add-on to "real life," but as an exercise of continual striving, can become the foundation of a truly human mastery of life.

Music in the Waldorf Kindergarten

Margret Constantini

From *An Overview of the Waldorf Kindergarten* (WECAN 1993)

Editor's Note: In his lectures and books, Rudolf Steiner describes a series of "Post-Atlantean" cultural epochs which include: Old Indian; Old Persian; Chaldean-Babylonian-Egyptian; Graeco-Latin; Fifth Post-Atlantean (the current cultural epoch).

One reference for understanding these cultural epochs is Rudolf Steiner's *Outline of Occult Science*, Chapter 4, "The Evolution of the Cosmos of Man."[1]

What is meant by musical education in the kindergarten? Certainly one understands that the musical abilities with which each child is born, but which often rest hidden within, must be guided and nurtured. Then the musical element proves to be a rich source of strength for the entire life of every single child.

Now one can also say that every child is born a musician. There is no unmusical child. This can be seen in the child's joy of his own movement. But when present-day children come to kindergarten at the age of four years, their musical abilities are often already buried under the noises of the environment, the many different machines all around them, canned radio music, the impression of television, and so on. It is truly hard labor for the teacher to free the child's musical abilities—often it is no longer possible! That is what it is all about: to make the ears of the children, which have been inundated by noise, more receptive to the gentle tones of music that are appropriate for them.

In doing this, it is important above all that the teacher strives to permeate the kindergarten with the musical element—not just with the music itself. I include in this a harmonious arrangement of the room: a use of color shades which are alive on the walls and objects in the room; the use of toys which are carefully selected made of suitable materials and that stimulate imaginative play; and the well-structured rhythm of each day. However, it is especially important that the people around the child live in harmony amongst each other. Of course music itself must be nurtured in living experiences. Because the child is an imitative being, it is the task of the teacher to find an approach suitable for the child. To begin with, the teacher needs to develop a clear, steady speaking and singing voice of her own, worthy of being imitated.

In order to find a starting point for the musical education of the young child, one would have to study music history in the various cultural periods because every child experiences all the cultural epochs in a shortened form in his development—precisely so in the area of music.

It is very difficult to comprehend the changes in the cultural epochs, because music is a question of Man's inner experience and therefore cannot be grasped in physical manifestation. In Rudolf Steiner's lectures on music and eurythmy, he refers to many things which personalities such as Julius Knierim and Heiner Ruland among others have worked out. For example, in his lecture, "The Inner Nature of Music and the Experience of Tone," Rudolf Steiner refers to the Atlantean Epoch where musical perception was related to the seventh (the interval between the tonic and the leading note).[2] Heiner Ruland has now precisely described in his book, *Expanding Tonal Awareness*,[3] how the Nature-Seventh-Music was built up, how it sounded, and what effect it had on man in the Post-Atlantean Epoch of Ancient India. Before this time man was not capable of hearing tones set apart because he was a part of world activities, and the music of the spheres was spread around him like a mantle. It is important for us to know that this Nature-Seventh-Music existed outside of the human being, that it moved circling outside man. It was experienced more in ecstasy, so to speak. One could say it was music that pushed man outside of himself.

Also in the ancient Persian Epoch (from 5067 B.C. to 2907 B.C.), where the musical experience of man was related to the sixth (the interval between the tone and the Submedian), music still lay outside of conscious comprehension.

The next stage in musical development lies in the Egyptian Epoch (from 2507 B.C. to 747 B.C.), in which the interval of the fifth (interval between tonic and dominant) could be experienced by man. This was the period in which man lost his natural relationship to the spiritual world, but thereby slowly became capable of consciously comprehending the earthly world through his senses. The laws governing the course of the sun and the constellations with the twelve signs of the zodiac revealed themselves to man. Everything that was formerly infinity and that lay outside of the earthly realm now became comprehensible, capable of being experienced in space. This stage in the cultural development of man corresponds to the birth of our children today on our earth. When they are born into our world, they come out of the unconscious-spiritual world and want to enter into the conscious world, but at first, perceive the world unconsciously with the senses.

Now this is all reflected in the experiencing of the fifth. A breathing in and out of what weaves musically around man begins and grows in him as sense impression. In experiencing the fifth, man touches the earthly world. In the Egyptian Epoch the fifths sounded as if they were vibrating around a central tone. The central tone was known as the sun tone, the tone which lay closest to the sun, that had the brightest sound, the tone by which man oriented himself, from which a great force emanated. In present times, all our music orients itself around one single note, the "A," which no longer emanates the great force of former times, but is used for tuning instruments. Listening to the "A" one has the brightest tone perception. Couldn't one assume that this central Sun tone has remained right through to the present day as our "A" note? Whenever this Sun tone "A" was experienced as a central tone, then one fifth vibrated geometrically upwards and one downwards; the central tone lay in the middle.

This is where our musical education of the small child begins. The ninth, which results from the two fifths around the center tone, is the tone-realm of the young child. All songs with these two intervals swinging around the central note are called pure fifth songs (in German, reine Quntenlieder).

Now one can again raise or lower by a fifth. Because those tones are beyond the capacity of the human voice they have to be shifted by one octave into the previously described realm of the ninth. Then we get the tones that we need for music in the mood of the fifth.

You reach the seven tones of the children's harp if you let resound the upper and lower tone of the two fifths again.

Now one should describe briefly the different between music in the mood of the fifth and pentatonic music. The music in the fifth is pentatonic in so far as it also does not contain half steps. But the pentatonic music is based on five tone systems which even when the tonic note itself is missing, suggesting the feeling of a tonic note by using upward or downward scales or sequences. Almost all folk cultures had pentatonic scales, which has this floating sound because of the absence of half steps. The pentatonic forms the bridge between music in the mood of the fifth and music based on the tonic.

Because we as adults are no longer living in the Egyptian Epoch today, it is not too easy for us to immerse ourselves in the mood of the fifth so that the small child can imitate our example. We adults have difficulties with songs in the mood of the fifth because they are still objective and do not speak to our souls or emotions. A lot of practice is needed. But practice is rewarded. The mood-of-the-fifth songs which the children can sing right away have a healing effect. The children become calmer, quieter, and begin to play harmoniously; their behavior becomes more balanced.

About the Use of Instruments in the Kindergarten

The singing voice of the teacher is certainly the most important instrument in the kindergarten, because the child can directly imitate it. In practice it is important that one always really begins on the same tone and sings in tune, because in this way the child learns to orient himself musically.

In regard to the use of instruments, each kindergarten will be a little bit different. But in almost all Waldorf kindergartens the Choroi children's harp is used because it possesses a gentle tone and works intensely on the children. As soon as an adult strums the strings gently, the children become quiet and listen. Because the children's harp has no resonating body it is most in keeping with the mood of the fifth. The instrument should be played by the teacher. If the child wants to strum over the strings once, then of course, it should be allowed. On certain occasions, the kantele or lyre are also played in the kindergarten.

The pentatonic Choroi recorder is used by the kindergarten teacher when, for example, the shepherd plays his flute or when the children are doing a little dance.

IV. Activities

At certain times the children are also given an "instrument" in the hands, which they are allowed to play in an informal and free sort of imitation. For example, in the circle time when the birds in the forest are calling, the woodpecker gets a finger cymbal, the nightingale a glockenspiel, the cuckoo a cuckoo's flute. The children are allowed to use bells often: when the first flower rings in the spring, the lily of the valley blossoms in the forest, the bell flowers are swaying, or when during Advent the bells call Mary to come to the heavenly kingdom.

The question whether one may also sing the "usual" diatonic songs in the kindergarten I would like to answer simply, "yes," above all because they are almost always traditional songs, folk songs, circle games, or Christmas songs, which in a certain way create a musical connection to the activities at home and the outside world. Also each cultural epoch is a preparation for the following cultural epoch.

The music in the mood of the fifth, however, is most in keeping with the child's development and has a healing effect that counteracts the copious inundation of "musical noise" of our times.

Notes

1. Rudolf Steiner, *An Outline of Occult Science* (Anthroposophic Press 1972). Also published as *An Outline of Esoteric Science* (Great Barrington: SteinerBooks, 1997).

2. Rudolf Steiner, *The Inner Nature of Music and the Experience of Tone*, Lecture 5 (Great Barrington: SteinerBooks 2015).

3. Heiner Ruland, *Expanding Tonal Awareness: A Musical Exploration of the Evolution of Consciousness—from Ancient Tone Systems to New Tonalities* (London: Rudolf Steiner Press 2014).

The Mood of Early Childhood: Music in the Kindergarten

Nancy Foster

From *The Mood of the Fifth* (WECAN 2013)

This essay considers mood-of-the-fifth music in the context of the early childhood experience as a whole, and how this music supports the overall mood we wish to create in the early childhood classroom.

For inspiration in our work with music for early childhood, we may ponder Rudolf Steiner's statement that "song is an earthly means of recalling the experience of pre-earthly existence."[1] With this statement in mind, we will feel a responsibility to bring music into the early childhood setting not only with joy, but also with respect. How can we fulfill this responsibility?

Just as a plant has meaning and reality only in the context of earth and cosmos, so music and movement may best be considered in the context of the early childhood experience as a whole, by recalling the mood we are seeking to create in our classroom. We wish to provide an atmosphere in which the child can feel truly recognized as a being who has come into earth existence from a sojourn in the spiritual world. This is, of course, not spoken to the children, but the recognition is there in our thoughts, words, and deeds.

It is also our intention to nurture the quality of early childhood sometimes called dream-consciousness—a whole-hearted devotion to all that is in the surroundings, an un-self-conscious participation in life.[2] Rudolf Steiner tells us that ". . . the inner soul-being of the child, with all that he has brought down from pre-earthly life out of the world of soul and spirit, is entirely devoted to the physical actions of the other human beings around him. And this relationship can be described in no other way than as a religious one."[3]

The child's religious devotion is not the quiet inwardness we associate with the adult's religious devotion; certainly it can be a quiet condition, but it can equally well be lively and boisterous. It is the whole-hearted immersion in all that surrounds the child, which is the characteristic quality we wish to encourage and support, in contrast to an analytical, self-aware approach in which the child senses a separation from the surrounding environment, a state of consciousness appropriate to a later stage of development.

We can support the child's immersion in the life around him or her—the quality of dream-consciousness or religious devotion—in a number of ways. In working with imitation instead of instruction, we allow the child to enter into activities in a natural way. The child may imitate the adult outwardly—for example, making the same gesture, or the child may simply absorb the gesture without doing it, but later imitate the gesture. For example, parents often tell us that their child has done all the circle gestures at home, though at school the child did not seem to participate at all. The child will also, however, imitate the inner activity or mood of the teacher. Our heartfelt involvement in whatever we do is taken up by the child, whether or not the child is outwardly imitating us.

We can further nurture dream-consciousness by bringing archetypal activities of life into the kindergarten, allowing plenty of time for creative fantasy play, and providing an environment of beauty and order. We seek to provide a rhythm for the early childhood day which will make dream-consciousness possible. This rhythm, most often described as in-breathing and out-breathing, could also be compared to a pleasantly rolling landscape. Hills and valleys are necessary and life-giving; but we hope to avoid dramatic precipices! Finally, our choice of music can be an important source of joy and of a healthy breathing rhythm, and a support to the child's natural tendency to enter activity with devotion.

Music and the Consciousness of the Young Child

The history of music is also the history of the incarnation and evolving consciousness of humanity. The human being's changing experience of self in relation to the cosmos finds an expression in the changing experience of music. In essence, it can be said that the human experience of music, and human consciousness itself, have moved from an expanded, less-incarnated condition, to one that is more contracted, more deeply incarnated.

Rudolf Steiner tells us[4] that in the time he designates as the Atlantean epoch, human beings were formed in such a way that the substance of their bodies was much more delicate than it later became. The human form was still mobile, and human beings were still given up to an experience of unity with the cosmos. The soul element stood in a different relationship to the world than that which we experience today. Human beings had no consciousness of the self as a separate entity; they experienced themselves to be "in god" rather than "in myself." At this time, Steiner tells us, music consisted of intervals of the seventh; human beings actually could not experience smaller intervals.

Major Seventh:

In the experience of the seventh, human beings felt transported into the realm of the gods. They did not experience themselves as making music; rather, their experience was, "I live in music made by the gods."

In the Post-Atlantean age human beings began to descend more deeply into the physical body, and the interval of the seventh began to be "faintly painful." They still felt at one with the gods, but to a somewhat lesser degree, so that the experience shifted from "I am in god" to "god is in me." During this time, human beings developed a capacity for, and preference for, experiencing a sequence of fifths.

Sequence of Fifths Intervals:

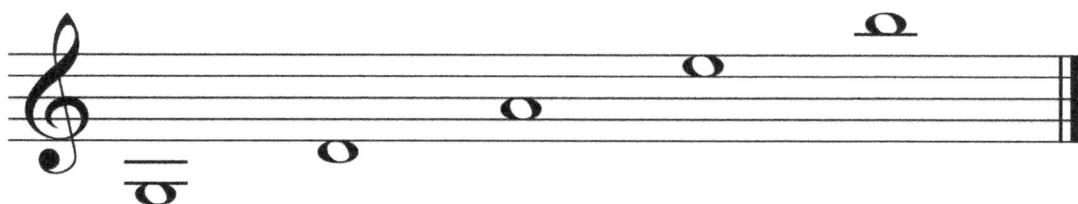

In the interval of the fifth, human beings still experienced a unity with the gods, but rather than feeling drawn out of their bodies in an exhalation, as in the seventh, they experienced both inhalation and exhalation, a breathing between inner and outer. They felt themselves to be "soul and spirit within their bodies."

Experiencing the interval of the fifth, human beings felt, "The higher beings think, feel, make music in me." This is, in fact, a description of the kindergarten experience of religious devotion to the surroundings, of being at one with the environment in a condition of total imitation or empathy, a breathing between inner and outer.

Eventually, in the fourth Post-Atlantean epoch, the "aptitude" for the interval of the third—major and minor—appeared.

Major Third | Minor Third Intervals:

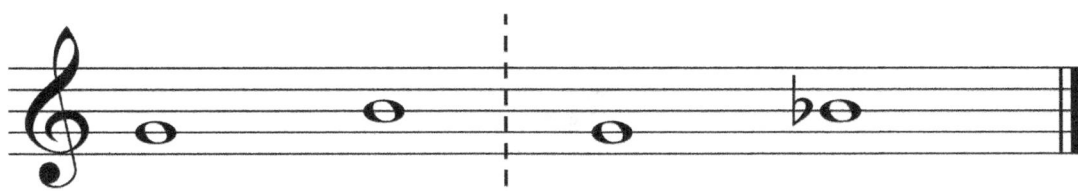

The experience of the third called forth an awareness of an inner condition, in which the human being felt the self within, distinct from the surroundings. Human beings thus felt that they themselves were singing; they felt themselves as earthly beings. In this way, humanity was gradually descending from the spiritual into the material world, and also, on the soul level, into a sense of individual selfhood.

Based on this overview of human evolution, we can see that music based on the experience of the fifth will meet the developmental stage of early childhood. We owe a great deal to the work of Julius Knierim, who brought this idea into practical application in working with children. Dr. Knierim used the expression "mood of the fifth" to characterize the experience of music based on this interval.

Music in the mood of the fifth swings or balances around the central note a above middle c, creating a mood of purity, openness, and objectivity. This configuration of fifths can be presented as images:

Balanced motion around the a:

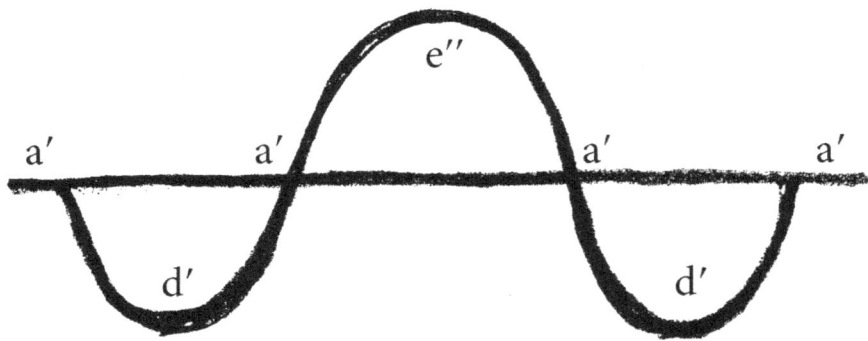

Lemniscate with a as center:

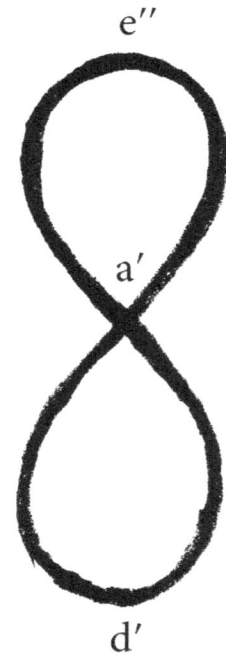

A melody based on the above images might sound like this:

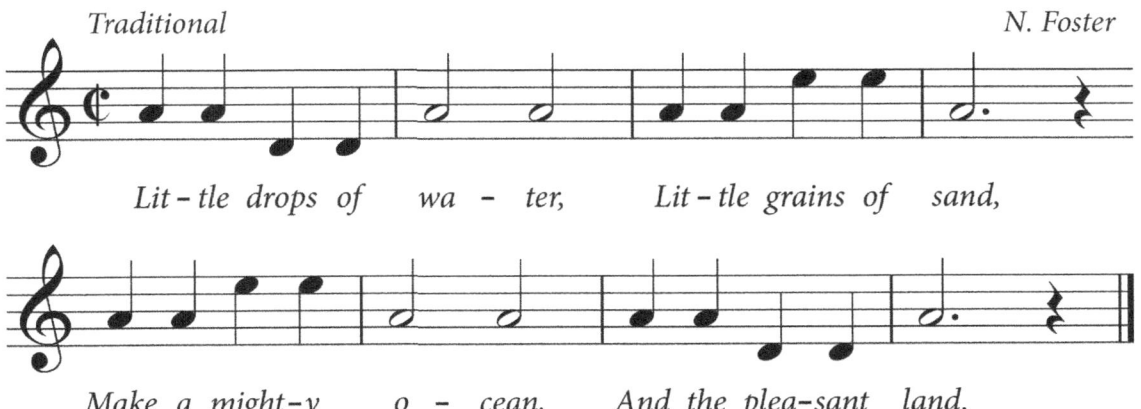

Traditional   N. Foster

Lit-tle drops of wa-ter, Lit-tle grains of sand,
Make a might-y o-cean, And the plea-sant land.

More varied, but still suitably simple, melodies can be created by adding other notes, still balanced around the a and still within the overall framework of the two fifths, a down to d and a up to e. The notes g and b are most easily added. (A lower e and upper d can be used as passing tones, but care must be used not to contract the framework of two fifths—d to a to e—into an octave—lower d to upper d). Images for such melodies might look like this:

Balanced motion around the a with g and b added:

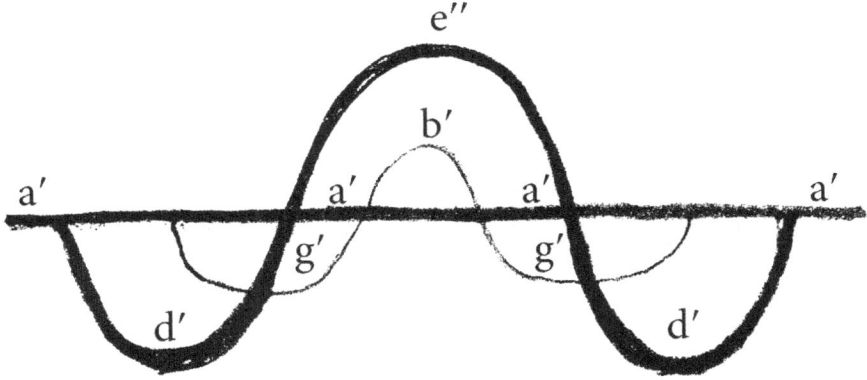

IV. Activities

Lemniscate with a as center with g and b added:

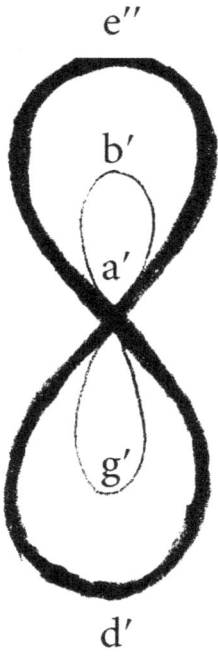

Using the same nursery rhyme as above, we might then compose a melody that would sound like one of the following examples:

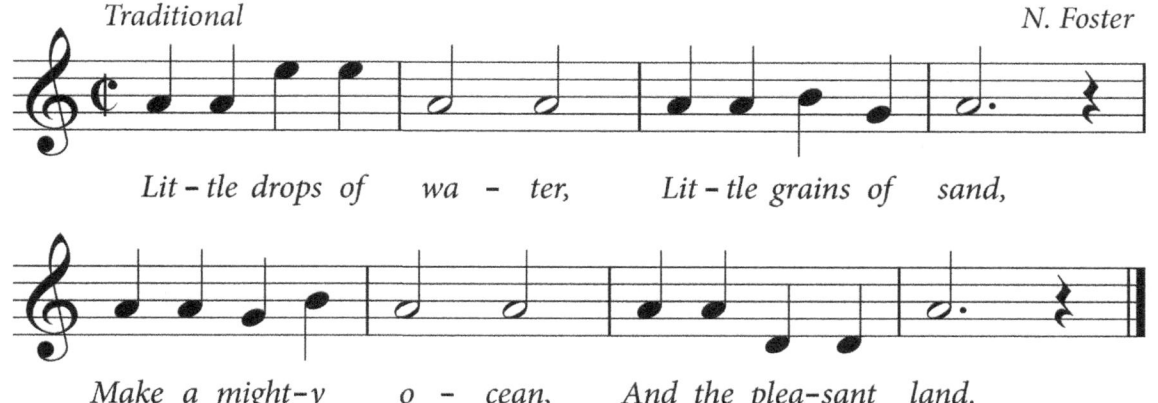

For adults, these melodies may seem strange or unappealing at first; it takes time to become used to their sense of purity and objectivity. They may even give us a feeling of emptiness. Bearing in mind our adult consciousness, this is understandable. Even for many children, this music in the mood of the fifth may not come easily at first, since they have most likely already been exposed to other kinds of music. In our times, we have all been bathed in a sea of tonality, so to speak, and this music based on fifths is very different. Nevertheless, if we understand the relationship of the mood of the fifth to the consciousness of the young child, we can see how important it is that children be allowed to experience this kind of music.

For those wanting to become familiar with music in the mood of the fifth, a helpful approach is to choose one song that you will sing with the children every day, perhaps at story time, or as a morning song at circle time. Gradually, as you become more comfortable with this kind of music, you may add more. The first step is to learn to understand why mood-of-the-fifth music is important for the young child; out of this understanding will grow the wish to become comfortable with it and introduce it to the children in your care. In the process, if the qualities of mood-of-the-fifth music are kept in mind, you can do much to bring this "mood" into whatever music you choose.

Songs based on the framework of the two fifths as illustrated above are in a suitable range for the young child's voice. For adults, this may present a challenge, but with practice, and by singing with a light "head tone," most people can achieve this voice range. It is a great help to the children's singing, and good training for their developing sense of pitch, if the teacher is consistent in beginning songs on the same pitch each time, as much as possible. If a correctly-tuned children's harp is kept nearby, for example, at least the first song can be started on the proper note. Even if the teacher is not able to maintain this through the whole circle play, it is at least a beginning. Adults' sense of pitch can also be developed! In any case, it is good to avoid slipping into a low voice range, since this is hard for children to imitate and often causes them to sing harshly.

The teacher's tone of voice can contribute much to the mood of the music. Singing in a clear, light tone will help to focus the children without overwhelming them. They will feel "invited" to sing and, just as in storytelling for the young child, dramatic effects will be avoided, so that a mood of joyful serenity will leave the children free to participate wholeheartedly in the music we bring.

Our own enjoyment of singing is a great gift to the children. As Rudolf Steiner said, "The joy of children in and with their environment must therefore be counted among the forces that build and shape the physical organs. They need teachers who look and act with happiness and, most of all, with honest, unaffected love. Such a love that streams, as it were, with warmth through the physical environment of the children may be said to literally "hatch out" the forms of the physical organs."[5]

In our striving to work with mood-of-the-fifth music, let us always remember to cultivate love and joy as we learn from the children what nourishes their devotion to all that is around them.

Notes

1 Rudolf Steiner, *The Inner Nature of Music and the Experience of Tone*, (Great Barrington: SteinerBooks 2015), p. 35.

2 Rudolf Steiner uses the term "dream consciousness" in the following passage from "Education and Spiritual Science," Cologne, Dec. 1, 1906: "Our dream consciousness is a residue of the Atlantean's normal pictorial consciousness, which could be compared to what a person experiences in vivid dreams during sleep. But the pictures of an Atlantean were animated, more vivid than today's most fertile imagination. Furthermore, Atlanteans could control their pictures, so that they were not chaotic. We see an echo of this consciousness when young children play, endowing their toys with pictorial content." Steiner, *The Education of the Child* (Great Barrington: SteinerBooks, 1996) p. 66.

3 Rudolf Steiner, *The Essentials of Education*, Lecture 2 (London: Rudolf Steiner Press 1982), p. 37. See also *The Child's Changing Consciousness*, Lecture 3, (Great Barrington: SteinerBooks, 1996), p. 47.

4 Steiner, *The Inner Nature of Music and the Experience of Tone*. See also Rudolf Steiner, "The Riddles of the Inner Human Being," Lecture given on May 23, 1923. An extract from this lecture is available as "The Creation of a Michael Festival out of the Spirit" in *The Festivals and Their Meaning* (London: Rudolf Steiner Press 1996).

5 Rudolf Steiner, "The Education of the Child in the Light of Anthroposophy" in *The Education of the Child*, p. 22.

Circle Time in Early Childhood

Nancy Foster

This essay, in slightly different form, appeared in Dancing As We Sing *(Acorn Hill Waldorf Kindergarten and Nursery 1999; distributed by WECAN)*

Let us form a ring
Dancing as we sing…

Circle time (sometimes called ring time) can be experienced as the heart of the early childhood group's morning—the organ through which all the morning's activities flow, harmonized in a rhythm of expansion and contraction. The mood of the morning affects the children's experience of circle time, and the experience of circle time rays out into the morning. Indeed, the circle is a microcosm of the life in the early childhood class, which is in turn a microcosm of life itself. We seek to bring archetypal activities of life and experiences of the natural world to the children. We also seek to support the dream-consciousness of the child—that ability to live completely in the moment in an unselfconscious, participatory mood. Thus the material we offer in circle time will have qualities which support these goals.

One of the great gifts we receive as teachers in the realm of Waldorf early childhood is a deepening and enriching of the experience of the course of the year. For busy adults, it is all too easy to become caught up in the pressures of "clock time." Through singing and moving with the children in seasonal circles, we nurture their natural, heartfelt participation in all that lives in the world of nature. At the same time, we rediscover our own connection with that world and the spirit that weaves in and through it. With the children, we enter the world of the natural cycles of time, as experienced in music and movement. This experience is nourishing to both children and adults, and helps to create the mood of joyful serenity that we seek in the early childhood group.

The circles found in printed materials are merely so many words and notes on the page until they are brought to life through human voice, movement, and gesture. The particular way in which a teacher carries this out is, of course, a matter of individual creativity; there can be no "right" or "wrong" way. It is possible, however, to offer a few thoughts and guiding ideas, based on experience with mixed-age kindergartens and with nursery groups. I hope they may help teachers create and work with circles and find a satisfying way to bring them alive for the children in their groups.

Many circles are created primarily on the theme of the seasons, but story or fairy tale circles are also of value. In either case, a key characteristic of circles is the development of a unified theme, rather than the presentation of a miscellaneous collection of songs and verses. The circles generally have a story-like quality, with a beginning and end, offering a feeling of completion. This sense of the whole can be strengthened through appropriate movement and gesture.

It is a wonderful gift for the children if much—though not necessarily all—of the music in a circle is in the mood of the fifth. This music, which swings and balances around the note "a" above middle C, creates a sense of pure objectivity and openness. For adults this can at first feel strange and uncomfortable, leaving us somehow empty. We will benefit from taking time to understand and experience why this music is appropriate and healing for the young child, who still lives in a condition of pure openness and receptivity to all the surroundings, in the dream-consciousness of wholehearted participation, of empathy.

For those who wish to learn more about the mood of the fifth, references are listed below. What is most important for the child's experience, however, is that the teacher enjoy the music. This enjoyment can be cultivated simply by learning and singing the songs and becoming comfortable with them. The teacher's voice, too, can help to create this mood of openness and empathy. A light, clear, tone in a range that centers around the "a" is most suitable for the children to imitate, and has a selfless quality which supports the objectivity and purity of mood-of- the-fifth music, even if a particular song is not in the mood of the fifth. Attention to the consonants, both in singing and speaking, also helps the children to participate, since these give form and pictorial quality to the words.

The young child is a being of movement—we become concerned if we observe a child who is awake but motionless for very long!—and each child has a particular style of movement. In circle time it is the teacher's task to bring the children into harmonious, nourishing, enlivening movement and gesture. Gesture is formed movement, movement that creates a picture; we could also say, movement with inner content. It is gesture that communicates the inner and outer qualities of whatever we encounter in the environment. How much more deeply we experience the form and quality of a tree, for example, if we try through gesture to "become" that tree! If this is so for an adult, we can see how much more so it must be for the child, whose experience of the world is still so new. Pondering this thought can give us a sense of our responsibility to bring true gesture to the children.

To find suitable gestures for circle time, the teacher will want to strive to develop a genuine relationship to the world of gesture. This can be done, first, by taking the time to observe the world, trying to penetrate to the essence of what we see. For example, observe how a plant grows. What is the "gesture" of a sprouting bulb? of unfolding leaves? of the spreading branches of a tree? Observe the movements of craftspeople and workers: how does the blacksmith hammer the iron? How does a farmer swing the scythe? How does Mother or Father sweep the floor? Observe animals: what is the quality of a squirrel's movements? How is the butterfly's flight different from that of a bee? Then we can imagine how we could convey these qualities in gesture, so that the children, imitating, can feel how it would be to be a growing plant, a farmer working in the field, or a scampering squirrel. We can try also to become conscious of our own gestures and relation to space in general, not only in circle time; this awareness can help us to bring a quality of gesture worthy of imitation.

The experience of eurythmy is invaluable to a teacher of young children, since it develops sensitivity to the world of gesture. While only a trained eurythmist can bring eurythmy to children, teachers who have experienced eurythmy can certainly be inspired by it. What we may call "kindergarten gesture" arises from a different source than eurythmy gesture. While eurythmy arises out of the inner quality of tone or speech—from the sounds of words, which have archetypal power—kindergarten gesture arises from the qualities of the surrounding world as we see it and relate to it. The same creative force works in the sound of the letter "b" as works in the protective, enfolding gesture of a big blue blanket; thus, the gestures for both may appear similar although they originate differently. And this gesture may be used in a circle whenever there is this enfolding quality (for example, when the snail creeps into its shell), whether or not there is the sound "b." The essential point is that the teacher is not imitating eurythmy, but rather is creating pictures of the outer world that deepen the child's experience of that world. If our gestures are life-filled, if we truly experience the reality of our gestures, we give the children a treasure of great value in today's mechanized world.

These remarks about gesture, while of course greatly over-simplified, may help in understanding that we wish to help the children be something rather than describe how something looks. In addition, we can see that gesture involves more than just putting our arms in a certain position. Rather, we wish to create movement around us and experience gesture as a living reality.

In working with kindergarten movement and gesture, a basic element is the experience of polarities. The alternation between contrasting poles brings a sense of joy and well-being to the children. Perhaps the essential polarity we experience as human beings is that of expansion and contraction. This polarity is found literally, of course, in our breathing. The importance of polarities in movement and gesture becomes obvious when we imagine the feeling of holding the breath too long, or of being out of breath. Moving between expansion and contraction provides a kind of inner and outer exercise, helping us to find a healthy, mobile balance within and around ourselves. In kindergarten movement and gesture this polarity can be experienced in a variety of ways: in tempo (fast/slow); in size of gestures (small/large, whole-body/fingers); in direction (up/down, in/out, right/left); in motion (standing still/moving; starting/stopping); in mood (serious, sad, dreamy, quiet/jovial, humorous, vigorous, playful); in gravity/levity (walking/skipping or jumping); and group/individual (moving in a circle as a group/each individual turning around).

As we work on developing movement and gesture for a circle, we may try to be aware of providing an experience of these polarities, of creating a balance. One pole calls for the other; if the children are kept at one for too long, they will become weary or they may "explode," as if they had been holding their breath. I have found it is essential to plan the transitions between poles. These transitions are even more important than the movements or gestures themselves; as in music, it is in the intervals that something really happens. For example, how will we bring the children from standing to sitting? Do we need to add a transitional rhyme or gesture? If we expect the children to change from one pole to another too quickly or too frequently, they will become tired and frustrated and are likely to become disruptive. A quick change can add welcome humor on occasion, but in general children need help with the transitions. For example, if they are galloping ponies, stopping to pull on the "reins," and saying "Whoa!" as part of the circle helps them to stop without confusion and disruption, while avoiding instruction that would interrupt the flow of the activity.

To help children to imitate our gestures, it is good to begin the gesture or movement slightly ahead of the words. By anticipating, we are reflecting the reality that the forming force creates the sound, and we allow the children time to follow, so that they do not become frustrated. Most children genuinely want to imitate, and this practice will make it possible for them. Repetition is also a help. Especially when a circle is new, it works well to repeat each song or verse (or sometimes each section of a verse) so that children can experience the images more deeply and have an extra opportunity to imitate the movement or gesture as well as the words. This gives them a deep sense of satisfaction, of mastery. Later, perhaps, as the circle becomes quite familiar, we may omit some or all of the repetitions. This then offers a greater challenge and keeps the experience alive in the teacher and the children.

It is good always to strive toward simplicity of movement and gesture and to avoid using too many gestures. Too many or over-complicated gestures may cause the children to become silly or wild, because they cannot keep up with what is being presented. A large repertoire of gestures is not necessary. Rather, we can focus on using a few clear, meaningful gestures with suitable transitions. This will create the most satisfying experience for the children.

For the sake of older children in the group, we may wish to add new polarities or more complicated movements or gestures as a circle becomes familiar. For example, if we have been walking in the woods, we may later skip through the woods instead, or add skipping to our walking. Or, if we have been jumping in a puddle, we may change to hopping in on one foot and then the other, or whirling as we jump. Adding small challenges does wonders for maintaining interest and participation for children who are nearing readiness for first grade. Finally, and most important, the teacher will want to be well-prepared. It is very helpful to practice the circle many times before we bring it to the children so that it becomes part of us, and so that the inevitable distractions of the classroom situation will not interfere with the continuity of the experience.

In circle time, it is good to have times of moving in circular form without joined hands. This allows more freedom of movement, especially if we want the children to move quickly—galloping, skipping, striding, etc. In addition, this allows movement without the disruption of children not yet able to hold the form of a circle with hands joined. In my experience, nursery groups are rarely if ever able to move in a hands-joined circle, since they have not yet achieved the necessary conscious relationship to space. They are happy simply to "flock," moving in the same general circular direction as the teacher, but each in his/her own particular orbit.

Even in mixed-age groups, there may not be enough "circle-ready" children until after Christmas to be able to enjoy holding hands. It is important for the teacher to know the group before attempting to introduce this kind of movement. Instead, we may simply walk in a circle, hands at our sides, or we may hold the arms above as if carrying a large, light, golden ball. This offers a satisfying polarity between the sense of gravity in walking and the sense of levity in the awareness of the light-filled space above. In general, we like to move clockwise in the early childhood circle; the opposite direction may occasionally be taken briefly to bring a bit of humor and surprise, or if we are "returning" from a "journey."

It is a good thing to end each circle time with a brief period of silence and stillness, so that the movement, gesture, and music can re-echo in the children and be digested. This moment, which can be profound even though quite brief, may be brought about through the use of a particular rhyme or finger game, or even by having a short rest before moving on to the next activity of the day.

May these ideas help to bring circle time to life in an artistic way which will nourish the children in your care. This artistic quality, which can live throughout the early childhood morning, is beautifully characterized in "The Essentials of Waldorf Early Childhood Education" by Susan Howard: "In the early childhood class, the art of education is the art of living. The teacher is an artist in how she perceives and relates to the children and the activities of daily life. She 'orchestrates' and 'choreographs' the rhythms of each day, the week, and the seasons in such a way that the children can breathe freely within a living structure." In circle time, this orchestration and choreography appear in heightened form—the heart of the morning.

IV. Activities

Understanding and Fostering Healthy Creative Play

Joan Almon

From *On the Play of the Child* (WECAN 2012)

Play is a fundamental activity of childhood, and the playful child is generally viewed as a healthy, active child. After a child has been ill, parents will often describe the seriousness of the illness in terms of whether the child was still able to play. "She was really sick and couldn't play at all," or "He was sick but was up playing," are comments often heard from parents. There is scientific research to support this view, showing that play is linked to children's healthy physical, social, emotional and mental development. The absence of play becomes a serious problem in children's lives.

There are many types of play, ranging from simple play, where young children handle materials such as pots and pans and other household objects, to make-believe play, where two or more children play out complex stories together. This can be in a single play session or over many days. One sees the same types of play among children all over the world, and one can speak of a common language of play. Children from different cultures, for example, can happily play together without knowing a single word of one another's spoken language.

At the same time, one sees differences according to children's age and development, gender, and individual natures. Culture also plays a role. Among cultural differences, for instance, one sees that European children playing "mother" will push their dolls in prams, while in Africa they tie their baby dolls onto their backs with colorful cloths. Children imitate what they see around them and at the same time play bubbles up from deep inner wellsprings.

Even in situations of war or poverty, most children continue to play, although children suffering from serious illness or trauma may stop playing, at least for a time. What does it mean, then, that one hears in the U.S. and elsewhere that play is disappearing from childhood—that there is no time for play or that children have forgotten how to play? There are rising rates of physical and mental illness among children, and it may well be that this is related directly or indirectly to the loss of play. The World Health Organization, for instance, has sounded an alarm that mental illness among children may increase by 50% by the year 2020. At the same time, many countries are concerned about the increases in childhood obesity and related illnesses. Because play is so linked to children's healthy development, its absence must be taken seriously.

Waldorf early childhood educators have recognized the disappearance of play from childhood for some time, but increasingly we hear concern from other educators, psychologists, and doctors. A child psychiatrist in the U.S., for example, recently wrote of a fifty percent reduction in children's play over the past twenty years. Interviews with experienced kindergarten teachers in the U.S. brought forward two common answers: there was considerably less time in their curriculum for play now than ten years ago, and when they gave children time to play, the children did not know what to do. A professor whose area of study is play noted a similar response. She asked early childhood educators in a workshop how many had children in their kindergartens who did not know how to play. About ninety percent of the two hundred teachers raised their hands. Experts are beginning to speak out about these problems in an effort to alert parents, educators, doctors, and government officials. Organizations are also forming which are focusing on the importance of play, such as the Alliance for Childhood.

One naturally asks why play is disappearing, and there seem to be several answers. One is the amount of media children watch, and this includes television, films, and computer time. The average time for a child in the U.S. to sit still in front of a screen is now between four and five hours per day outside of school time. This is time when children are not engaged in play, but it is also time when children are absorbing other people's images. This limits the development of their own imaginations.

Another factor is the growing emphasis on early learning. Using the U.S. as an example, five-year-olds are often attending all-day kindergartens where they may spend ninety minutes a day on early reading, sixty minutes on mathematics, and devote time each day to science and social studies activities, yet have no time for indoor play. Five-year-olds in many places in the U.S. are expected to enter kindergarten knowing their alphabet, basic sounds, numbers and much more. To prepare children for this, most preschools focus on teaching academics to three- and four-year-olds. Often, young children are tested on what they have learned in these early years so the stress on academic achievement becomes considerable.

A third factor is the growing amount of time young children spend in organized activities rather than in child-initiated play. Many young children are taking classes in gymnastics, sports, dance, music and other subjects. Some attend several classes a week after they return from their regular pre-school programs, leaving almost no time for unstructured play.

Perhaps the greatest consideration is that parents feel a need to see their children get ahead in life and push intellectual awareness and organized activities from the earliest ages, undervaluing play and discouraging children from engaging in it. Early childhood educators frequently complain that parents insist on teachers pushing early academics even though they, the teachers, do not think the children need this push. Reaching the parents to help them understand the critical role of play in their children's healthy development is probably the most important single step we can take in bringing play back into children's lives.

An additional consideration with play is the role of imitation in stimulating play. Children need to see adults engaged in meaningful work, for it inspires children to play. Yet today's children see very little real work in their environment. When helping children who can't play, it is astonishing how quickly play can be reactivated once children are exposed to real work, whether it is cooking, gardening, carpentry or the like.

The absence of play can have serious consequences for the development of a child's imagination and creativity. Without play children are less likely to be able to form their own independent ideas. This in turn can have an impact on society, for democracies rely on citizens being able to think creatively and independently. On the other hand, totalitarian regimes do not tolerate such independent thinking and strive to hinder its development. If one wants to prepare children for life in an active and thriving democratic state, then it is critical that we help them play creatively when they are young.

For all of these reasons it has become very important that people recognize the vital role of play and do all they can to bring play back into childhood. The insights of Rudolf Steiner regarding play and the experiences in Waldorf kindergartens can be a great help in awakening an understanding of play and in inspiring us all to work on behalf of play.

The Healing Power of Play

Joan Almon

From *On the Play of the Child* (WECAN 2012)

As a Waldorf kindergarten teacher I had the opportunity to travel around the world for Waldorf education and to meet many teachers, parents, and children in different countries. I was in Tanzania, Africa, a few years ago, and there was a Waldorf school with two kindergartens. One of the teachers had already been in a Waldorf teacher training in East Africa, and her kindergarten was going very nicely. The children were playing quite well.

The other teacher was quite new to Waldorf education. She had only started a month before and was not yet in a training course. She was very gifted in playing with children, one on one, or with a small group of children, but she truly did not know what to do with twenty-five children. And you know how chaotic a kindergarten can be if the children are not playing well. When I went past her room that first day I could hear the sounds of chaos. I knew them well from my own early years as a teacher. On the second day, I was going to have a couple of hours to be with her in the kindergarten, and I thought: "What can I do in two hours that could help her?"

The next morning, when I entered her room the children were outside playing, and I said to her: "Usually I bring sewing with me when I visit a kindergarten so that I have work to do in front of the children, but on this trip I did not bring my sewing kit. Do you have some work that I could do, such as making a doll, or repairing a play cloth?" She looked very puzzled and said: "Oh no, I do all of that work at home in the evening." I was shocked and replied, "No, no, in a Waldorf kindergarten we do that work in front of the children to inspire their play." I looked around her room for something that I could do when the children came in. There weren't many supplies in the kindergarten, but the children were making little pom-poms with yarn and cardboard, and she had a little basket of leftover yarn pieces. They were quite small, perhaps only a half-meter in length.

When the children came in, I was sitting at a table winding tiny little balls from the yarn, singing a song about winding the yarn. As each ball was finished, I set it down forming a little circle of balls. This is a little trick that I learned from Freya Jaffke years ago. When you want to engage children in play, you can slowly create a little circle of stones or wood pieces for them. Quite often, by the time the circle is finished, the child has an idea for play and is ready to continue on his or her own. I did that often in my kindergarten when a child did not have an idea of what to play, and it nearly always helped.

So I made these little yarn balls, and all the children gathered around to watch. What happened next was amazing to me. When the circle was finished the children turned like a flock of birds and went into every part of the room and began to play. They took chairs and made a bus, they built shops with play stands, and they made houses.

There was one boy that the teacher had pointed out to me the day before, saying, "He cannot play at all; he only hits children and disturbs their play, or he stays by himself." He now built himself a little play area with a table and some little pieces of wood on top. He also put a small cabinet behind him. I don't usually ask children what they are playing, but in this case, I wanted to understand him a little more and only had this one chance.

After a while I went over to him and asked: "What are you playing?" He answered, "This is an airplane and I'm the pilot." I helped to build up his play space with some playstands and cloth to give him a greater sense of protection and asked him what was in the cabinet behind him. "The television," he answered. I had suspected that television viewing was part of his problem, and now I was fairly sure. The teachers were so happy to see him playing at last.

What was especially beautiful, though, was that the next day when I stopped by to say goodbye on my way to the airport, the children were again deep in play. There was that wonderful hum in the kindergarten that comes when children are deep in play. The little boy who had played pilot and who had been so unsocial was now taking the pom-poms that still had holes in the middle. He put yarn through the holes and made necklaces for the children in the class. He had found a way to connect with them. He went from one child to the next, giving each of them a necklace to wear. The power of children's imitation and the real work of the teacher are a powerful combination which lead children deep into the world of play. They can also bring children back to play if they have forgotten how to play.

Imitation in early childhood is an incredible gift. It is a gift that the children bring down to earth with them. When we human beings are in the spiritual world, we breathe our way out into the hierarchies, we take them into ourselves. This is how we learn from higher beings.

This capacity to flow out into the hierarchies is a capacity we bring down to earth with us. In the heavenly world we interpenetrate with higher beings. When we bring this to earth we call it imitation. The child has the ability to breathe into us and "take us on." Imitation is the basis of the religious life of the child, a religious life which includes the spiritual world, but is very focused on the earthly world. Imitation is the child's way of communing with others.

There are indications from Rudolf Steiner that we kindergarten teachers are like priests in the kindergarten. One can easily misunderstand that indication. Normally, the priest is at the altar, looking up, as it were, to the spiritual world. We are at the worktable bringing spiritual impulses down into the earthly world. This is the world into which children are incarnating, and we are there to help them. They bring wonderful gifts with them. One is the ability to meet us in the world of imitation, to enter deeply into us, to try us on as if we were a kind of clothing for them to enter into us as we bake, or sew, or do woodworking. As we work they enter into us, not just our outer gestures, as important as they are, but they enter into our whole inner mood and being.

Maybe you have experienced in your kindergarten what I experienced, that on some days there was a kind of nervous energy in the room. The children were playing, but their play didn't have that deep hum of the kindergarten. I would look around from my work area, to see if someone was creating a disturbance, but no, they were all playing. Nobody was really disturbed, and yet there was a nervousness in the air. Finally I learned an important lesson: that when I experienced that nervousness I needed to first look at myself, at my own inner mood. Often I found that I had grown nervous and was not calm and focused. I was listening to the class while I worked, but I was not fully focused on them or on my work. I was thinking of other things. When I became attentive again, the whole class became quieter and more focused in their play.

Young children are so open to our every mood, and we live together with them in an intimate way through their capacity for imitation. They take us in, they breathe into us, and we can help them to grow and flourish. We can help them to become full human beings.

There is something else that lives strongly in the child and is a gift of the hierarchies, a gift for the child's incarnation. It is a deep wisdom that lives in each child and shows them what they need for their path of incarnation. One sees it already in the infant. How does that little baby, lying there on its stomach, know that it needs to lift its head and look around? Yet every healthy baby does that at a certain point. How does a baby know, when it is on its back and rather helpless, that it needs to fling its arm over and turn itself over? No one is teaching this to the baby. It's not even imitation in the direct sense, because it is not seeing people do this.

Yet a baby of six months old has a deep inner wisdom that it is time to turn over. I often think of Gordon, a little six-month-old baby whose family lived with us for a month. I used to come home from kindergarten every day and relax by watching Gordon on the rug on his back trying to turn over. It took him the whole month to learn to turn over. Every day, over and over, he'd fling his arm over trying to turn himself. He'd do it dozens of time, perhaps hundreds of times, but never with a hint of frustration. Finally, one day, he did it.

To us it felt like an enormous deed. But for him it was normal. He practiced it a few times more as if to be sure he could do it, and then he seemed ready to take on the next step of development. In this sense there is no pause in your development when you are little. You just keep going from one step to the next. All the while there is a tremendous inner wisdom that guides you from one step to the next.

When we see children at play, we also see this wisdom at work before our eyes. We see it in the normal development of play, but it is clearest when a child has a problem in life and uses play to resolve that problem. I want to give you a few examples, and I am sure you will know many, many more from your own experiences.

There was a little boy who came into my kindergarten who was about four years old, and the first thing I noticed was that he had an unusual voice. His speech was well developed, but his voice was that of a baby or a very young child. It didn't fit his age of development. I had not experienced this situation before, and I wasn't sure what it was that I was seeing in him. I watched his play, and every day he played in the same way. He took six or seven stumps and he'd make himself a small round house with the stumps standing up. Then he'd go into the house, and he'd put a cloth cover over the top of the house. The house had no doors and no windows. Every day he built the same house and spent almost all of his playtime in it.

I had a conference with his mother to try to understand what was happening in his life. She also was very concerned about him. He had been fine up until age three and a half. Then a baby sister was born, and at first he was fine about that as well. But when the baby was about six months old and was in a very cute stage, it seemed that everybody was drawn to the baby and not so drawn to the older child. At that point he began to regress, to go backwards and to develop a form of baby language. He also wanted to drink from a bottle again. One day when I looked inside his house, I saw that he was curled up like a baby in a womb, and I thought: "He has made himself a womb; he has gone as far back as he can, as if he was still inside his mother."

It concerned me but my sense was that he knew what he was doing, and that something was in a growth process in him and not stuck. I felt I needed to give him time to work through this. It took about two or three months in which he played the same way every day. My assistant and I watched over him and did not let the other children disturb his play.

After a few months a day came when he left a little opening in his house. It was not very big, but it was important. Then, a couple of days later, he made a bigger opening, and then he went out looking for a friend. He found a lovely boy named Bill and brought him into his house with him. There they played for a few days. Then the house seemed too cramped, and it began to grow. It grew bigger and bigger, and other children could come in. Slowly the child's voice came back to normal. Young children have a wisdom about what they need. They cannot verbalize it to us, but they often show us their wisdom through play.

Here is one other example. There was a four-year-old girl who came into my kindergarten. She was very sweet and very playful. The only thing that concerned me about her was her voice, but the problem was in the opposite direction of the little boy I described. Hers was not a baby voice, but a high-pitched, nervous voice. I have to admit that her voice got on my nerves. It was hard for me to open my heart fully when she would approach me. Something in me would draw back as she approached me, and I had to work to overcome that.

One day she brought me one of our little knot dolls, just a simple little cloth doll. With it she brought a thin play cloth, a very long cloth, at least four meters long. She asked me to wrap her baby, and my first reaction was: "She should go and get me a smaller cloth." My second reaction was: "Let's wait and see." And so I took the doll and I took the cloth and I began to wrap the doll, very slowly. I thought: "Soon she will be impatient, and then I will go faster." Slowly, slowly, I swaddled the baby. She was not impatient. She seemed to take in every gesture, every wrapping of the baby. She waited till the last bit of cloth was used and then took her baby doll back again. After that, her voice came down into a normal range. It was as if she herself needed to be wrapped, as if she was too exposed to the world, and it was making her nervous. Through this simple wrapping of the doll and all that went into it, I think she now felt wrapped and protected.

I want to tell you one more story, and it goes in a slightly different direction. In this case I felt the children were showing something of their development, but it was going in an unhealthy direction, and I had to decide what to do about it.

Two little boys, Brendan and Thomas, were good friends and played together every day for several years. Now they were five years old. Brendan, a radiant, large-headed child, was very playful. He was an exceptionally imaginative and social child. Thomas was a little more drawn into himself and was a little more stressed by life. But he was also a very sweet child. They played happily together and with other children. When they were about five-and-a-half, you could see their intellects beginning to wake up. Children at that age often, out of themselves, become very interested in arithmetic, in mathematics. In my experience, the girls often become interested in infinity, and will have huge philosophical conversations about infinity, while the boys become interested in mathematical problems. Brendan and Thomas woke up to arithmetic at the same time, and often, over the snack table, they would throw arithmetic problems at each other. It was playful, and I let it be.

IV. Activities

In their play, however, they entered a phase of very intense activity with each other. They went to an area where there were playstands forming a house-like structure, and they took over that area. Usually the playstands were moved and rearranged into new houses, shops, puppet theaters and much more. But they took over this area and did not move the playstands. Instead, they took a basket of ropes and tied ropes on the top of the play stands. They used many ropes, and tied many, many knots. You know how children can get into tying knots at that age. I don't know at what age they learn to untie knots, but it is not in the kindergarten. Clean-up became difficult with so many knots to be untied, and I will confess that I finally put a pair of scissors in my pocket to quietly cut through the knots.

Every day they played this way, and they would not let anybody else into their play. It was a picture for me of the awakening intellect in the boys, like a spider spinning a web of thoughts. Gradually I felt this intellectual development and all these knotty thoughts were holding them in and pressing them down rather than allowing them to grow and flourish. They were awakening to thinking, but their thoughts were not taking them out into the world. These thoughts were not leading them toward an interest in others. This was a form of intellectual development that was isolating them, as if they had climbed an "ivory tower" and cut themselves of from others. I began to grow very uncomfortable about their play.

One morning, before they came, I took the basket of ropes and I put it high up on a shelf out of their reach. I expected the boys to be very upset, even angry. They came and asked me for the ropes, and I said to them: "Today, the ropes are going to rest." What I felt in them was not anger but a huge relief. They were not at all upset. They actually seemed grateful, as if they were relieved of a burden they could not overcome by themselves. That day they went and played by themselves in the house, but the next day a few children came into the house and played with them. After a few days, they were again in a normal flow of play with the children.

Then they came to me and asked for the ropes. What was I going to do? I trusted that they were now in a new place, and I brought the ropes down and gave them to them. Now a whole new play developed. They took the ropes and used them as telephone wires, and they connected all the play-houses in the kindergarten. They linked all the children together into one large social network. All that thinking and intellect that had felt trapped inside was now working itself out into a large social body. The other children helped, as well, to create this phone system that united all their houses.

For me, this was a real lesson that even when one fully appreciates the wisdom of children's play, one still has to practice a kind of discernment, a subtle form of judgment. Not all play is equally healthy for children. When is the play supporting the child's blossoming and growing, and when is it taking hold almost like an addiction, a habit that's not healthy?

It is not always easy to discern what is healthy and what is not in children's play, but as Waldorf teachers we can cultivate discernment through our inner work, our schooling path as adults. I think of many wonderful exercises that Rudolf Steiner has given us that help develop our inner capacity for discernment, for telling the difference between one thing and another. I would like to describe just one of those exercises. It is one where he says: "Observe the plant world, that which is blossoming and growing, and that which is fading and decaying."

You can practice this outdoors or even indoors when you watch a bouquet of flowers in your own room. Perhaps there are flower buds in the bouquet, and other flowers that are just starting to open, while others are in full bloom, and still others are fading and decaying. You can sense the tremendous capacity to grow in the bud and the strength of growth in the opening flower. But as the flower passes its peak, its petals thin and begin to droop. They are no longer so life-filled and gradually they drop off. Over and over you do these exercises and gradually you sense in a child: "This child is in a budding, opening process, or this child is drooping and not thriving. Or perhaps this child is fading, but it feels appropriate, as if it is shedding an old skin and making way for a new one."

I would like to tell you one more story about Brendan, the little boy with the ropes. He went on to a public school, and I lost track of him until about five years ago. Then there was a big article about Brendan in the newspaper. He was about seventeen years old, in the twelfth grade of a public high school. From the article you could see that he was a wonderful, warm young fellow. But he had a severe health problem, and this problem was that he had used computers so much that he had intense pain in his wrists and arms. The pain was so severe that he could no longer hold a pencil or pen to write. Someone had to sit next to him to take notes for him in class. He was not allowed to use a computer, and even opening a door was extremely painful for him.

The journalist, knowing that Brendan was going to go to Harvard University the next year, called the health service at Harvard to ask: "Do you have other students with this problem?" The University said: "Yes. We've didn't have this problem in the past, but right now we have about a hundred students on campus with this problem. They developed the problem from using computers too much." In Brendan's case I wished so much that someone would have seen that he was trapped in his relationship with a computer and helped him out before he did himself such harm. For me it was as if he had spun a web again and gotten stuck in it. Finally the world of computers had to be closed, at least for a while, to let him breathe into the world again. It's hard sometimes to see these things and to say no to a child: "No, not now, this is not the right thing, this is too much." But that is part of what we learn as teachers, and we need to help parents learn it as well.

IV. Activities

Play is a force that allows children to grow in every area of their being. It is a foundation for all their learning, and it allows them to explore every aspect of life, including those that hold real sorrows and problems for them. Therefore it's a huge tragedy that we hear from all sides that play, creative, open play, is disappearing from children's lives. This is a theme that I am very actively working on in the United States through the Alliance for Childhood. In this first stage of our work we are gathering stories from teachers, and I will tell you just one.

A professor of early childhood education in Boston told me of a workshop she did at a NAEYC conference. It was a year after 9/11 and she was asking the teachers if they saw an increase in violent play in their kindergartens. There was an uncomfortable buzzing in the room as they began to speak with each other. She asked what was wrong, and one teacher spoke up and said: "The problem is not that we see more violent play, the problem is that we no longer see children playing at all." She asked if others had a similar experience and about ninety percent of the two hundred teachers put up their hands.

The Alliance then did a small study where graduate students asked experienced kindergarten teachers about play. Two things became clear. One, the curriculum of our kindergartens in the U.S. no longer allows any time for free play. Most of our kindergartens are now full-day kindergartens, from nine o'clock to three o'clock. Reading and writing, mathematics and science, fill the children's day, and these five-year-olds have no time for play. The other thing that became clear was that when the teachers gave children time to play, the children did not know what to do. "They have no ideas of their own," said the teachers.

We then went in search of more research. Was there any quantitative research about the disappearance of play? That was our question. We found one excellent researcher who had studied the lives of children by asking teachers and parents to keep a diary for a day, writing down every thirty minutes what the children were doing. Thousands of these diaries were collected, and all of the answers were very clearly coded so you could see how much time was spent eating, how much time was spent sleeping, and how much time was spent playing. We asked her if she had found a decline in children's play and were astonished when she said, no, she had found an increase. "How is that possible?" we asked. "Everyone is telling us that there is a loss of play."

Then I had a thought and asked, "What do you include under play?" She answered, "Outdoor play, make-believe-play and computer play." Aha. Computer play had increased considerably over the five-year time period, so we asked her if each of the forms of play had been coded separately? She said they were and we asked if she would separate the different types of play and look specifically for changes in the time spent in make-believe play. We found that time spent in indoor creative play had indeed decreased significantly in the five years of the study.

Though we may not always know the figures, from all sides we hear reports that there is less and less imaginative play taking place in children's lives. The Alliance for Childhood has received funding for research to help fill in the picture. Meanwhile, we are addressing the real challenge: "How do we bring play back?" We're working with a very skilled "playworker" from London's Adventure Playgrounds, and with her help we've been carrying the message of play into children's museums, parks, preschools and kindergartens, and many other venues. I'm happy to say there is growing interest in play although there is a long way to go before it is restored to all children's lives.

While play is still alive in many countries, we hear reports of its fading away. So often what we experience in the United States is like an epidemic that goes around the world. The disappearance of play will also will go around the world unless we find ways to change the situation. We need to become fully active in support of the spirit of play.

I often ask myself: "What can we do?" I think of the things that we can do—and I mean "we," because all of you as Waldorf early childhood educators are experts in play. Sometimes you don't realize how much you know about play, but you have real expertise in this area and can use that expertise to help rescue play. What could that mean? In the first instance it can mean workshops for parents on play so they become strong in their support of play for their children. My favorite workshop that I did for parents was where I brought them into the kindergarten and let them play. It was a unique experience for them and one they valued.

In this workshop the parents did not only talk about play, they actually played in the simplest ways. They built houses, dressed up, played with dolls, and much more. At first they were self-conscious, but gradually they relaxed and really played. Afterwards they said they were astonished to realize that this type of play was still alive in them, for they thought it had died out long ago.

Also, I've helped to organize Play Days, and can recommend these. This is where you create a play situation, indoors or out, on a Saturday morning, let's say, and you invite in the public so that children and adults can come and play. You don't do this for the sake of bringing in more families to your school, although that might result, but really to support play itself, to help people understand the importance and the joy of play. Play is a joyful human experience, and we've lost the sense for that. Play Days show parents the importance and fun of play (see Note).

There are many other things that can be done to support play and help bring it back. If you like to write, then write an article for your newspaper or a local magazine about play.

What if all over the world, in the two thousand Waldorf kindergartens, one deed was done each year just for the purpose of supporting play? And what if we brought along friends from other kindergartens, non-Waldorf kindergartens, and encouraged them to do the same? I think we could stop this decline of play. We could reverse this tendency. I know we are all so busy with what we are already doing, but my biggest concern at the moment is that if we do not find ways to become active in support of play, then its disappearance will spread and grow, and year by year children will play less and less until they have forgotten how to play altogether. And with that loss will go one of the most powerful elements in children's development and one of the most important forms of healing that children have available for themselves. This loss of healing will happen at the very time when new illnesses, psychological illnesses, are growing intensively in children. Already the World Health Organization has issued a kind of call saying that by 2020 there will be an enormous increase in mental illness in children around the world. Mental illness is growing rapidly among children, and play is a strong "medicine." It can lower their stress levels and help them deal with their problems, yet it is disappearing just when children need it so badly.

Children need play for a dozen reasons, for a hundred reasons. It is their doorway to growth and learning, and it is their doorway to healing. Now we need to make sure that it remains a strong part of their lives.

Note

For information on planning Play Days, visit the International Play Association online at ipausa.org and ipaworld.org.

V. Language, Storytelling, and Puppetry

Language, storytelling, and puppetry offer an incredibly rich and deep well of wisdom for teachers of young children.

Susan Weber writes about the acquisition of language and the importance of speech for the young child. Daniel Udo de Haes, in his essay titled "Story-Thread and Language for the Toddler," turns our attention to the role that picture books play for the toddler. He also writes of the importance of nursery rhymes and play songs.

Fairy tales are deeply healing and their narratives and images provide children with a rich tapestry of imaginative ambrosia. In his essay on fairy tale language, Helmut von Kügelgen writes about the spiritual wisdom contained within fairly tales.

Rudolf Steiner writes: "There is nothing of greater blessing for a child than to nourish it with everything that brings the roots of human life together with those of cosmic life. A child is still having to work creatively, forming itself, bringing about the growth of its body, unfolding its inner tendencies; it needs the wonderful soul-nourishment it finds in fairy tale pictures, for in them the child's roots are united with the life of the world" (see Note).

After this overview on fairy tales, the essays hone in on certain specifics that offer examples as how to deepen our understanding of fairy tales. Ruth Pusch writes about witches, and of how exploring the deeper meaning of the tales shows us something of the mystery of evil, while Joan Almon offers guidance in choosing tales for children of different ages, based on their appropriateness for various developmental stages.

Additional essays in this section describe marionettes and puppetry in the context of a Waldorf kindergarten. Helmut von Kügelgen writes about Rudolf Steiner's efforts to establish a marionette theater, quoting his words about this endeavor: "We must do everything in our power to help the children to develop fantasy."

Note

Rudolf Steiner, *The Poetry and Meaning of Fairy Tales*, Ruth Pusch, trans., ed. (Spring Valley: Mercury Press 1989).

Fostering Healthy Language Development in Young Children: A Journey in Relationships

Susan Weber

From *A Warm and Gentle Welcome* (WECAN 2008)

The development of speech and language in the young child is truly a marvel, full of wonder for those who accompany its unfolding. We know intuitively that speaking arises from a mysterious place, one that has fascinated linguists for a long, long time. The Gospel of St. John begins with the very image of language development: "In the beginning was the Word." The creative energy of the Word is understood, in Rudolf Steiner's description, as a formative power, building even our physical bodies. It is no wonder, then, that coming into language is of such monumental importance, and that the adults in the young child's environment have such a profound influence on this process. The Word is a powerful force. Poets, writers, orators, and each of us change the world through our speech. Language is the gift the gods give to humanity for our creative activity.

This creative force of the Word can be experienced in the child's earliest expeditions into language. The child's magical made-up words, concrete descriptions of the world around him, and unique phrasings wake up our own hearing. The Word is fully animate to the child and each word contains a world within it: "I thought 'boxing' was a word that hit," a young child said to his mother. Backhoe becomes "hackbow," butterfly becomes "flutterfly."

At each stage of the first seven years of development, children delight us first with babbling, then with the utterance of "Mama" or "Papa," followed by words, names, phrases, and increasingly complex syntax enriched by an ever-broadening vocabulary. Daily experience brings every detail of the child's environment into words. Many steps unfold as the child's language capacity grows. Eventually, our kindergartners greet us with their rhyming word play, their interest in riddles they scarcely yet understand, and their extraordinary memory for each linguistic turn of phrase in a complex fairy tale.

But what comes in between? Most importantly, what is it that draws forth the child's ability to work, play, and live as a speaking human being? As with other capacities that unfold during the first three years of life, speech requires not only human relationship and example, but also the existence of forces within and beyond the child herself. Initially, the adult leads the child into speech and language through intimate relationship. Within this sacred space, the adult both speaks and listens, enabling the first communication through spoken language to come forth.

Clearly, for language to emerge there must be an "I" and a "Thou," adult and child. Over days and months, a foundation of nonverbal communication is built: a listening to one another without a single word. Is my baby hungry, or tired, or cold? Is mama coming to get me now? Is she happy to hear me? Will she feed me? The parent learns early to differentiate the language of crying, and also to observe and read the gesture of her child: Is she still hungry for another mouthful or has she turned her head away from the spoon, signaling that she is full, satisfied? Does she wish to be picked up from her crib? The baby stretches out her arms in a gesture of active openness, a gesture that tells a whole story. The child, too, learns to read the gestural as well as verbal communication of parents and caregivers.

The more sensitive and rich these elements of interpersonal communication are, the more deeply does the child become a communicating being. The adult welcomes the child by creating a spiritual space into which the child enters and dialogue arises. When the adult speaks with interest, warmth and respect, the child listens with her whole being. Without question, the adult's speech toward the child is central to this phase.

Gradually, the child's speech unfolds: he takes hold of his world and, as Karl König describes so artistically, words "rain down" upon him. Dialogue between adult and child about daily life, their mutual interests and activities, remains central. Tenderly the child begins to speak. But at first it is as if this capacity to express words is a secret between parent and child. Parents often say, "But he speaks so much at home!" And truly, the child's home—that protected space that is the child's world—is the mystery center in which the miracle of language blossoms. Step by step, the child will gradually select other adults with whom to speak—a grandparent, a neighbor, a playgroup leader, a friend's parent.

If we observe closely, we will see that young two-year-olds do not often converse with one another. One child will speak to the other, but the second child is seemingly deaf to the words, as if the child were not speaking to him. As adults, we still remain the primary language partners and models. Seen from the context of Rudolf Steiner's description of the twelve senses, our sense of the word has developed through the presence of our Ego. This enables the possibility for real listening. Whereas before the child said "I" to herself at around age three, this sense is not yet adequately active to enable true listening to the other.

But let us peek in at a group of four- and five-year-olds. As a community of speakers, they almost seem to exclude the adults. They now have a secret language among themselves! As the adults, we have receded into the background.

Language acquisition is a gradual process, individual for every child, with its numerous delicate transitions unfolding either quickly or slowly. The path is wholly individual, not unlike walking. Tremendously subtle linguistic structures have been built, and linkages have been created within the brain, the speech motor mechanism, and with the outside world. Invisible word-threads have been woven with the whole surrounding world, creating a tapestry that belongs solely to the child himself. We recall the stages:

✦ *Babbling*: the baby's earliest babbling encompasses all the sounds of the universe and all the language groups of the earth;

✦ *Selection*: the baby gradually selects out the phonemes of his own language, and sounds that he does not hear in his environment fall away;

✦ *Encapsulation* of meaning in words, then phrases, then "telescopic" phrases of noun and verb that express a complete concept.

All of these stages occur within the context of adults speaking to children. When does this most naturally occur during infancy? During those moments that arise out of personal relationship. And where is this relationship most logically and naturally expressed? It is within the activities of daily care—diapering, feeding, dressing, bathing. Emmi Pikler, through her work as a family pediatrician and later at the Pikler Institute in Budapest, recognized this aspect of the child's life as primary for the activation of many developmental themes for infants and toddlers. Magda Gerber also brought these insights from her experiences with Dr. Pikler to North America through her work in the United States at Resources for Infant Educarers (RIE).

Can any of us picture carrying out these basic caregiving tasks in silence? It is not easily imaginable. Observe mothers with their infants and young children. If we hear and observe silence, our pedagogical intuition is alerted, actively searching for a source, a reason, a path to understanding the genesis of this unnatural behavior.

The adult continuously expands the child's language through natural dialogue, embellishing and extending the conversation as the child's language becomes ever more expressive.

Those who have studied the work of the Pikler Institute and RIE cannot help but encounter in themselves a deep interest in the unfolding of language. The work of RIE often brings questions from Waldorf early childhood teachers about "talking to children," since we have been encouraged to work with the young child out of imitation, artistically and through gesture, to guide the child through his will and engagement with life. With children from three to seven, we can understand this way of working. However, with the child who is just coming into language or has not even begun to speak, something different is needed. The child's language organism awakens through stimulation from without, and we are the source of that stimulation.

Rainer Patzlaff's booklet, *Childhood Falls Silent*,[1] offers a compelling description of the situation for many children. In this booklet, Patzlaff cites research in which the physical imitation of the motor mechanism of speech from one human being to another was observed:

> *With great surprise kinesthetics found that the listener answers the perceived speech with just the same fine motor movements as the speaker unconsciously performs, also incorporating the whole body and with a delay of only 40 to 50 milliseconds, precluding the possibility of conscious reaction. Condon, the one responsible for this discovery, describes the astonishing synchronicity of movements in the speaker and listener as follows: "Figuratively speaking it is as if the whole body of the listener was dancing in precise and flowing accompaniment to the perceived speech." ...It is as if both speaker and listener are moving in a common medium of rhythmic movement. And this applies only for speech sounds, not for noise or disjointed vowels, as repeated tests have proven ...A two-day-old baby in the USA reacts to spoken Chinese with the same minute movements as to spoken American-English.*[2]

At the Pikler Institute in Budapest, the caregiver develops her intimate relationship with each child not only through her touch and the sharing and playfulness that occur during caregiving times together, but also through her voice. In a musical, natural way, the caregiver engages the child with rich, rhythmic language; she speaks to the preverbal child from earliest infancy, and he responds with his eyes, his gestures of collaboration, his interaction. This is precisely the activity Patzlaff describes as essential for human development. "Whether we recognize it or not, we have an effect on the physical body of the child through the spoken word and we consequently influence the emotional and spiritual possibilities for the child's development later in life. Which of us is aware of this immense responsibility when we talk to a child?"[3]

How do we support the unfolding of language? This is a critically important question in our times, during which children experience so much 'mechanical' language but less and less human discourse. Patzlaff details the decline in language capacity of children over the past several decades:

> *Joachim Kutsche found some bitter words for it [speech falling silent] in the magazine* Der Spiegel *(38/1993): "Whether at home at the dinner table or in the car on the road, in German families (what's left of them), people don't converse. At most functional instructions are still in use: "Don't be so late!"; "Leave that!"; "Hurry up!"; and the binary answers of the little ones: 'Yes.' 'No.' 'Yes' ...end of conversation.*
>
> *... In 1997 a leading insurance company felt compelled to publish a book with the title* Talk To Me! *with the sole purpose being to stimulate parents to speak with their child!*[4]

The advent of the ubiquitous cellular telephone, hand-held movies, and recorded stories for little children in the course of the fifteen years since this research was shared only increases the urgency of our need to engage with our children through language. Clearly, children learn to speak by being spoken to. The musicality of the adult's speech with the infant bathes the child in the Word, introducing the holy capacity that makes us human. In the earliest stages of language development, it is essential that the adult speaks to the child. We are the source of language!

We serve forever as models for children's language development, but in the later years of early childhood our role is transformed. As kindergarten teachers especially, the functional aspects of speaking recede and the artistic aspects—storytelling, poetry, recitation—come forward more strongly. The children speak with each other! Our stepping back creates the opportunity for listening to the child, for ensuring that he feels seen and heard as the individual he is becoming.

Our task as educators and caregivers is to understand and differentiate the kinds of speech that we offer to children in relation to their developmental stages. Language is an essential tool for providing the child with orientation in time and space, and in the early years, language together with gesture is intrinsic to guiding children.

One can picture a caregiver approaching a young child with the intention to pick him up for a diaper change. The adult's thoughts are clear, her intentions far along the path into will activity. But the child may be unaware of the adult's intention, and when the adult arrives, the child is only then entering into the process of participating in this caregiving activity. For the child to engage himself fully and comfortably in relaxed and happy anticipation, he needs time to prepare himself. He must change his focus, let go of involvement with his play or another activity, and recognize both the adult and the anticipated diapering. No matter how intimate the relationship, if the adult unexpectedly picks up the child without making eye contact and verbal contact, the child's startle reflex may be activated and he may express distress or, in a somewhat older child, resistance. Repeated activation of the startle reflex in this way may cause a child to sustain a high stress level, which over time interferes with healthy well-being in numerous ways. Alternately, when the adult approaches the child slowly and uses her voice to indicate her presence, when she orients the child through words and gesture about what will happen, the child now has a "response time." These precious seconds—the waiting, the respectful pause—make all the difference: "Hello, Sadie, I'm here for you. It's diaper time."

This simple, natural and direct approach is deeply integrated into the caregiving practices that have evolved at the Pikler Institute. Soft, melodic, musical speech accompanies all caregiving activity, serving to engage the child delicately, stimulate his own language development, and build the relationship between adult and child.

These conversations do not involve the kind of aimless chatter or premature conversations that draw a child out of his doing by bringing unneeded consciousness to his activity. But the older child who has unfolded a life of fantasy and imagination is a very different being from the infant or toddler just beginning to savor the joy of language, the power of speaking, and the intimacy of words exchanged with others.

With toddlers, the adult's language is also crucial to helping them navigate situations involving conflict with other children. Children need to know boundaries and to receive strategies for problem-solving from the adults around them. Once the period has passed in which distraction is effective as a strategy for guiding behavior, young children want and need to engage their peers and adults in conflict, to test their emerging feeling of self and to understand themselves in the context of social relationships. As adults, we help children navigate this transition through our loving support and our gift of language. We express boundaries for appropriate and inappropriate behavior through speech, and through our words we offer simple solutions for toddler conflict.

As adult speakers in the child's environment, we are the bridge that enables the child to unfold her full humanity. Rhythm, cadence and the metric forms of the mother tongue are offered throughout the child's waking hours as invitations to step further into living relationship with others. We pass to the child the gift of language once given to us. Through our activity as human beings who speak with one another, the holy journey begins.

Notes

1 Rainer Patzlaff, *Childhood Falls Silent: The loss of speech and how we need to foster speech in the age of media*, (Spring Valley: WECAN 2007).

2 Ibid., p.8.

3 Ibid., p. 10.

4 Ibid., pp. 2-3.

Story-Thread and Language for the Toddler

Daniel Udo de Haes

From *The Creative Word* (WECAN 2014)

A good picture-book, one that depicts cheerfully and without a story the simplest things and actions, will help us to find a healthy way of "interpreting" the pictures for the toddler. We can simply let him see and hear what the picture itself wishes to portray; for instance: "This is a man… and this man is chopping," and we can make gestures to accompany this sound: "Chop, chop, chop! He is chopping wood." Later, perhaps after several months, we can connect these three thoughts thus: "This man is chopping wood, chop, chop, chop!" Inevitably an event or action, however insignificant, contains a first little tale. But it is the action that is emphasized rather than the things. Similarly we can proceed from images like "woman," "pump," "water," to "This woman pumps water," again with gestures and emphasizing sounds.

Most of the time we quite naturally carry out this "interpreting" of a particular picture with the same intonation, gestures and sounds. This repetition is good for the child. He feels profoundly connected with our presentation, which is indeed a miniature "incarnation process" for him: his soul finds embodiment in these sounds and gestures. Constant change would have a disturbing and disquieting effect. We shall often be reprimanded if we do it "wrongly," that is, differently from previous occasions. "No!" I once was told off, "No, not chop, chop. Chop, chop, chop!" Indeed a great difference! We are not even allowed to alter the words. If we have once spoken of "wood," we may not on the next occasion say "logs."

We may still observe this characteristic in the four- or five-year-old, and we shall have to bear it in mind when we repeat fairy-tales, for example. There, too, we should not introduce any changes into the chosen words or into the facial expressions and gestures with which the child has formed a connection.

Many of us will be able to remember how wonderful it was and how good it felt to have the same words and gestures repeated again and again. We looked forward to what was to come, and grew into it when the moment duly arrived: the dark voice in the dark wood, the croaking voice of the witch, or the quacking of the little white duck. Only later can the child develop a little more independence from these earliest embodiments of his soul-life.

Now when the first signs of a sense for stories have begun to show in the toddler, we can start very gradually to take these things further—even though the fuller development of this faculty comes only with the five-year-old. Continuing with the given examples and keeping to the same pictures and the same voice, facial expression, and gesture, we would be able to say, for instance: "This man chops wood for his wife: chop, chop, chop! Now the woman pumps water, sh-sh-sh! And here," (next picture), "she lights a fire, ff-ff-ff! And now, (another picture, though every picture should of course be looked at quietly for a long time), "she hangs the pan of water above the fire until the water boils, bubble, bubble, bubble!" and so on. Like this we make a quite natural and gradual transition—which should not be too quick—from the sounds of words to their meanings and a simple story.

We can, so as to keep the first impressions completely pure and unmixed, also take other picture-books and select those in which a certain coherence of narrative begins to appear: two little ducks that go out walking and swimming and have all sorts of adventures, a little boy who goes picking blueberries, and so forth, until finally the child of kindergarten age can be told fairy-tales.

While the story is told it is possible for the child to look at the pictures. In a larger group, for instance in a play-group, this is obviously not often practicable. But here it is particularly important to allow the older ones the opportunity of freely developing their imaginations. However, at home with one or two little children of this age, we can look at pictures during the fairy-tale, provided that they are really beautiful and speak to the child's world of dreams. I recall vividly an illustration by Gustave Doré of the entry of Tom Thumb's family into the dark wood, father in front with his big axe, which called forth experiences which have played a large part throughout my life. The children should not look at the pictures until after the story is told, for they will have already formed their own imaginations which would be disturbed or replaced by the pictures from the book.

It should be stressed that our own feelings and experience should guide our looking at picture-books and telling stories to children. One point to watch, especially with the youngest toddlers, is that we do not look at too many pictures one after the other. This is because a surfeit of images disturbs the quiet intimacy that belongs with each picture. Then, as each picture-book breathes a completely different atmosphere, looking at more than one book at a time may have a confusing effect, especially at bedtime. So it would seem good that we restrict ourselves to one picture-book which can then bring a mood of total peace and dedication.

It is also good if in the course of some days we look again and again at the same picture-book, just as later we tell the same fairy-tale over and over again. This helps the development of a profound relationship with the pictures, and later to the fairy-tale. Thus we should regard it as a good and healthy sign if the child asks—even for weeks at a time—for the same picture-book or fairy tale. This shows how deeply he experiences what he takes in, and we should satisfy this longing. Just as in a religious service for adults the repetition of certain words and actions makes for the deepest effect, so impressions of the pictures and fairy-tale images become ever more intimate and deeply rooted. We shall also be able to observe the extent to which joy in repetition grows continually and how healthily this works on the inner growth of the child.

Unfortunately there are few picture-books which are really good for the toddler, allowing both the things and the simple events of life to speak for themselves, and as yet having no story-thread. There are plenty of illustrated fairy-tales and other stories, but books with pictures for the toddler are few and far between. If we look with the child of this age at the same books over and over again, there is no need for a large number of books.

However, if these cannot be found, one possibility is that we do the drawings ourselves, preferably while we are telling the story and draw with the child watching. Of course many people think—"Oh, I can't do that at all and I couldn't learn it either!" There are, however, more possibilities than most of us think. The point is, after all, that through our simple sketches we awaken the imagination and sympathy of the child. And if we draw with faith and without heaviness, not wishing to do it better than we are able, we shall often feel that it works like magic. I cannot draw at all, and yet the child is fascinated—it is as if miracles are born from my fingers.

What fascinates children is not how well we can draw but the fact that our scribbles, which they imbue with their own fantasy, call forth their inner recognition-experiences. Through this, the toddler's longing for the earthly world will be awakened in a more lively manner than through any picture-book, and in the same way their trust in being truly understood and able to find their way in life will be strengthened. There are many clever artists and painters, and there are many who are clumsy but who nevertheless are able to offer children exactly what they need, having the ability to awaken their memories of the world from which they came.

However inadequate the adult's sketches may be from an artistic point of view, they bring something which a child's picture does not have. This is a certainty that the nature of the child's quest for the earthly world is understood by the adult.

And when adults try to open themselves to the source of the child's soul and to share in that longing to enter into earthly life, then they will be able to offer children what they are looking for.

It is our conviction that starting from this respect for things and this love for the child, almost every adult would be capable of bringing children what they need in this realm.

For instance, say slowly, drawing at the same time: "Look, this is Mother knitting by the fire, and this is Puss playing with a ball of wool; Father is feeding the dog and Rachel is watering the plants," and so on, so that all that happens there, and also every person, every object—the ball of wool, the knitting-needles, the watering-can—speaks its own language. That is what is important for the toddler.

Another possibility is that we manage to find picture-books which come as close as possible to the goal that we set and which we then describe, omitting the narrative-content. We simply relate what we see, without making too much of it, and we speak our words calmly and clearly: "There swims Mother-duck with her ducklings: quack, quack, quack, peep, peep, peep!" For the slightly older ones we can embellish our interpretation a little, as we did with the man and the woman: "Look, there swims the Mother-duck with all her ducklings and Mother-duck says: 'Quack, quack, quack, little children, are you all here?'—'Peep, peep, peep, yes mother, we are all here!'" and so on. In this way we leave out the actual story.

And when we turn to a new picture—unless the child does this himself—we need not begin immediately with the interpretation, but may first allow time for what is there to speak itself, and offer the child the opportunity to take everything in calmly. This should be done also every time the picture is looked at again. Then after this period of undisturbed looking, we may begin a little conversation about it, which the child or we may start, and in this way the things can begin to express themselves also in our words.

Thus everyone will be able to find the best way of avoiding or removing the unnecessary thread of narrative for the toddler.

Once my grandson, a young toddler, managed to do that through his own highly original initiative. He was with his older brother (also still a toddler) on my lap, and we all were looking at a picture-book, a version of a fairy-tale that was not really suitable for toddlers. It had caught his attention because of its beautiful colors, and, as it was taken out of the cupboard by the eldest brother, I had no wish to disapprove and preferred, rather, to try to look at it in toddler fashion. But through my attention being concentrated on the elder who was nearly of kindergarten age, little bits of the story kept creeping in. The little one would not accept this, and his solution—which I would never have thought of—was suddenly to turn over six or eight pages at once, then ten back, and so forth. This was precisely the help I needed to keep completely to the picture itself and abandon all story.

The brother was entirely content with this, even though he would have been able to cope with something of a story. Later I heard that the two had been looking at picture-books in this way also at home, with the younger brother taking care how the pages were turned and the elder giving his commentary about every picture that happened to fall open. Thus we can use any book with simple and beautiful pictures for toddlers.

For the little child it must be a curious experience in his early years to discover how people address one another with words. We should once put ourselves in his place. He observes how, through word-sounds, people create a certain relationship with one another. When one person has uttered some of these strange sounds, the other answers him with some more. The meaning of these sounds remains hidden from the child. He understands the things around him without the help of words, but the word-sounds of people he does not comprehend. Speech itself is to him a world rich in mystery, but the words themselves cannot yet reveal their meaning. Through divergence into many tongues and through the development of the intellect, their sounds have moved so far from their source that they can no longer be recognized. Because of this, the meaning of ordinary human words—for all the fascination and effectiveness of their sounds—is for the time being unknown territory for the child.

But certain words—like "spray," for example—do give us an experience through their sound of what such a thing does. Other examples are words that we have already mentioned: water, stream, dash (as of waves), roar (as of the sea), murmur (as of a stream), wind; all of which express in their sounds something of their meaning and of what happens. These onomatopoeic words are best for the little child, and we should show them to their best advantage through a clear and natural pronunciation. Poets, too, will often express themselves in their sound-paintings through these words.

Examples of this sort are common, but unfortunately are usually spoken carelessly and only seldom come to prominence. This externalization, this dull and sloppy daily use of the spoken word, is the chief reason why the step from the imaginative-experience of his surroundings to the understanding of human language is so great and so far-reaching for the young child. It is the step from an inner participation in the phenomena to a more external intellectual understanding: an inevitable process. Nevertheless, so far as we are able we should fashion healthy forms by speaking as calmly and naturally as possible through the living sounds of the words. A curious and important part is played here by sound-expressions such as jingles and nursery-rhymes, where the inevitable first beginnings of a story-element are rendered "harmless" through being made so delightfully nonsensical; here word-sounds can come to the fore in a lively way. Remember how we used to delight in nursery rhymes, such as "Humpty-Dumpty sat on the wall," and "Hickety, pickety, my red hen," and "Eeny, meeny, miny, mo." The playfully childish content is ushered in "on a bed of sound," and despite the narrative element that is prominent in some of these, a melody can further strengthen this living and dreaming into the sounds.

V. Language, Storytelling, and Puppetry

These nursery-rhymes and play-songs have the great virtue of being able to help the child to bring into the intellectual realm of present-day human language the rich picture-language of things and actions, adorned with sound, melody, and nonsense and allowing it to live on afterwards beneath the surface. They protect the child from too early an external understanding of words, preserving the mystery of the sounds. They are the sacraments of the little child, in the sense that where Communion helps us to regain the spiritual element in our earthly environment, the "sacrament" of the nursery-rhyme helps the child from early on in life to guide the spirit into the very heart of his existence.

Fairy Tale Language and the Image of the Human Being

Helmut von Kügelgen

From *Love as the Source of Education* (WECAN 2016)
Originally published in *An Overview of the Waldorf Kindergarten* (WECAN 1993)

"Fairy tales are healing to the soul of a child."

The fairy tale originates in the childhood of humanity; it has its roots in another state of consciousness. It opens its treasure to the consciousness of today's adult only when he or she can appreciate that our manner of thinking has evolved, and that the history of humanity touches us most deeply when we understand it as an evolution of consciousness. A dreamlike, experiential consciousness that radiated feeling and was filled with images preceded our present-day, scientifically critical, observant, awake consciousness, which is filled with ideas. Mankind's knowledge of the spiritual world, of creation, and of the meaning of the earth, of fate and life's task were imprinted by the ancient mysteries on the imaginations of mythology and the inspirations of religious traditions. Thus, the truth of what lies behind the sun, moon, and stars, and in animals, plants, and stones, would still be told through imagination and human prayers. They also tell of what is revealed in the twisting paths of human life and in the struggle with all that is downgrading, violent or tempting, and of what, as the essence of humanity, steps from being unborn into existence and sees again its immortality in death.

The fairy tales are the remains of these mystery languages—and the children are passing through these stages of human consciousness. For this reason, they live with the fairy tale images and are warmed and fulfilled by them again and again. In the mysteries, one learned and practiced a direct spiritual view of the forces and models behind the senses. Out of this source of truth, from which the ancient cults of the world religions were also created, the fairy tale speaks to the unreflecting, experiential consciousness of the children; and the child creates the formative forces of his inner humanity from this source. For that reason, Rudolf Steiner, who showed to the modern, scientific consciousness the methods of exercise and meditation to gain anew the power of spiritual perception, speaks of the fairy tales as healing to the soul of a child. Cosmic forces of structure and growth shape the child's body into its increasingly earthly and solid form. These same forces operate in the outer form of spiritual facts in the fairy tale images, and nourish the child's healthy life forces. He says, "The human soul has an inextinguishable need to have the substance of fairy tales flow through its veins, just as the body needs to have nourishing substances circulate through it."

Education is inextricably linked with the image of the human being. In modern times, the teaching of education has developed pedagogy as a science and, above all, as a methodology and an art of teaching (didactics). In the nineteenth century, the demand for a more psychological and philosophical foundation in pedagogy addressed the growing uncertainty of educators. With increasing conflicts between generations, the traditional ways were not working.

Thus, Johann Friedrich Herbart's pedagogy resulted from his philosophy; however, from the point of view of human soul forces, his philosophy essentially only took imagination into consideration. For this reason, the reform pedagogy at the turn of the century spoke much about "the whole person." Alfred Lichtwark spoke about experience and feeling, and Georg Kerschensteiner, and the direction of the Worker School, spoke about the will to form. The impulses for an artistic high school curriculum and for the pedagogical islands of the country boarding schools, where the teachers were supposed to be companions and educators as well as lesson-givers, came particularly from the youth movement.

The concern with the interests of youth and the wish to understand more than the rational aspects of human life challenged teachers to include the extensive life of the soul in their teaching. There were also demands from the school administration and home that teachers take their educational task as a forum for the distribution of career and social prospects.

Psychology and anthropology at the turn of the twentieth century could not expand upon what Herbart, for one, had accomplished concerning the forces of the human soul. The reality of the feeling life and the will was not accessible to the scientific, materialistic consciousness. It was there that Rudolf Steiner was active. He broadened the realm of human experience by showing "results of observation of the soul according to scientific methods"—thus the subtitle of his book *The Philosophy of Freedom*, "the basis for a modern world conception"—and thereby he recognized the reality and lawfulness of feeling and will in the life of the human soul. Now an "anthropology as the basis for pedagogy," especially as an impetus for an expanded striving for knowledge, could be presented—this was called by Steiner anthropological spiritual science, or anthroposophy. The body, soul, and spirit of Rudolf Steiner's comprehensive view of humankind became the foundation for Waldorf pedagogy. They also proved his power to renew cultural development in medicine, agriculture, art, curative education, religious life, etc. One aspect of this renewed view of the world and humankind was the development and extension of consciousness. Another was the extension of the ideas of Darwin and Haeckel to spiritual development. Yet another was that he made accessible to westerners the clarifying concepts of karma and reincarnation.

When properly understood, fairy tales reveal answers to the ultimate questions about our outer and inner lives and needs. Even those of us who do not experience with artistic sensitivity the full meaning of the fairy tales can gain a clearer comprehension. Preparatory work for this can be carried out. The modern adult must earn his love for the child. Because the traditions of heartfelt relationships no longer exist, he must earn his inner comprehension of the whole of humankind in its childhood. Thus it is still worthwhile to create anew the fairy tale mood and the fairy tale reality.

"Poetry heals the wounds that the intellect inflicts," says Novalis. By this, he means there is a deeper truth than that which the unspiritual, rational, scientific method has to offer. Every explanation for children of the fairy tale age, and even beyond, should be interwoven with this poetry. The sorry statements about cell division and chromosomes, which in their time must also be learned, express nothing of the truth about the preparation for human birth. Heredity, human love, and the spirit of the ego seeking its destiny are involved. Heaven and earth have a share in it as well. Raphael filled the blue background of his Sistine Madonna, out of which Mary carries her child into his earthly life, with the faces of the unborn.

Whoever has been present at the moment when a small human body ventures forth, painfully, from the mother's body into the light of this world, knows the worrisome question: will the life of the soul, with its first breath and its first cry, move into this body not yet capable of life? He or she also knows the joyful moment when, with the rhythm of breath, the soul moves in, and the birth is completed. The small lump of earth is loved and animated by God's breath—the picture of the biblical creation story reveals itself in its radiant truth: God blew the breath of life into Adam.

The desire for truth ought not to be an excuse to deliver unspiritual explanations, especially concerning the riddle of humankind—which engages us with its own fate in the most moving way when a new, small person seriously changes the destiny of a family or a circle of concerned people. The touching certainty that the infant is led to the earth on the wings of spiritual messengers ought not to be exchanged for the half-truths of materialistic biology and the belief that human existence begins with the birth of the physical body! The fairy tale of the stork is true. Its new interpretation in the material world, its sentimental or cynical mocking from the point of view of the "naked ape," has destroyed the power of the symbol.

We are grateful to the old revealing wisdom for the true fairy tale. It speaks figuratively of change, enchantment, and resolution—and with this, again and again, of the secret of humanity. Fairy tales depict the spiritual origin of people, their trials, their life phases, their triumphs and disappointments. The child can immediately sympathize. All the "cruelty" that we see in the dance around the wolf drowned in the well is for the child no more or less than the blessed victory of good over bad. This victory confirms in the child the trust with which he is so wonderfully equipped for his first steps along the path of life. The fact that the adult depicts such pictures gives him strength to deal with the disappointments that come with the first encounters with the bad in this world. Fairy tales teach children that the bad must be struggled against.

A healthy child aged three or four will listen to the fairy tale of "Star Money" a hundred times with ever-increasing sympathy. This child experiences an imagination, a painting for the soul in the fairy tale. It is only the intellect, not the feeling or will, that is ever done with a matter in which it has once taken an interest. We stand before art, imagination, and religious truth ever stirred anew; we are elevated, and the impulse of our will is strengthened to its best.

Each person—child and adult alike—needs a field of activity for his inner life, for his willing, feeling, and finally also for his thinking soul. If I do not present the child with the images and the language of the fairy tales, then the contents of his soul will be supplied by idle talk. Car makes and money concerns, trivial, unimaginative bits of everyday conversation will fill his soul, resulting in a field filled with weeds.

As children's vocabulary grows, so does their capacity for experience. With growing capacity for experience comes joy in creativity, the inner kingdom. The fairy tales which are told over and over again are acted out by the children; they live and deal with the vital fairy tale characters. Thus it happens that the "fairy tale children," in their first year of school, have a decisive advantage over their peers who have been deprived of the fairy tale world. They experience with greater differentiation; they experience more; they can express themselves more fully either in words or through art. They are open, can listen better, and display greater pleasure in creative endeavors. They form their thoughts into well-structured sentences containing unusual words from their vocabulary.

And what are the fairy-tale films serving up? They are turning into fixed, industrially manufactured pictures, the imagination which blossoms from the lovingly spoken descriptive words, from the fairy tale mood. They are shackling and destroying the imagination. It is best not to send your children to any film before the age of twelve—and then only to cultural or travel films. The fairy tale films break into the sanctuary of the child, and with the suggestive form of the picture's effect, they stamp stereotypes onto the children's souls. The adults themselves who have seen such a film can scarcely rid themselves of this imprinted image and create, once again, a living, imaginative picture of the lonely, Prussian king. A child who has had to see Disney's *Snow White and the Seven Dwarfs* is cheated of the ability to feel the real forces in nature and to experience actively and creatively the spiritual reality in the world of the senses.

The child is not an unfinished adult. She is a person whose state of consciousness allows her to be nearer to the spiritual reality than the adult. "If you do not become like children..." means there is no going backward. The child, who is of the "Kingdom of Heaven," still lives unconscious and dreaming in its guardianship. The adult who is supposed to become like the child, and will possess the Kingdom of Heaven in the days to come, is the person who has achieved knowledge of the spiritual world. In the language of the fairy tales, child and teacher have a language in common.

What to Do about Witches

Ruth Pusch

From *An Overview of the Waldorf Kindergarten* (WECAN 1993)

At the word "witch" we think almost invariably of the horrid creature in the gingerbread house, who tempted little children into her power. To see her more plainly, we need only to look a few pages further in the Grimm's Fairy Tales, to "Jorinda and Joringel"[1]: "A crooked old woman, yellow and lean, with large red eyes and a hooked nose, the point of which reached to her chin… she could lure wild beasts and birds to her, and then she killed and boiled and roasted them. If anyone came within one hundred paces of her castle, he was obliged to stand still and could not stir from the place until she bade him be free. But whenever an innocent-looking maiden came within the circle, she changed her into a bird, and shut her up in a wicker-work cage, and carried the cage into a room in the castle. She had about seven thousand cages of rare birds in the castle."

Such thoroughgoing cruelty, malice, and inhumanity is surely not for children's hearing or reading? How can we allow such impressions to strike terror into the heart of a five- or six-year-old? Even if we call the figures in a folk tale—prince, good fairy, giant—only symbols, and even if bad fairies and witches are symbols of evil, should children have to be confronted with it so early and in such frightening images?

It is a problem that challenges the parents and teachers who love to tell the old stories to their children. It is a problem that has to do with the fact that Rudolf Steiner in his wisdom put fairy and folk tales at the very basis of the Waldorf School curriculum. And he said that the adult who tells the tales should have first made an effort to understand the hidden meaning of the tale. Does the "meaning" of the witch somehow soften the impact of the figure?

Let us look more closely at her various shapes and appearances. There are "big" stories and lesser ones, and in all the more important tales there seems to be either a stepmother ("Mother Holle," "Cinderella") or a witch ("Hansel and Gretel," "Rapunzel"). There are two major stories here in which there is a variation: in "Little Snow White" the stepmother is the witch; in "Sleeping Beauty" one cannot be quite sure that the Bad Fairy (called in Grimms' one of the Wise Women) is a witch, though she seems to have familiar characteristics: her anger, her opposition to "Good" in the other Wise Women, and her accomplishing of what appears to be a cruel deed in letting Briar Rose prick her finger and fall asleep for one hundred years.

What witches do seems to vary considerably. The Jorinda witch changes lovely maidens to birds; the Rapunzel witch keeps only one maiden shut away in a tower. Snow White's stepmother tries to strangle her with bright-colored laces and poison her with comb and apple. The gingerbread-house witch wants to cook and eat Hansel and Gretel. Foundling Bird's witch, an old cook, wants to put him into boiling water. In "The Six Swans," the witch, who is a beautiful queen, makes silken shirts and with them changes the six little princes into swans. "The Old Woman in the Wood" changes travelers to trees and seems to hold their souls shaped as rings in her hands. This is a colorful lot of nasty creatures and one wonders what good they do in the world to have acquired immortality in these never-to-be-forgotten stories.

One step toward understanding witch-nature is the close relationship of stepmother to witch, especially in "Little Snow White." The lovely queen, the real mother, receives her child and blesses it with a name as it comes into the world "as white as snow." But a stepmother comes to take her place.

Beneath the German *Stiefmutter* (stepmother) lies the meaning: stiff-mother, someone who is hard and rigid. The All-Mother who created and watched over us in ancient times has been replaced by Mater-Materialia, matter. Mankind has had to forsake the knowledge of divine powers and plunge into a completely physical existence. A child, too, goes through the same "fall": losing its unconscious life-forces that are woven by protective beings, and becoming awake only to the material world around him.

Hermann Beckh, a priest of the Christian Community, wrote the following in an article, "On Snow-White," published in the magazine *Die Christengemeinschaft*, 1924/25: "The stepmother is hard, physical matter, through which the temptation to envy and pride can enter a pure, light-filled soul. We know that it is the crystallization and hardening of light that has created matter. In this are held the forces of hate, in contrast to the forces of cosmic love active in the warmth of the sun. The wonderful mirror into which the stepmother gazes is the moon-related mirroring power of matter which awakens egoistic self-knowledge and envy in the heart."

But why does Beck say that the forces of hardening enter a pure, light-filled soul? Surely the stepmother exerts her power in ever-widening spirals until Snow White finally succumbs?

Ah! We have come to the moment when the fairy tale reveals its inmost meaning. Novalis was one who recognized it—a creator of fairy tales himself. "All the figures in a tale are but parts or aspects of a single synthetic person, the human being per se." Carl Jung has said it, too: that the "various personages of a dream or a fairy tale can be seen as different aspects or qualities of the protagonist." In a lecture about *The Portal of Initiation* Rudolf Steiner speaks of the many soul-aspects of Johannes standing in their allotted places on the stage in the final scene, the Sun Temple. We can remember how closely this first Mystery Drama corresponds to Goethe's fairy tale of the Green Snake.[2]

Editor's Note: Rudolf Steiner completed four plays, often referred to as the Mystery Dramas. This series of plays depicts the mysteries of reincarnation and evolving karmic relationships over the course of several lifetimes. *The Portal of Initiation* is one of these.

We realize then what a fairy tale really is. It is we ourselves; it concerns our Self; it is a picture of our very being in its struggle to become a human being. The soul yearns to become spirit and can do so only through the pain and battle of physical existence. Why does the Stepmother within us send us forth "in winter, when everything is frozen as hard as stone" in a dress made of paper, to fetch her a basketful of strawberries? Because she knows that there is healing for us—for her—in pain, pain that can be heightened to compassion.

Indeed we carry within us many, many layers of our past, the sequence of our "becoming." In various lectures Rudolf Steiner has enumerated them all. There are the giants, the memories of the time when we were larger, stronger, less individualized, not yet clever; sometimes they rise to haunt us. There are the Enchantress, the Wise Women, Mother Holle, the Old Kings, who seem to belong to an age of wisdom. The late-comer is the clever little tailor who knows how to get the better of any stupid giant and who can be of use even to a mighty King. He became part of us at the end of the Middle Ages, when our modern epoch began, growing ever smaller and cleverer: a picture of our present soul nature.

In the medieval scenes of the second Mystery Drama, *The Soul's Probation*,[3] a tale is told by Dame Kean about the origin of evil. It was the time of transition from one epoch to the coming modern age, and the teachings of occult groups at that time—such as the Templars in the play—wished to prepare for "future shock" with images of the battles to come, battles that every individual would have to wage with ahrimanic powers of hardening, coldness, mechanical thinking, abstractness, fear. Hence the appearance in all parts of the world of fairy and folk tales with similar motifs.

Hansel and Gretel, archetypes of childhood, are forced to leave "their father's house," a phrase that reverberates. "In my Father's house are many mansions…" but this one has become poverty stricken. And the father, weakened, has to follow the decision of "the woman" or stepmother to leave the children—alone and free—in the forest, a world of confusing terror.

Now they have to meet the even harder, greedier, colder character of the witch. She is deceptive, too, and snares them with sugar and the promise of little white beds. In the physical comfort they find in her house, they "think they are in heaven," but in a trice this turns into a prison. The witch is a more powerful version of the stepmother.

The battle begins; it is one all face and we have to fight. In physical existence our spirit, like Hansel, is shut into a small skull-cage and it may not lose hope. It must have the initiative to try to deceive the deceiver: hold out a little animal bone instead of a plump finger. And like Gretel, our soul-nature must be patient in the service required of it, in order to help the more helpless brother. Compassion, patience, and something greater is required. Gretel's copious tears, flowing from the very beginning of their troubles, must be arrested. A decisive deed is necessary; water must be conquered by fire. Only a moment is allowed Gretel to awaken to her opportunity—and she is ready. "Marvels are many, but none more marvelous than man!"

In the Grimms' tale the battle is short and decisive; for most of us it is a constant and consuming one. Simply the fact that we are born into this modern existence places us in the witch's power. As soon as we are conscious of the world, we find her in it. And we know, even as small children, that her power imprisons us and brings hate and coldness too close. She sometimes lurks in an older child's grin; she frightens us in the angry tones of an adult; she can suddenly stare out of our beloved mother's eyes (don't we all believe at one time or another that this isn't "our real mother" but a stepmother?). A child cannot be sheltered in any way from the power of the witch; this is the tragedy of our life of knowledge today. But the love of parents and teachers can bring living imaginations to their children, aware that the spirit wants to fly, like Hansel's white bird, and the soul wants to find its white duck to carry it across the water to its father's house. And more than anything, it will bring that dramatic moment of the soul's awakening to the joyfully listening child, the assurance that every child can meet and subjugate the witch.

That is the strength of fairy tales. They are filled with promise. The weak cannot be strong; evil can be turned to good; the ugly can become beautiful; Cinderella can become a princess, the frog a prince. Every human being can rise to his true stature. Even the smallest child can realize this and rejoice at future victories.

The adult who understands the underlying meaning of a tale tells it, of course, differently from those who have not considered its significance. A good "teller of tales" will not make the dramatic moments horrifying (as Disney loves to do) but keeps to a matter-of-fact tone of voice. It is important not to arouse fear but to be engaged in understanding the fear already in the child. "This tale I am telling you," one must seek to say, "is to show you that everyone in the world is a poor lonely child lost in a deep forest, but see! whatever it is we have to meet there, we can be ready for, and we will be able to deal with it!"

After all, Snow White finds the good dwarves and then her prince; Beauty rescues and transforms her Beast; Cinderella's slipper really fits only her foot; Rapunzel's tears bring sight back to her face. A fairy tale is not cruel, it is consoling. It has the power to awaken meanings, as George MacDonald said. We must only do our best to understand one or the other of those meanings, and we must understand the children we tell the tales to and the needs of those children. The "big" tales we have talked about here are assigned to the first grade curriculum and can wait for their telling until a child is almost six. None of them should come to a child too early. In Kindergarten certain tales, carefully chosen and carefully told, can be given to children one knows well. As songs or marionette plays, they are helpfully intertwined with music and rhythmic movement.

Bruno Bettelheim in his *Uses of Enchantment*[4] has described the wonderfully positive effect fairy tales have on children. It is not wholly his fault that he understands the needs of children better than the highest meaning of the tales. It is actually only spiritual science and the work of Rudolf Steiner that can provide this meaning. But an effort to reach a spiritual understanding of the world around us is like lifting a determined sword to cut through a hedge of sharp thorns and, finding it open to our entrance, like the Prince, for whom the hedge was covered with flowers and who then found his way through the sleeping castle and up the steep stone steps into the place where Briar Rose was waiting.

Notes

1   The Brothers Grimm, *The Complete Grimms' Fairy Tales* (New York: Pantheon Fairy Tale and Folklore Library, 1976), no. 69.

2   See Rudolf Steiner, *Three Lectures on the Mystery Dramas* (1910-1911) (Great Barrington: SteinerBooks 1983).

3   See Rudolf Steiner, *Four Mystery Dramas* (Great Barrington: SteinerBooks 2015).

4   See Bruno Bettelheim, *The Uses of Enchantment* (New York: Vintage Books 2010).

Choosing Fairy Tales for Different Ages

Joan Almon

From *An Overview of the Waldorf Kindergarten* (WECAN 1993)
Updated by the author for this publication

Author's Note: Since the time of this essay's original publication, many fairy tales from Asia and Africa have been included in Waldorf preschools and kindergartens.

Fairy tales collected by the Brothers Grimm are numbered from 1 to 200, corresponding to their numbering in Grimm's Fairy Tales as published by the Pantheon Fairy Tale and Folklore Library, formerly an independent press, currently a division of Random House.[1]

A list of sources for most of the fairy tales mentioned here appears at the end of the essay.

Deciding which fairy tales are appropriate for which age group is a problem that faces every kindergarten teacher as well as every parent who wants to offer fairy tales to children. Over the years, with the experience of actually telling the tales to children, one develops a "sense" for this, but in the beginning some guidelines may be helpful.

Among the fairy tales, there are stories of varying degrees of complexity. At the simplest level there is the "Porridge Pot," while a considerably more complicated story is the beautiful French tale of "Perronick," the simpleton in quest of the grail who must overcome seven difficult obstacles. The latter is a tale for elementary school children, perhaps just as they are leaving the world of fairy tales around age nine, while the former little tale is a delight to three-year-olds as their first fairy tale. They enjoy hearing of the little pot, so full of abundance, which overflows (for lack of the right word). At this age, the children themselves have a sense of life's eternal abundance, which one child expressed to her mother in this way when told she did not have enough time to take her out to play: "But Mother, I have lots of time. I'll give you some."

In almost every fairy tale, there is either a problem which must be solved, such as how to get the porridge pot to stop cooking, or a confrontation with evil, which can take many forms, such as the Queen in "Snow White" or the various monsters that Perronick encounters. The milder the problem, the more appropriate the tale for younger children, and conversely, the greater the evil, the more appropriate the tale is for older children.

V. Language, Storytelling, and Puppetry

Another aspect of fairy tales is that the hero or heroine must undergo certain trials or go on a complex journey before succeeding in his or her quest. In the original version of the "Three Little Pigs," the pig is nearly tricked three times before he is able to overcome the wolf. Three is a number that frequently arises in relationship to the challenges of the fairy tale. In this case, the tasks are not portrayed as very ominous, and the pigs handle them with a good deal of humor, making it a tale well-loved by four-year-olds. In the "Seven Ravens," the daughter must first journey to the sun, the moon, and the stars in order to restore her brothers to human form. This tale speaks well to five- and six-year-olds. An even more complex tale is the beautiful Norwegian tale entitled "East of the Sun and West of the Moon." Here, too, the heroine must go on a great journey to redeem her prince, and the journey takes her first to the homes of three wise women. She is then aided by each of the four winds. Yet even when the north wind blows her to the castle east of the sun and west of the moon, her work is not yet completed, and she is further tested before she is able to marry the prince. This is not a tale for the kindergarten, but rather one for the first grade or beyond, when children's own inner struggles grow more complex and they are nourished by the more complex fairy tales.

With these thoughts in mind, I would like to divide some of the tales commonly told in Waldorf kindergartens into categories of complexity. This is a somewhat dangerous business, for the fairy tales are so alive that they do not rest comfortably in one category or another. Even as I divide them up, I find myself constantly switching tales from one category to another. In the end one makes one's decisions very much within a particular group of children or with an individual child in mind. Please accept these divisions lightly, as mere indications, and take the time to develop your own judgments in this area. You may find it helpful to read a few stories from each category as a means of understanding the different levels of complexity.

1 The three-year-olds in the nursery or mixed-age kindergarten are very satisfied with little nature stories, or with a simple tale such as "Sweet Porridge." The older threes are often ready to hear the "sequential" tales such as the tale of the turnip. The turnip has grown so large that Grandfather cannot pull it out by himself, so one after another come to help him: Grandmother, grandchild, dog, cat, and finally mouse. All together are then able to pull out the turnip. One finds many tales of this sort. Songs that also fall into this category are "I Had a Cat and the Cat Pleased Me" and "Had Ga Ya," which is sung during the Jewish holiday of Passover. Such sequential stories and songs have the added advantage of being relatively easy for a beginning storyteller to learn. A collection of tales for this age group includes the following:

- ✦ Sweet Porridge (*Grimm's Fairy Tales*, 103)
- ✦ Goldilocks and the Three Bears (a Russian tale)
- ✦ Little Louse and Little Flea (*Spindrift*[2])
- ✦ The Turnip (a Russian tale)
- ✦ The Mitten
- ✦ Little Madam (*Spindrift*)
- ✦ The Gingerbread Man
- ✦ The Johnny Cake (English)
- ✦ The Hungry Cat (Norwegian, *A Lifetime of Joy*[3])

2 The next category of tales is slightly more complex, but the overall mood is usually cheerful and without too much sorrow or struggle. The fours and young fives are usually quite comfortable with these tales.

- ✦ Three Billy Goats Gruff (Norwegian)
- ✦ Three Little Pigs (English)
- ✦ The Wolf and the Seven Kids (*Grimm's Fairy Tales*, 5)
- ✦ The Pancake Mill (*Let Us Form a Ring*[4])
- ✦ Mashenka and the Bear (Russian, from *A Lifetime of Joy*)
- ✦ The Shoemaker and the Elves (*Grimm's Fairy Tales*, 39)

3 In the next category come many of the tales which we normally associate with the term "fairy tale" and which we think of in relation to five- and six-year-olds. These tales contain more challenge and more detail. The main character often sets out in the world with a simple task to perform such as in the "The Miller's Boy and the Pussy Cat." Although obstacles are encountered, they do not weigh too heavily on the soul of the individual. Such tales include:

- ✦ The Poor Miller's Boy and the Cat (*Grimm's Fairy Tales*, 106)
- ✦ The Star Money (*Grimm's Fairy Tales*, 153)
- ✦ The Frog Prince (*Grimm's Fairy Tales*, 1)
- ✦ Mother Holle (*Grimm's Fairy Tales*, 24)
- ✦ Little Red Cap (*Grimm's Fairy Tales*, 26)
- ✦ The Bremen Town Musicians (*Grimm's Fairy Tales*, 27)
- ✦ The Golden Goose (*Grimm's Fairy Tales*, 64)

- The Spindle, the Shuttle, and the Needle (*Grimm's Fairy Tales*, 188)
- The Hut in the Forest (*Grimm's Fairy Tales*, 169)
- The Queen Bee (*Grimm's Fairy Tales*, 62)
- The Snow Maiden (Russian, *Plays for Puppets*)
- The Seven Ravens (*Grimm's Fairy Tales*, 25)
- Snow-White and Rose-Red (*Grimm's Fairy Tales*, 161)
- Little Briar-Rose (*Grimm's Fairy Tales*, 50)
- The Princess in the Flaming Castle (*Let Us Form a Ring*)
- The Donkey (*Grimm's Fairy Tales*, 144)
- Rumpelstiltskin (*Grimm's Fairy Tales*, 55)
- Little Snow White (*Grimm's Fairy Tales*, 53)
- Hansel and Gretel (*Grimm's Fairy Tales*, 15)

4. The final group I will include here are those fairy tales well-suited for six-year-olds making the transition to first grade. This is a time of stress for children as they lose their baby teeth and a develop a sense of departure from the heart of early childhood. (Fortunately they still have a few more years before they make their final "fall" from Paradise.) Tales in which characters have a personal experience of suffering or sorrow meet this new phase of inner development in the children. Often these tales are not told in the kindergarten at all but are left for first grade.

- Jorinda and Joringel (*Grimm's Fairy Tales*, 69)
- Brother and Sister (*Grimm's Fairy Tales*, 11)
- Cinderella (*Grimm's Fairy Tales*, 21)
- Rapunzel (*Grimm's Fairy Tales*, 12)

A frequent problem that troubles kindergarten teachers is how to select tales for a mixed-age group. If there are three-year-olds present as well as six-year-olds, will the more advanced tales harm the little ones? My own experience and that of other teachers is that this is not a problem provided the story is appropriate for some of the children in the group. This is an interesting phenomenon that seems to work as follows. In a mixed-age group with children three to six, one can choose a tale for the five- and six-year-olds and the three- and four-year-olds will be attentive. They may seem less focused than they are with a simpler tale, but they rarely grow restless (though it sometimes helps to seat the youngest ones near the teacher or the assistant). On the other hand, if one would tell the same complex tale to a group of only three- and four-year-olds, one would find that they do not attend to it well and easily lose interest. It is as if there is no one in the group who can "carry" the story for the others. In a mixed-age group one can also create a balance in the tales by telling some that are appropriate for the younger children. The older children generally do not get bored with the simpler tales, for they are now old enough to see the humor in the sequential tales or simpler fairy tales, and they will laugh at the humorous parts while the little ones listen with full seriousness.

When choosing a fairy tale, another factor to take into account is whether a fairy tale is generally well-known in the society, even if it is known in an incorrect form. When a tale is well-known, children often seem ready to hear it at a younger age than they otherwise might be.

The final consideration, and probably the most important one, is the storyteller's own relationship to the story. Sometimes a storyteller loves a tale so much that the story may be told to children who are generally too young for it. It is as if the storyteller's love of the tale builds a bridge to it. Thus, I knew one teacher who loved "The Seven Ravens" so much that she told it year after year to class after class of three- and four-year-olds, a feat I would not undertake. When this love of fairy tales is coupled with an understanding of them on the part of the storyteller, doors are opened to the whole realm of life in which fairy tales are true and live forever. In the telling of fairy tales we too are nourished and brought back into this realm. Rudolf Steiner describes the fairy tales very beautifully when he says, "Much deeper than one might imagine lie the sources whence flow genuine, true folk tales that speak their magic throughout all centuries of human evolution."[5]

Notes

1. The Brothers Grimm, *The Complete Grimms' Fairy Tales* (New York: Pantheon Fairy Tale and Folklore Library, 1976
2. Wynstones Press, *Spindrift*, (Gloucester, UK: 1999).
3. Bronja Zahlingen, *A Lifetime of Joy* (WECAN: 2005).
4. *Let Us Form a Ring*, Nancy Foster, ed. (Silver Spring: Acorn Hill Children's Center 1989).
5. Rudolf Steiner, "Folk Tales in the Light of Spiritual Research," February 6, 1913. This lecture is currently out of print, but we hope to see the publication of several lectures on fairy tales by Rudolf Steiner in the near future.

Further Resources

Peter Christian Asbjornsen, Moe, *A Time for Trolls* (Norway: Arthur Vanous Co. 1992)

Marionette Theater: Posing a Task for a Socially-Oriented Education

Helmut von Kügelgen

From *Love as the Source of Education* (WECAN 2016)
Originally published in *An Overview of the Waldorf Kindergarten* (WECAN 1993)

The struggle for the legal security of a freely chosen, humane education for preschoolers demands spiritual decisions that parents and teachers can no longer avoid. Independent of these efforts, however, we must not neglect the concrete questions of the creation of a counter-balance against a civilization inimical to children.

Whatever can be done to offer children enlivening soul nourishment must be begun. In the late fall, children are more and more withdrawn from nature—insofar as they can reach it at all—and are brought into the house and indoor occupations. It is also the time for the first thoughts about Christmas and Christmas presents, so the educational experience should lead to understanding with the heart and to action.

How incongruous it must have seemed in the year 1917, in the tragic last phases of the First World War and in the beginning of his open political and social activity, that Rudolf Steiner should have been concerned with the establishment of a marionette theater. But he devoted his full attention to this theater. The task of this marionette theater was to give a concrete example of the spiritual impulse of Middle Europe against the flood of western ways. In Rudolf Steiner's house at Motzstrasse 17, Berlin, a day care center was established by the Berlin branch of the Anthroposophical Society with financial support from the state. The children there were from four to twelve years old; their mothers worked and their fathers were in the military. The story of this theater has been told by Helmut Vermehren in No. 74 of *News of Anthroposophical Work in Germany*, Christmas, 1965. The following paragraphs are taken from that article:

> *For this center, several anthroposophical friends now built a puppet theater. The moving force was the painter and sculptor Leonhard Gern. It was he and Hedwig Hauck who asked Rudolf Steiner for advice about the realization of their ideas. Rudolf Steiner seized immediately upon this invitation. He explained that the marionettes must hang on threads and be directed from above; only such marionettes were appropriate for the presentation of fairy tales.*

> *In the course of time, he gave many indications, and he was often present at the rehearsals. The stage, which was a sliding one, had three curtains in different colors which were raised one at a time to lift the action on the stage completely out of worldly,*

prosaic connections. The marionettes were not controlled with the usual crossbar but rather with strings tied directly to the fingers. Rudolf Steiner showed how the marionettes were to be used. His advice was clear: 'Marionettes cannot speak!' The fairy tales must be read to the children, and the narrator—who should look 'pretty'—should sit nearby on a chair, similar in style to the chair of God in the Oberufer Paradise Play. The tale should be read quite simply and naturally, and the different creatures and people characterized with the voice. He himself gave many examples of this.

Rudolf Steiner laid special emphasis on the right style and color of the costume fabric. Once a gold embroidered fabric was needed for the garment of a prince. Rudolf Steiner was shown five samples and selected a fabric with the remark that this one was well suited for showing the image of the Ego. Another time, he wanted a dark gray garment for the wicked fairy, while for the other wise women he selected garments in the colors of the rainbow. In the dwarves one should avoid any caricatures; they should, however, have a special liveliness.

During rehearsals for 'Sleeping Beauty,' after many experiments, there arose the possibility that the thorn hedge should be transformed into a rose hedge from above down. Steiner remarked, 'In fairy tales, after all, even the roses grow down from heaven.' The scenes in which the prince goes around the castles were painted on veils; these pictures were then lit up by a spotlight as they passed, one after another, across the background. Sometimes Rudolf Steiner took up a paint brush and corrected the stage scenes.

He was especially interested in the stage lighting. There should be, for example, a strong red illuminating the stage scene each time the wicked queen appears. He was concerned about the smallest details with this purpose in mind: 'We must do everything in our power to help the children to develop fantasy.' This was the basic attitude which he instilled in the hearts of those working with the marionettes. One has the distinct impression that in this work Rudolf Steiner had before him something of the future. The hint which he gave in this connection, that 'the marionette theater was a remedy for civilization's damages,' attained through the events described a special importance.

On this stage, performances were given until the end of the first World War. Stories presented were: 'Sleeping Beauty,' 'Snow-White,' 'Hansel and Gretel,' and 'Rumpelstiltskin.' Steiner was always at the rehearsals, giving advice and being actively involved. The direction of the plays lay in the hands of Leonhard Gern, who also made the marionettes. Hedwig Hauck made the costumes and selected the fabrics which were laid before Rudolf Steiner. The music for the plays was composed by Leopold van der Pals. It was played before the curtain was raised and also during transformations and other important moments, such as 'Mirror, mirror on the wall...' Helene Gunther, later Mrs. Hansen, played the piano. The performers were Wilhelm Selling, Hedwig Hauck, Anna Samweber, Miss Knipsel, and Lore Schumann. The latter—a cousin of Kathe Kollwitz—painted the stage scenes and helped with the development of the stage in special ways. The narrator was Eva Groddeck, later Mrs. Putz. Rudolf Steiner said to the players: 'Doesn't she herself look like a fairy tale?'

With the end of the war in 1918 there also came an end to this theater. When Hedwig Hauck went on to the first Waldorf School in Stuttgart, Marie Steiner telegraphed to her that she should bring the marionette theater with her to the school. But this stage did not again develop a new life.

It does not help much to rage against television, whose mighty influence on the education of children can be observed with the greatest concern. One correctly understands Rudolf Steiner's efforts for a marionette theater as a "remedy against civilization's ills" when one sees in it the beginning of a genuine cultural movement such as has arisen around the Waldorf kindergartens. Independent stages in establishments such as Rudolf Steiner houses, Waldorf schools and kindergartens should reach a growing number of children besides those actually in the kindergartens.

This picturesque, educational medium, the living play imbued with inner imagination and fantasy, should be offered in many styles as a way of activating the creative powers of children. The joy and animation of young viewers, who gladly turn their attention and love to the marionettes performing the fairy tales, develop in the course of a child's education into building stones for life.

The Waldorf school movement is not without experience in this area. In the Free Waldorf School in Hannover, the marionette plays were nursed along for many years in the handwork and artistic classes. The Stuttgart-Kräherwald Waldorf School, and later Marburg, developed a puppet stage as part of the handwork classes. A large number of kindergartens have arranged performances which attract more children than just those enrolled in their own groups. It depends on the initiative of individuals and the readiness of their colleagues and the school association to support these initiatives.

There is here a concrete task for all who want not merely to discuss preschool education, but to do something about it with full consciousness.

The Pedagogical Value of Marionette and Table Puppet Shows for the Young Child

Bronja Zahlingen

From *A Lifetime of Joy* (WECAN 2005)
Originally published in *An Overview of the Waldorf Kindergarten* (WECAN 1993)

The creative form-giving power of fantasy reveals itself to the careful observer as a soul force, which in the first seven years of life and in many ways even up to the ninth year appears completely intertwined with the forces of growth. During the development of the wisdom-filled organization of the human body, the flowing streams of life and the shaping, form-giving powers work in a certain polarity. They are unified, however, in unity through the ever-working, breathing power of the middle sphere of man.

Tender soul powers are released step-by-step from the life forces and become visible in the child's play, until with the change of teeth, they are ready to be used in the free shaping of concepts. This allows the child to enter school for actual learning, which, however, must still be imaginative and full of pictures. At the same time the forces of memory can be guided and used more consciously.

From where does the living fantasy receive its power, the tools for its use? It is the senses that open up the world to the individual being that wants to unfold. In the beginning, they work in unison. The young child appears like one great sense organ which opens itself up to the impressions of the world as a unity of body, soul, and spirit; it does not yet consciously decide for one or the other impression, but must in the truest sense of the word "embody" all the impressions which the world makes upon it.

At the birth of a healthy child, the different bodily organs are present with a quality that fits a human being, but their lasting and individualized shape is formed on the whole during the first seven or even nine years (apart from those organs which begin to ripen in puberty). After that point, soul experiences are mostly working in the functioning rather than the shaping of organs; growth still continues until the human being comes of age and is in the position of experiencing a soul and spiritual development which is less tied to the body and its organs.

Now let us return to the young child and his senses. (Rudolf Steiner introduces us to the vista of twelve senses in several of his works; see Note.) These senses are gradually differentiated as to their particular quality. They do not, however, like to be completely isolated. The shape of a colored surface, for example, can be understood through inner movement; whatever looks beautiful to the eye is expected to also taste good. The aroma of Christmas cookies will at the same time bring forth in a magical way the memory of the sound of bells, lights on the tree, shining faces, and a sense of true well-being. Through the unity of several senses, the experiences of the soul become richer and more colorful. If the senses act in isolation, the soul is in danger of being impoverished. If, however, through a handicap it becomes necessary to educate the senses in a more isolated way, one will have to give the soul additional experiences in other ways.

Actively, the young child unites with the outer world through his senses. Through the quality of the impressions made on the individual sense organs, he shapes and forms these very organs, making them active and strong, or dull and passive.

To come to a better understanding of the development of the senses we can link ourselves to Goethe's words: "The eye is built by the light for the light." If we want the eye to develop the ability of clear sight and sensible perception of colors and forms, we have to guard it in this formative phase of childhood from too-strong, glaring experiences of light and color. That which moves and changes too quickly, which the eye has to take in but cannot even follow, will possibly create a misforming of the organs of sight.

It is even worse for the ear, which we are not able to close voluntarily: here the consequences work even more deeply into the inner being. We understand the consequences brought about by the pleasant qualities in sounds, music, and language, or by their opposite, namely inorganic, penetrating, monotonous noise. A very similar situation exists with the other senses. In our world today only very few children can grow up in the quiet of a garden. Town and countryside are equally flooded by an overflow of sense impressions, which change and alter incessantly, and very many children, therefore, have to suffer from outer and inner restlessness.

So as educators we try to create at least some special times for inner quieting, for a deeper breath and concentration. An example of such an opportunity is the play with table puppets or marionettes, which children experience first as observers. Out of this observation, rich impulses can grow for their own play. We build up a scene with pieces of colored cloth, materials taken from nature such as stones, wood, pine cones, unspun wool, and such like, and simple home-made standing dolls or animals of wood or soft material. We move the figures in an appropriate way while we tell the story. Or we can create a scene fitting to the content of the story with colored silks or veils. Amidst great expectation, what is mysteriously covered at first is gradually unveiled, and the eye meets a meaningful wholeness. Simple marionettes of silk wander through the colorful world. They walk from house to forest, over the sea and sometimes to sun, moon, stars, and even sometimes up to the mountain of clear crystal glass. As they move over the surface of the scene using its length, breadth, and depth, the observing child can inwardly unite immediately with the experience of space, while on the television only deception of the eye is at work. Here inner activity is created that works in a refreshing and enlivening way into the very breath and blood circulation. Color, movement, gesture, and language shape a unity, and fitting music can envelop the soul in warmth and safety. It can also give joy and pleasure.

A little world that is a whole, and which can be fully realized, is given to the child. The child is part of the events because it can share in them through adding, out of its own fantasy, to that which is given to the sense impression as an impulse. For young children we do not need any technical tricks. The whole event is present as in a picture. As it is happening without a break or an interval, it brings about a pleasing harmony of experience. The other day, after a performance of "The Seven Ravens," a father remarked, "You know, the children become so good."

One finds that the adults, too, cannot resist the magic of such a play. The child in us loves to reenter this world of creative imagination, which releases a higher vision out of the sense experience.

Last but not least we would point out something rather essential in this kind of puppet play where the person who is leading the dolls remains visible. Not only can we then perceive the reactions of the children and possibly take them into consideration, but also our appearance does not worry the children. Life, body, soul, and spirit still exist as a unity in children. For example, it is only the detachment of the adult that enables us to read the most horrendous reports in the newspaper while at the same time enjoying our lunch; the young child, on the contrary, will even eat up food he does not like as he, so to speak, opens himself heart and soul to something nice you are telling him—his open mouth follows! Children's pleasure and displeasure are visible right down to the tips of their toes; they can seem to be twice their normal weight if they do not wish to be moved.

While thus engaged in building and developing their bodies, children form tendencies toward good or ill health, depending on their physical and soul experiences. The very functions of their organs are influenced by the warmth and friendliness we offer, even by our inner striving and moral intentions. Somehow, little children seem to see right through us.

Note
See Rudolf Steiner, *An Outline of Esoteric Science* (Great Barrington: SteinerBooks 1997).

VI. Working with Parents

Parenting is hard. The bombardment of information, the reality that many parents live far from their extended families, the hectic and chaotic pace of life—this and more contribute to the challenges of parenting. It is not uncommon for parents to be filled with fear, anxiety, confusion, and feelings of loneliness when confronted with the awesome and sometimes overwhelming task of raising their children.

Rudolf Steiner described our current epoch as the time when mankind is developing the consciousness soul.[1] He spoke extensively of the consciousness soul, and the social challenges that accompany its development. In a lecture on October 10th, 1916, Rudolf Steiner said in relation to the challenges of modern life:

> ...Through the consciousness soul man is much more an individual, a solitary traveler through the world. And the tendency people now show to withdraw into themselves is becoming [a] more and more pronounced characteristic of our time. The hallmark of the consciousness soul is the urge towards an isolated life, secluded from the rest of mankind. Hence the difficulty of getting to know one another, especially of establishing confidence...[2]

Many parents feel insecure and alone in their parenting struggles. As teachers, we have a wonderful opportunity to bring confidence, warmth, love, compassion, and understanding to the parents we meet. We can accompany the parents on this journey with their children in a supportive way, offering guidance and encouragement. We can build trust and support each other with courage.

In the following essays, the writers offer pictures of what it means to work with parents today, and how we can best do so. Kimberly Lewis offers insightful tips encouraging joy, acceptance, and the gift of time. She urges teachers to practice active, compassionate listening in their interactions with parents.

Louise deForest explores the consciousness soul and Rudolf Steiner's six basic exercises in relation to working with parents. In all of the challenges we face with parents that might bring fear, confusion, alienation, and powerlessness, we can bring equanimity, positivity, open-mindedness, and sympathy. Louise writes: "Martin Buber once said 'all living is meeting.' In our working with parents, we have the opportunity to overcome our sympathies and antipathies and replace them with true interest in the human being who stands before us."

Lauren Hickman writes about creating community and conversations with parents, making conscious connections. Margaret Ris encourages teachers to be sensitive, open, and respectful with parents, offering non-prescriptive guidance. Dialogue, conversation, and modeling ways of behavior can be effective with parents. She offers specific proposals for parent meetings and she draws from the ideas of Rudolf Steiner, Magda Gerber, and Emmi Pikler.

In the final essays of this section, Ruth Ker and Nancy Blanning give specific suggestions for activities for parent meetings and tackle the issue of discussing first grade readiness with parents.

Notes

1   Rudolf Steiner describes a path of development for humanity and for the individual which includes stages referred to as the Sentient Soul, the Intellectual Soul, and the Consciousness Soul. See his book *Theosophy* (Great Barrington: SteinerBooks 1994) for further exploration.

2   Rudolf Steiner, "How Can the Destitution of Soul in Modern Times Be Overcome?" Lecture given on October 10, 1916. The only known English translation is available from the Rudolf Steiner Archive (http://wn.rsarchive.org/Lectures/GA/GA0168/19161010p01.html).

Reflections on Working with Parents

Kimberly Lewis

From *Gateways* Newsletter Issue 58 (WECAN 2010)

For decades, pioneers in the field of parent education have been quietly creating exceptional methods of working with parents. Since having my own baby far from home at the age of twenty-three, I have made a life study of parent education. As a new mother in a small workers' community in the middle of the Saudi Arabian desert, I was fortunate to find La Leche League leaders who introduced me to the "mother-to-mother support" model. This blessing inspired me to learn what I could about parenting the very young child and to bring this knowledge to other parents.

Today, in the parent-child classes I teach, I draw on my in-depth studies of the diverse disciplines of La Leche League, anthroposophy, Waldorf education, the work of Emmi Pikler in Hungary, and the work of Magda Gerber in Los Angeles. In an attempt to integrate and synthesize the best and most essential ingredients of each of these models, I have come up with a number of approaches that I use in my classes with good results. Here are some of them.

Be worthy of imitation

In my parent-child classes, I have discovered that, just like the children, parents can more easily internalize what I'm teaching when they have a model. So I try to model for them what I believe are the most important aspects of healthy childcare in the early years. I model optimal behaviors when I interact with the children, and perhaps more importantly, I also model them when I interact with the parents. The parents get to feel the effects of these approaches first hand.

Offer unconditional acceptance

Parents often hold an image of their future child in their mind's eye and then become disappointed or embarrassed when their actual child doesn't match up to this image. So I try to teach unconditional acceptance of the actual child in the present moment. I believe the child is always right in doing what he or she is doing (I might not endorse it, but the child has a good reason for doing it). The same is true of parents. They are doing the best they can. I can't expect them to be different in that moment. Acceptance is the starting point for understanding. It allows me to ask the right questions and discover the root of the behavior so I may offer guidance and support.

Create joyful, one-on-one interactions

During snack, I try to model for the parents what it looks like to give 100% attention to the children during moments of care. I wash each child's hands slowly and gently, giving my full attention to the child and to the task. I offer each child just the amount of food he or she is willing to eat. The parents, too, need similar one-on-one time with me. To be seen completely by another person is one of life's great joys. I try to find a time during our morning when I can circulate among the parents and check in with each of them for a few minutes.

Keep them warm and well-nourished

For the children this means a warm room, warm clothing, and wholesome, natural food. For the parents this means human warmth, deep respect and spiritual nourishment. By creating a safe and beautiful environment, one nourishes the parents. We bring the wonders of nature into the classroom; we light a candle at snack time; and we honor the festivals of the year. These rituals and traditions are touching elements to the parents.

Allow them to progress at their own pace and in their own time

I teach the parents to give their children time to progress through each stage of development at their own pace—without being pushed or prodded. This goes for the parents as well. Every parent comes to class at a particular moment in his or her own life's journey, and this must be respected. Some parents know that Waldorf education is going to be a part of their family life even before the first day of class. Other parents warm to it gradually. Still others take what they find useful and then follow their paths in separate ways.

Give them the gift of uninterrupted free time

Just like children, parents love the time, space, and freedom to do whatever they are moved to do without interruption. For parents, this usually means visiting with whomever and discussing whatever they'd like. I support them by making sure there is a time and place in our morning for open conversations. Even though it isn't a particularly long part of our morning (usually twenty minutes or so while we are outside), I think it's an essential ingredient.

Do less, observe more

While modeling purposeful work is ideal in the kindergarten, it needs to be re-examined for the youngest children. In my experience, sensitive observation is an equally important activity for parents of little children. At the beginning of each session, we do short periods of quiet observation (five minutes), and then very quickly we move into longer periods (at least twenty minutes). Most of our group discussions come out of these observation periods. Parents often try to accomplish too much when their children are little; what a blessing for them to discover they can simply sit, relax, and be with their children.

Don't put them into a position they can't get into themselves

Children as well as parents need to feel safe and at ease. With children, this has more to do with the physical positioning of their bodies. With parents it's mostly behavioral. The principle holds true for both. I don't put parents on the spot or ask them to do anything that might make them feel uncomfortable. And while I might give them homework to do over the week, it's always optional.

Allow them to do as much as they can themselves

The message I want the children to hear from their parents is, "You are capable. I'll stay close, but you can do it for yourself." The same is true for the parents. For example, I'm not likely to try to soothe a crying child if the parent is right there doing his or her best. I offer my presence and that is enough. However, if the struggle is too great, I will step in and make a change.

Practice active listening and compassionate speaking

With the children, I do a practice called "reporting." Rather than praising or correcting the children, I model for the parents the simple act of reporting back what I see the children doing. The same goes for the parents. Instead of saying, "Don't do that," or "Try this instead," I simply report what I see and describe the situation. For example, I might report, "You've moved your baby onto her belly. She's having difficulty moving her head. Her arms and legs cannot move freely. When she was on her back, her movements were more fluid."

These ideas and tips are some of what I've learned in my study and practice of parent education. In the past, I co-moderated an online discussion group for families and teachers who work with children under four. The group was a good forum for sharing ideas, experiences, and questions. I look forward to finding new ways to encourage continued musings and discussions on parenting.

Working with Parents: A Different Perspective

Louise deForest

From *Gateways* Newsletter Issue 64 (WECAN 2013)
Originally published in the UK Steiner/Waldorf early childhood education journal, *Kindling*

Many years ago, when my two youngest children were still very small, I would occasionally visit a friend of my mother's named Mrs. Robb. She was quite active in those days; at that time she was the oldest living survivor of the Titanic and was much in demand to give interviews, visit talk shows and tape her memoirs for different maritime museums. She was in her mid-nineties when I met her and she lived alone in the village where my mother also lived. She was losing her eyesight but still remained active in her small community and had many friends. I considered myself one of those many friends. Because we lived quite far away, I would see Mrs. Robb only every four to six months. The children and I would knock on her door and she would open it with a big smile on her face. She would kiss the children, give me a hug and invite us into her lovely home. She bustled about as she gathered things for tea, telling me the freshest news from town and recounting amusing anecdotes from her latest round of interviews. Finally everything was in place—the tea was brewed, cookies were on the plate for the children, and we were all comfortably sitting on the sofa with the late afternoon sun streaming in through the windows. As Mrs. Robb poured out the tea for us, she said, "Now, tell me dear, just who are you?"

I find myself often wishing that parents in our schools would receive the same warm welcome I received from Mrs. Robb, basking in a sense of well-being and feeling as if they are already our friends. Instead, too often, they are met with closed doors, with dos and especially don'ts, and opinions and judgments about the "right" way and the "wrong" way to parent their children. Each year we teachers open our hearts and our classrooms to new groups of children starting on their journey into life, but often we forget to do the same for their parents. Too often, parent evenings are seen as a chore, and it is not unusual in our schools to blame parents for the difficulties their children may have. And yet, if it weren't for the insight, courage, and sacrifices of our class parents, many of us would not be able to practice our vocations. They enable us to fulfill our destinies as Waldorf early childhood teachers!

There is much talk these days about the different kind of child coming into our classrooms and we have worked hard to adjust to this change. We have changed our rhythms of the day, we have incorporated much more movement into our circles, adjusted our snacks for those children with allergies, and spent long hours researching different syndromes to better understand these little ones. But there is also a different kind of parent these days: a parent who asks questions, who is not content to take our word for anything, who demands more information, communication, and answers. And this is just the way it should be. We are in the Fifth Cultural Epoch and humanity is striving to develop the Consciousness or Spiritual Soul. Our task at this time is to develop ourselves as individuals, becoming, in the process, ever more antisocial. We are asked to develop equanimity in the face of the unknown, in the face of the breakdown of all familiar forms, and we must increasingly rely on our inner lives to give us any sense of security. All of us increasingly experience alienation in our thinking, isolation in our feeling life, and powerlessness in our will. Choices have to be made that have consequences for every human being alive, yet our relationships are more and more impersonal. However, if humanity were not faced with this difficulty in mutual understanding, the consciousness soul would not be able to develop. It is a trial we are going through, but an essential one.

And, as is true in each cultural epoch, we are also sowing the seeds for the next epoch, one that Rudolf Steiner tells us is significantly different from the world we know today. In the Sixth Cultural Epoch, Steiner tells us that there will be three areas of major difference from our present times. The first is that belief in the spiritual world will be a given for the humanity of the future; the second is total freedom of thought. One will not be bound by organized religions, family perspectives, traditions, or social mores. And the third major difference is that we will achieve such complete empathy with the other that our own personal well-being will be completely dependent on the well-being of others. If one person is hungry or suffering, their hunger pangs will be ours; their suffering we will feel.

There are some meditative exercises that I find helpful when working with parents. These are called the Six Basic Exercises or Subsidiary Exercises. Rudolf Steiner gave these as preparation for leading an active meditative life, but I have found, after thirty years of working with them, that one never graduates from them. These exercises keep us oriented and, over time, allow the "I" to work less on keeping the body, soul, and spirit together and more on refining the spiritual essence of who we are. They involve exercises in five areas: concentration (our thinking), will, equanimity, positivity and open-mindedness. And the sixth exercise is in harmonizing them all. You do the exercises one at a time, adding more as you become adept at the ones before until you are doing all of them all of the time. Rudolf Steiner suggests beginning with one, doing it for a month, starting over each time you forget or are unable to complete it before beginning the second exercise. It took me years before I was doing more than one at time!

I want to look at these exercises from the perspective of working with parents.

Thinking: How am I thinking about the parents I work with? Is there warmth in my thoughts? Am I interested in who they are? Do I have critical thoughts as soon as I see them? How do I speak about them with my colleagues, or my partner at home? Is there kindness in my thoughts about them? When I have an antipathetic reaction to a particular parent, do I realize that this says more about me than it does about them?

Will: Do I have the will forces to find parents the help they need if I cannot provide it? Can I have yet another conversation with a particular parent when I am already tired, without feeling resentful? Do I have the will to do the research to better understand a child or parent in my care? Can I write a thoughtful, honest, and fair report for a child at the end of the year? Do I have the interest to call a family, even when their child has not done something wrong? Do I have the will forces and imagination to look beyond the outer behavior of a child or parent to see the being of that person? Can I do for my parents what I would want a teacher to do for me and for my family?

Equanimity: Can I respond, rather than react? Responding to a difficult situation means that on a human level we are both left free; reacting is on a much more animalistic level and leaves all parties unfreed. Can I develop within myself a center of calm, no matter what? Can I not take things personally but rather ask myself what the other is thinking? Am I professional enough to move away from my sympathies and antipathies? Our own feelings say nothing about the other; they only express our own limitations. Feelings are really outside of who we are. Can I not allow myself to be rushed into things, no matter the deadline? Rudolf Steiner tells us that the only way we can move into the future, meet evil and survive is through the development of inner tranquility.

Positivity: Have I found something that I can admire and respect in each parent? Can I give the parents (and find within myself) a positive picture of their child, no matter how difficult he or she is in the classroom? Can I embrace even the most difficult and unpleasant situation knowing that within it lies the potential for my growth? A dear friend of mine and a master class teacher once said to me, "When you see trouble coming down the road toward you, drop down to your knees and give thanks, for you are about to learn something important."

Open-mindedness: Are we open to new ideas? Are we open to other ways of doing things? Waldorf teachers are famous for believing that we are the ones who have found the truth and are doing the best work with children, and we are very often disinterested in the work going on outside of the Waldorf movement. Can we develop interest in different ways of working? Can we truly say that we are free of prejudice? New manifestations of truth must find us ready at any time to receive them. Can we look beyond all the tattoos and piercings of a new parent or colleague and find the human being within? Can we accept a parent's perspective and thoughts with the same enthusiasm as we carry our own? For those of us who have been in Waldorf schools for a long time, can we accept what the younger generation of teachers brings to this work even when it is different from what we expected? Can we recognize the gifts each generation brings? How open are we to differences of opinion in our personal and professional lives? Are we so afraid of conflict that we become defensive or retreat?

Of course, in this age of fierce individualism, conflicts will naturally arise. What can we do? One might ask oneself a series of questions:

What is the problem? Essentially, that just means taking time to not react but to think about what has happened and to identify the issue.

How did this come about? What were all the steps that brought you to the present situation? This is really looking at it etherically. It is never about placing blame but about recognizing all the nuances of a situation and our own part in it.

Why did this problem happen? And here we have to put ourselves into the motives of another... and our own motives. Honesty is really important here.

Who is the person doing this? Here we are reminded of the sacred mystery of the other. Which part of me is responding to this situation? My higher self or my lower, more personality-bound self? And why?

What is being asked of me? What am I being asked to develop within myself through this particular situation? This is perhaps the most important question to look at. If we believe in the Laws of Karma, we have to know that the big things that happen to us in our lives have been orchestrated by ourselves. Where do I need to grow? What do I need to let go of, however comfortable it may be? We can never change the other, as we well know through our personal relationships; we can only be responsible for ourselves.

Looking at a problem in the above way moves the problem in us and makes it less fixed. It allows us to look at it with perspective and objectivity and helps us to remove our personalities from the mix, allowing understanding to flow. Any time we fail a parent, we have also failed the child.

Martin Buber once said, "All living is meeting." In our working with parents, we have the opportunity to overcome our sympathies and antipathies and replace them with true interest in the human being who stands before us. It is not struggle but the rendering of assistance that truly promotes progress. Many of us have had the remarkable blessing of meeting Rudolf Steiner's anthroposophy and working and living with his insights. But with this blessing comes a responsibility: we must take anthroposophy personally! Anthroposophy offers the opportunity to revolutionize our way of living through a path of doing. It offers nothing less than social renewal, and with it, the respiritualizing of the human being. It is our task and responsibility to be the midwives of a new age. In truly meeting the parents who come to us, we can participate in this new birth.

Conscious Connections

Lauren Hickman

From *Creating Connections* (WECAN 2014)

Empty streets. Quiet neighborhoods. Everyone gone. A lone mother tends her child. Relatives who once flocked to her home to see the new baby have long since gone. Her identity changed forever when she became a parent. She longs for connection, but her pre-baby peers have busy lives and little time available to socialize. She turns to the Internet for answers about her child's development and for connection with others through texts, Twitter, and Skype, looking at the screen in her hand while watching her little one.

My then-sixteen-year-old son walks into my parent-and-child class one day. He sees me on the floor with the parents of pre-walkers, guiding an observation. At home that night he challenges me; "Mom, do those people know you are ripping them off? I would never pay anyone to play with my baby!"

This is the world we live in today. With families and friends widespread, yet linked by cyberspace, we long for connection, and yes, we even pay for classes that replace the loving extended families of days long past. Advice gleaned from grannies and aunties while watching a baby learning to explore the world is rare.

Now is the time to create conscious community and intentional family. We are no longer bound by the ties of blood, race, or religion. We are both blessed and challenged by the myriad choices facing us today. How can a family navigate creating connections, sharing joys and tragedies, nurturing each other along the way?

I have worked to create a safe place in my parent-and-child classes where these connections can begin. I help parents to learn to trust themselves and to tap into the greater wisdom that is deep within and manifested in their intuition, a wisdom inspired by what cannot be seen, only experienced.

Honoring Vulnerability

As an early childhood educator, I have noticed that uncertainty and fear are common denominators for parents today. Parents are fearful that their beloved child will be injured or bullied, or not make it into the right school, the right college, the right career. With the fear comes judgment and misunderstanding.

I strive to normalize the daily ups and downs of raising a young child by talking about what to expect at different developmental stages. I give handouts and foster discussions at appropriate times. I begin by opening my heart and mind to the parents as they come to my classes, remembering my own days alone as a young parent. Each day seemed like an eternity, but somehow the years slipped by with lightning speed.

I remember when my own children challenged me and how others helped me when I desperately needed a break and some perspective. In my class, I notice when a parent's eyes are glistening with unshed tears, when she is close to the breaking point. I offer a cup of tea, a hug, words of encouragement, and some moor lavender oil or Rescue Remedy cream for the parent's pulse points. I honor the tears, letting the parent know that "tears release toxins; that is why you always feel better after a good cry. Some say tears wash the windows of your soul." I question gently until I can identify the underlying problem, and then we speak together to brainstorm an appropriate response.

One mother was very frustrated with her two-and-a-half-year-old daughter's behavior in class. She began to threaten the girl, telling her if she did not listen to her, she would take her home. She was upset that her daughter, who had been potty-trained for several months, had suddenly reverted to wetting herself. I asked if there had been changes lately, and the mother told me that she had just returned from a weeklong trip without her daughter. I pointed out that behavior regression was a normal response, and that the child was looking to see that the mother was still there for her. In the moment, the mother felt out of control and she feared she was doomed to a child who would always wet herself.

A hug, a hearty snack, and a walk to feed the school animals lightened the mood. The following week, the mom was delighted to tell me that all was well; they had reconnected with a few "home days" and potty training was back on track.

Clear Communication

During the first days of class, I encourage the parents to share stories of their child's birth, to the extent that they are comfortable. I have heard amazing stories of love and devotion, through adoption, through in-vitro fertilization, through difficult labors, and supporting children who were medically fragile. I have also heard stories of uncomplicated births and babies that slept through the night early on. Each child has a special story, and when shared, these stories bring the class participants closer together.

Naming potential challenges and stating expectations helps everyone to relax when the boundaries are clear. Even with the most loving intentions, parenting can be challenging.

Families are faced with so many choices, both personal and those offered by our modern society. How do parents choose what works best for their child, reflecting the values held by their family? Questions arise about health care choices, co-sleeping, bottle feeding, breastfeeding, pacifiers, immunizations, discipline, media, in-laws, spiritual paths, peers, nutrition, tantrums, sharing toys, what school to choose, sports, enrichment programs, and so forth. Emotions can be tender as parents step out into the world with their wee ones. Challenges to their parental choices form part of what they must face on a regular basis. Through these challenges, families continue to learn and grow as individuals and as parents charged with the incredible task of successfully raising children.

Children between the ages of one and four are incredibly contrary; one day they may be completely delightful and the next day nothing goes right. These shifts in mood occur regardless of how they are parented! In class I ask that we all be tender with each other and our different parenting styles. Even if one does not personally agree with the choices that others have made on their parenting journeys, I ask class participants to be open to and supportive of each other when a child (or parent) is having a difficult day.

Creating Community

I strive to create an environment where both children and parents are nurtured and cared for, slowing down the pace to one that is appropriate for the young child. It is my hope that by teaching about child development and doing observations, I can encourage the parents to learn together what incredible human beings their children are. In creating this environment, I ask that the adults try to leave the worries of the world outside the classroom—for instance, no discussions about the war in the Middle East or the car accident witnessed on the way to class in front of the little ones. Too soon the child will have to shoulder the worries of our world, and protecting them from adult conversations in their formative years helps them be strong when the time is right. Of course, if any parents need to discuss a difficult topic, I request that they please wait until the children are out of earshot, or make an appointment to speak with me after class.

We gather for a meal together, offering blessings for the food we share. Parents help in passing out the food. Once everyone is served, I ask if there is anything happening in the community for the coming week. We hear about events such as story time at the library, freecycling, hikes, train rides, and even some activities that are especially for adults (art shows, wine tastings). I encourage the parents to get together outside of class, starting a knitting circle or a walking club. I tell them about the "Grateful Dads" of Marin County who hike with their toddlers once a month. Through the supportive atmosphere, we network and build the longed-for connections. Play dates are scheduled, childcare trades are negotiated, and friendships are started. This is the true goal of my parent-and-child class: to empower the parents with tools for their journey that will carry on far beyond my weekly classes.

Many families come to the parent-and-child program without any particular religious practices. I have noticed that the school and the teacher have become the place for creating celebrations of life and, in many cases, death. I have coordinated blessingways for expectant mothers and memorial services for family members who have crossed the threshold. I have gone to vigils for children in hospitals and to visit newborns. Families look to me for guidance as they try to face difficult news. I help where I can and refer them to professionals as needed. Ultimately, I just strive to honor and bear witness to their lives, to the beauty of the human spirit, to the incredible mystery that each human being manifests. This is how I work to create conscious community.

A New Vision for Creating Partnerships with Parents

Margaret Ris

From *A Warm and Gentle Welcome* (WECAN 2008)

What new mother has not felt a flush of anxiety in the first weeks after the birth of her child? She realizes that she alone carries the responsibility for keeping alive this tiny, dependent and needy newborn. Not only must she care for him now without any real experience, she must also somehow assure that he matures into a decent, contributing member of society. What a prospect! It is not uncommon for mothers to feel this anxiety deeply in the immediate postpartum period, and for fathers, too, to experience it when they recognize the awesome responsibility inherent in parenting.

As Waldorf educators working with younger children for longer periods of time than ever, and offering daycare to working parents, we carry an increasing responsibility both for the children in our care and for their parents. In years past, the teacher might receive a child no younger than age three-and-a-half or four, after parents had become more accustomed to their new role. Kindergarten generally lasted for a morning of three or four hours, as a chance to play and socialize. Programs for children are now more a family need than a pleasant option. The dynamic has changed dramatically, and so compassion and support for parents have become ever more essential ingredients to our task of caring for the children.

Helping parents discover the art of parenting

When both parents and caregivers are able to focus on what is best for the child, the child will end up with the most integrated and wholesome experience. I would recommend that early childhood teachers and care providers adopt an attitude of partnership with parents, sensitively and non-prescriptively sharing practices and insights they have learned in professional training. Perhaps as we work professionally to cultivate the art of education and the art of childcare, we can also envision helping parents discover an art of parenting.

Ultimately, it falls to parents to sculpt the milieu in which their child develops. The influence of the parents' backgrounds and attitudes, the kind of environment they provide, and the caregivers they select will all influence the child. It can be daunting!

One of Rudolf Steiner's key insights about the young child is that he learns primarily through imitation. Another is that the little child absorbs sensory input in fine and exquisite detail and takes these effects into his very body as well as into his developing psyche. What the child sees, hears and experiences from the earliest weeks enters deeply into his developing self.

It follows that supporting a parent to be conscious of his or her own words, attitudes and actions will supply the child with the healthiest model of imitation. Making parents aware of this without alarming them or raising their anxiety or guilt requires extraordinary sensitivity. Parents are simply individuals, as we all are, with strengths, weaknesses, and foibles. They need not be perfect. Attachment studies have indicated that the most securely attached infants are not those whose signals were consistently picked up and attended to by the mother. Rather, children who experienced instances of disruption in communication followed by recognition and repair were more securely attached.[1] The process of attachment "disruption and repair" proved to encourage a certain healthy resiliency and confidence in infants. In a sense, it is as though these children were raised in a "cold hardy" atmosphere of attachment, rather than like delicate hothouse flowers in a highly controlled atmosphere. When their genuine needs, but not their every whim or whimper, were met, the children were able to encounter a greater array of responses, move through them, and experience a recurring sense of attachment after the "disruption" in communication.

The journey toward parenthood

New parents are also in a tender phase of their own adult development, and are undergoing a great deal of adjustment and learning. Supporting mothers and fathers in their experience of becoming parents—by informing, encouraging, validating, and inspiring them—can create a lasting and health-giving effect for the whole family. With intention and sensitivity, we can help parents become conscious of how to create healthy lifestyles and mutually rewarding relationships.

Parenting can indeed be a path for self-development. Just as the child learns to roll over, walk, climb, speak and sing, parents are also learning how to navigate and grow into their new roles. The child and his or her parents are in a parallel process of self development; however, the milestones of child development are well-articulated and recognizable in comparison to the parents' less defined process of adult self-development in the role of caregiver. Erik Erikson has identified the generative stage of adult social development as including family nurturing and career building, but writings on parental self-development are fewer.

Our love for the children in our care can expand to include love for the parents who have brought these children into life and who wish to provide them with the best possible future, although it may not be clear to them specifically how to accomplish that. Nowhere is this more important than in the earliest years, when the child is most impressionable and the parents most vulnerable.

A continuum of approaches to parent education

As parent educators, we have a continuum of tools for working with parents, from modeling ways of being with children to holding study groups and engaging in conversation to outright instruction. And perhaps the most beneficial approach may be to take the stance of helpful, but non-prescriptive, guides and supporters.

Modeling ways of working with children requires that the parent participate in a class situation to observe how a teacher/caregiver works with a child (for example, in parent-child classes, as a parent helper, or in a facilitated playgroup). Sometimes RIE (Resources for Infant Educarers) classes are formally structured as demonstrations. The teacher interacts with the children while the parents observe. Later they may discuss and process the new information and supplement the class time with readings.

Many approaches are less overt than this. Teachers in a Waldorf parent-child class often use an implicit, non-verbal approach to illustrate to parents ways they can relate to their children. A parent may or may not pick up on this. If they do absorb what has been modeled, this new approach might remain on the unconscious level. Mom doesn't quite know why she has started to speak in a more soft and melodious tone with her young child; she just took it on because it seemed to work when the teacher spoke in this way. Or Dad may consciously recognize the benefit of narrating a conflict between children instead of intervening, and adopt it openly—even soliciting others to try it, too, because it worked so well in class. Or a mother or father may never pick up on the subtle approach—instead they may pass the class time in a sort of reverie, appreciating the break from solitary caregiving or the chance to chat with other parents. The modeling technique, while an optimal way to interact with and teach the young child, is not necessarily the most effective teaching tool for the adult, whose learning mode has moved well beyond the imitative stage.

On the other end of the continuum, parent education via prescriptive instruction takes on a more authoritative aspect, as in the case of a doctor's recommendations (for example, "I recommend you feed her rice cereal mixed with milk at six months then add pureed root vegetables twice a day"). This more formulaic, one-size-fits-all approach can breed a kind of submission to expert advice and a reliance on external versus internal decision-making—or it can breed resistance and resentment. Parents in need of assurance often will gladly accept the advice of a trusted expert on physical or behavioral matters. And certain facts of child development need to be communicated to parents. But as we know, expert opinion on many childrearing practices has flip-flopped over the years, knocking the experts off their pedestals. Further, this style of parenting support can eclipse the opportunity for parents to develop their inner guidance—to become more conscious of what they are doing, to make wise choices, and to weigh the advice they receive in light of what is most appropriate for their family and lifestyle.

Today, there seems to be a call for a different path. It may be that we can best serve parents by offering guidance in the form of sharing ideas and by giving them opportunities to knowingly take up relevant ideas and practices of their own accord, because they make sense for them. This way parents have the chance to consider potentially helpful new ideas they may not otherwise have access to, digest and process them, try them out, and consciously integrate the ideas into their parenting styles. This happens best in a community of support, supplemented by written materials such as books, parenting articles, newspaper clippings, and so on, all of which serve to reinforce and ground the new material. Parents are seeking information—just peruse the parenting section of the local bookstore or check into a new moms' "blog." But information that can be received as empowering and non-judgmental (that is, non-prescriptive, sensitive, and conscious) is likely to have the most beneficial impact.

Deeper influences

How do we learn to be parents? We often simply do what was done in our childhoods—to us, for us, and around us. Many a parent has repeated the past, for better or for worse. How we were parented lives in us deeply, often unconsciously. Having the chance to unearth memories and raise awareness of how our previous experiences might color current behavior enables parents to see their way toward changing patterns. Selma Fraiberg and her colleagues vividly shine a light on the concept that "in every nursery, there are ghosts. They are the visitors from the unremembered past of the parents, the uninvited guests at the christening."[2] This dark scenario illustrates how the unexplored past can influence the present, particularly during early childhood. Unearthing the influences that live below the surface can only happen with a raised consciousness and remembered feelings. But Alicia Lieberman and colleagues posit that there are also "angels in the nursery," bearing messages of intrinsic goodness, unconditional love, and benevolence. These messages, passed from generation to generation, serve as protective shields of parental love and engender in the child deeply held, early experiences of safety, intimacy, joy, and pleasure that foster self worth and healthy emotional integration.[3]

We can be part of a gentle transformative process when we create a non-threatening platform for parents from which they can be encouraged to remember the past and explore the demands of the present, and from which they can see their own struggles within the context of challenges common to all parents.

Today's parent

Many parents I encounter today do seem to be looking for help. They are at times lonely, unsure, or stressed. Their relatives may be located too far away to be a regular source of support, or they may wish to be released from family conceptions about child rearing, and therefore have distanced themselves. Mothers are often used to working outside of the home and have a professional identity that evaporates when they take leave to be home with their child.

Mothers are frequently torn. There are financial as well as social insecurities involved with being at home with children. Some mothers cringe inwardly at leaving their children, but find themselves back at work to earn needed income or benefits. Mothers search the Internet, seek out self-help books from the bookstore, and look for other mothers pushing strollers to talk to. Despite the plethora of educational resources available to them, they seek living support—a community of peers or facilitators to help them navigate the shoals and shallows of parenthood.

But how can we go about providing helpful guidance to parents? How do we share the wisdom of insightful thinkers such as Rudolf Steiner, Emmi Pikler or Magda Gerber without being prescriptive or instilling anxiety over whether or not they are parenting the "right" way? There are, of course, numerous forms of effective parent support, and many paths by which to inform, encourage, and validate parents' innate wisdom. Our goal can be to facilitate an informed self-confidence. As Nina Barrett writes, "Self-confidence is perhaps the most important prerequisite for enjoying motherhood... and the secret is that no one knows the secret: we are each putting our motherhood together from scratch."[4]

One model of parent work

I offer one model that was used as part of a parent-child class I co-taught with Marilyn Pelrine at The Waldorf School in Lexington, Massachusetts. We supplemented the morning classroom experience with two evening meetings for parents per ten-week class. Tuition for the classes included the evening meetings, which covered many topics of family life, such as rhythm, nutrition, media influences, sleep, warmth, creative discipline, play, and healthy movement. These evenings were often presented within the context of the seasonal festivals celebrated by our Waldorf community, which reflected Christian, Jewish, and other traditions.

Every evening also included elements of thinking, feeling and willing in a structure akin to that recommended by Steiner for a morning main lesson class in a Waldorf school. For example, in December our parent evening focused on Warmth. We explored soul warmth as the human response to the divine gift of Light. We spoke of preparing to celebrate Christmas and Hanukkah, festivals of Light that illumine the darkest, coldest time of the year and through which an exchange of love and warmth occurs between people. We emphasized the inner experience of the gift of light during winter, as well as how to consciously bring warmth to the child's experience, both in terms of physical care and clothing and in our relationships. We created an opportunity for parents to quietly remember seasonal memories and then share them with the larger group, giving everyone the chance to recall his or her own family memories and see them alongside the memories and traditions of others. Then we had the parents work with wool to make a simple angel to bring home, a creature of light created using a medium of warmth. In this instance, we brought in the element of thinking through the discussion on the place of warmth during the season of light in the darkness, a chance to explore the feeling aspects of past family celebrations, and an experiential or willing activity by creating the angel to take home.

In early spring when the bare trees seem forever dead, yet invisibly the sap begins to run and thicken the buds, we spoke of the celebrations of Passover and Easter and their deeper themes of life arising from apparent death. We mentioned how the egg is a symbol common to both celebrations (the Easter eggs and the egg on the Seder plate) and how its crystallized shell contains new life within. At Easter and Passover, the retelling of an important story is essential to the celebration, so we emphasized the theme of storytelling and its value for children. We told them a story so they could experience its impact. We mentioned how telling actual stories from parents' own childhoods, as well as pedagogical stories and little stories to review the day, can deeply satisfy the child and also help move the child from one "place" or mood to another. Parents then paired up to co-create a story they could use at home to help their children move through a sticky part of the day.

Using festivals as anchors for the parent meetings helped us weave a thread throughout the year and introduce parents to the community and social life of the school. Most importantly, perhaps, we felt that working with the festival content helped connect parents with deep wellsprings of human cultural experience and with the seasonal changes in the natural world, irrespective of their own religious heritage. The three elements of the meetings—stimulating parents' thinking, exploring some feeling aspects in community with other parents, and creating something tangible—seemed to satisfy different people's preferences. It provided an integrating, non-threatening way of framing topics. We used the themes as cornerstones to the evenings, and carefully crafted the timing so that the meetings ran efficiently and ended at a reasonable hour.

The trust-building and learning that grew out of the parent evenings helped to strengthen our mornings together with the children. Sharing the adult time made it easier to reach parents more subtly through our modeling during class time with the children. And the fact that families often signed up for subsequent classes created an ongoing familiarity and sense of community among fellow parents and teachers. Many firm friendships among mothers and children grew from those early class times together.

While this approach may not work for every teacher, I offer it as an example of working with parents to accompany and inform their journey while maintaining a respectful attitude of partnership.

How Emmi Pikler worked with families

We may be inspired in this realm, too, by the example of Emmi Pikler. Dr. Pikler began her work as a pediatrician in Hungary in the early part of the last century, advising parents and caring for their children. As a pediatrician, she made weekly home visits to her patients to provide ongoing support to the mothers in her care. Her book, *Peaceful Babies, Contented Mothers*,[5] was written for parents to offer them an approach to childrearing that would nourish both the children and the mothers. Later in her career following World War II, she set up a residential home for orphaned children. This provided her with an opportunity to design and implement an approach to childrearing based on her core beliefs. She was given a building on Lóczy Street in Budapest in which to set up the home, and the Pikler Institute has been affectionately known ever since as "Lóczy." Pikler carefully chose and trained the caregivers who were to carry out her model of care, replacing all the original nurses because she didn't consider them to have the innate delicate sensitivity with the children that she sought. Pikler preferred to hire young women from the countryside who didn't come with the same intellectual and clinical training, but who operated from a more intuitive and gentle stance.

When devising her approach to caring for infants and young children in the orphanage, Pikler was conscious that she did not wish to create conditions that might interfere with the anticipated mother-child bond that would develop once the child was adopted. The caregivers gave exquisite attention to the child during caregiving, but were trained to refrain from extra displays of affection. Dr. Pikler seemed to be able to distill what was required for the creation of a healthy attachment without fostering a dependency in the orphaned child that would one day require painful disengagement. Trainees at the Pikler Institute learn the distinction: "The mother loves the child, so she cares for him. The caregiver [at Lóczy] cares for the child, so she loves him."

The pillars of care at the Pikler Institute are:

- exquisite presence and attention to the child's signals during caregiving, encouraging her active participation;
- ample opportunity for free movement; and
- astute and careful observation.

The success of this approach was validated by a 1972 World Heath Organization study that concluded that adults who spent their early years at Lóczy were as stable and healthy socially, emotionally and in terms of employment as adults who were raised at home.[6]

Pikler made no attempt to educate adoptive parents to continue the practices of the institute. Her aim—through careful, focused caregiving—was to lay the firmest possible foundation for healthy attachment and self-empowerment in the child, but she let adoptive parents supply their own version of affection and permanent upbringing. She recognized that love comes in many languages and flavors, and that by screening the adoptive families she could assure the children a secure home with ongoing parental love that would reinforce the children's basic sense of self-esteem and trust that her nurses had carefully fostered. The loving home would fill in the matrix of attachment that had been so carefully and consciously laid down from the first days at Lóczy and reinforced daily by the caregivers. The children had been given enough respect, time, attention, and opportunity for self-mastery to carry them into their permanent placements unscarred and ready to attach securely to a new set of parents. Emmi Pikler was decades ahead of her time in understanding that parents did not need authoritarian directives; instead she saw that what parents need are informed support and trust in both their innate parenting instincts and in their child's inner developmental sequence and wisdom.

Conclusion

Enlarging our scope of concern to include the parents of children in our care requires a new set of skills. These skills include sensitivity and courage to bring up all manner of feelings—and they also require a healthy dose of creativity and openness to the unknown. But the underlying motivations that have drawn us to our special work with children impel us to develop these new skills and share our insights. What has motivated us to work with young children has been our compassion for the child's dependent state, our respect for children as sensitive and spiritual beings, and our passionate recognition that the early years are critical to the entire lifetime of the individual. Let us see ourselves as partners with parents—not wiser or more capable, but, rather, having resources to share with them for their parenting journey. By respectfully creating a partnership with parents, our work in service to the young child can have a deeper and more lasting effect.

Notes

1. Beatrice Beebe, "Co-Constructing Mother Infant Distress in Face to Face Interactions: Contributions of Microanalysis." *Zero to Three Journal* (May 2004), pp. 40-46; E.Z. Tronick, "New thoughts on mutual regulation: co-creation and uniqueness–2002" in *Parent–Infant Psychodynamics: Wild Things, Mirrors and Ghosts*, Joan Raphael-Leff, ed. (London: Whurr Publishers, 2003).

2. Selma Fraiberg, Edna Adelson and Vivian Shapiro, "Ghosts in the nursery: a psychoanalytic approach to the problems of impaired infant-mother relationships," in *Clinical Studies in Infant Mental Health—the First Year of Life* (London: Travistock Publications, 1980).

3. Alicia Lieberman, Elena Padron, Patricia Van Horn and William W. Harris, "Angels in the Nursery; the Intergenerational Transmission of Benevolent Parental Influences." *Infant Mental Health Journal* (Vol. 26, 2005).

4. Nina Barrett, *I Wish Someone Had Told Me: A Realistic Guide to Early Motherhood* (Chicago: Academy Chicago Publishers, 1997), p. xiii.

5. Pikler, Emmi, *Peaceful Babies, Contented Mothers*, 1969, reprinted by *Sensory Awareness Foundation Bulletin*, Mill Valley, CA, no. 14, Winter 1994. See also Emmi Pikler, Friedliche Babys–zufriedene Mütter, Fourth Edition (Freiburg: Verlag Herder 2016).

6. Ruth Mason, *Respecting Baby: Dr. Emmi Pikler's Philosophy* and *Dr. Pikler's Parenting Concepts* (Los Angeles: Resources for Infant Educarers, 2000).

Working with Parents: Ideas for Parent Meetings

Ruth Ker and **Nancy Blanning**

From *You're Not the Boss of Me!* (WECAN 2007).
The authors note that this essay followed conversations with Tim Bennett, Louise deForest, and Barbara Klocek.

Wise teachers and parents realize that healthy development and happiness arise unconsciously within the child when those around him or her are all working out of the same intentions. The time that parents and teachers spend focusing on the children they share in common and developing a nonjudgmental interest in one another pays off mightily. These efforts build an abundance of warmth among parent, child, and teacher. In turn, this kindling of interest and warmth is what allows difficult topics to be addressed and trust to develop between the key people operative throughout the child's early childhood. Many insights are spawned out of the soul/spiritual substance that is created through this cooperative relationship. How many times have parents and teachers conferred together one day, and the next day the child they were pondering shows them the answer? Something invisible is at work here—spawned out of the efforts that the adults in the child's life have made to reach out for the betterment of the whole. Henning Kohler and others speak about these kinds of events arising out of the link that parents and teachers can cultivate with the child's and their own angels.[1]

We also know that the insights from anthroposophical child-rearing indications and Waldorf pedagogy can provide us with deeper understandings about child development and how to nurture the whole human being. This is something teachers want and need to share with parents, so that we can all work towards the same goals for the children. Yet we see daily that much of our culture contradicts these wholesome ideas. Waldorf schools are truly counterculture in this regard. Finding ways to share these insights without seeming "old fashioned" or "quaint" is a humbling challenge. In our urgent and passionate desire to protect and support healthy growth, we can also seem dogmatic and intimidating to parents when we do share our views.

The question then arises, "How is it that parents and teachers can best share the essential information?" The author of "Waldorf Education for the Child, and the Parent,"[2] herself a parent, stresses that there are many ways of making information retainable and many individual styles of learning. While we may find it effective to use the lecture format at parent evenings, we must be aware of how much easier and welcoming it is for parents to come to parent talks when the talks are full of warmth and lively examples. It is through these lively examples and true stories that the parents are able to reach into the topic being explained and find commonality with it. The examples allow them to "feel into" the situation. Taking this a step further, many teachers are finding much success when they provide the parents with an experience, where they can do hands-on things or actually momentarily dwell within what is being described by the presenter.

When we discussed the cooperative working of the parent and the teacher at our "Older Child in the Kindergarten Research Group" retreats, we agreed that we live in a time now where a new task confronts us as educators. The task is to create a new paradigm for our partnering work with parents. We would do well to hear the call to create new ways of involving parents in experiential learning. Perhaps the venue could be a caring circle, a discussion group where parents and teachers bring their own real-life scenarios to the conversation, a study group full of lively examples, or a well-planned parent evening in which the parents are actively involved in examples that teach the principles addressed. In any case, we are challenged to move beyond the top-down model to a more interactive model where the experience of the parents and teachers can co-exist and those involved can drink in more deeply the lessons involved.

As well as providing important basic information, parent meetings are a prime opportunity to strengthen the soul/spiritual substance of the adult social community. This ultimately benefits each child as an individual and the class as a whole. What we are able to enjoy together in our early childhood class meetings can be carried forward into the grade school, in the form of a class of parents that work well together on many different levels.

The following are some ideas collected from the working-group teachers. These are experiences that they and their colleagues have found effective for parent meetings. One common element apparent within these ideas is that the parents actually are involved in experiential learning. Some of these suggestions include a format that does not involve a lecture, and some have an experiential format woven together with lecture material. As we strive to work with the will of the children, so can we also engage the parents' will along with their thinking and feeling.

We live in a time now when humanity as a whole is developing the consciousness soul, and that motivates all of us to want to take things more deeply into the thinking, feeling, and willing parts of our souls. We also encounter each other at different times in our individual biographies. Someone who is learning during the ages of twenty-one to twenty-eight may want to experience the answers with his or her sentient soul, whereas the intellectual soul may be more operative between twenty-eight and thirty-five. The consciousness soul time in our own biographies spans the wide horizon of the years from thirty-five to forty-two. These previous seven-year cycles and their events provide the groundwork for the imaginations, inspirations, and intuitions that arise in the next twenty-one years of our development.[3] It's important for teachers to really know the ages and likely biographical phases of their audience in order to prepare the most nourishing parent meeting experiences. Preparing for a group of parents who are around twenty-five is very different than preparing for a group who are mostly over forty. There are many books on the life rhythms of biography, like the one cited below, that can be helpful reads for adults who are gathering together in community. Nevertheless, it is best to remember that when experience confirms what we are asking those in our audience to think, they will be able to hold more of a conviction for the idea. They will also be able to retain what they have learned and, if it serves their family, hopefully carry it into their home life.

Suggestions for Parent Meetings

The following are some ideas that we hope will nourish you and your community. At the first parent meeting, often held before school starts:

✦ Allow time for the parents to speak about themselves individually—saying their names and occupations, what is their passion or "bliss" for finding joy and rejuvenation in life. Remember to actively take interest in the parents as well as the children. This information sharing can happen as the parents are doing something with their hands to help prepare for the upcoming year. (This interest that teachers extend toward the parents can later expand into the parent-teacher conferences. Then teachers can allow some time to connect to what the parents expressed on that first evening and to ask the parents about themselves and how things are going now.)

✦ Parents decorate their child's birthday candle for that year and tell how they came to name their child. Later this candle will be used at the child's birthday celebration at school.

✦ The parents are asked to bring something from nature that represents their children. They can then explain what about this natural item reminds them of their children. All of these items are then assembled in the center of the circle as each parent first speaks about his or her child, and then places the offering on a table. By so doing, a class sculpture is created. If parents forget to bring something they can be encouraged to find something from within the classroom to add to the sculpture. It is remarkable to see that often the parents' classroom choice is exactly what their children choose as a favorite plaything when they enter school that first day.

◆ The teacher opens the meeting with an imagination of how each child has intentionally sought out his or her parents as being the perfect ones for their current life on earth. Then the parents are asked to choose two postcards (from a large collection the teacher has assembled)—one to represent the gift the parents already have that they can give to their children, the other to show what new qualities the children are asking of the parents to personally develop. Then the parents have the bonding experience of sharing around the circle their pictures and thoughts around these two topics.

Here are some ways that we could share some of the other important topics at later parent gatherings:

Schedule a three-, four-, or five-part parenting series. Give the series a lively title. Each meeting could address one topic such as rhythm, warmth, sleep, or other topics particularly relevant to your group. Include within the evening's presentation several ways that the topic can be experienced. Can those attending touch, manipulate, use their bodies in movement, see a picture, etc.? For example, have the room be too cold so that the parents cannot find physical comfort being there. Then ask the parents to pay attention to their reactions and how that affects their behavior and well-being. Then talk about young children not being able to monitor their own warmth organism, show the importance of physical warmth on the formation of the child's organs, and so on. Focusing on one topic alone allows the chance to deepen information and experience so that parents do not feel overwhelmed.

We want to speak clearly about what is good for the children but in a way that the parents do not feel judged. Carrying this intent into the next parent conferences, we can then make a point of expressing what we admire about their parenting. When affirmed in their parenting practices, often parents will feel freer to discuss their important childrearing questions.

With the topic of choices—As a prelude, when the parents have just arrived at the parent meeting, ask the parents in rapid succession to make all sorts of decisions, with no time to reflect upon them. This can give them the experience of how fatiguing and taxing it is for children to be bombarded with choices. (Thanks to Eugene Schwartz for this idea.) Also ask them how they would feel if they were airplane passengers and the pilot came onto the loudspeaker and asked, "Would you like to fly at 28,000 feet or 35,000 feet?" (Thanks to Dorothy Olsen for this idea.) With respect to leaving the decision to the children as to which school they would like to go to, ask the parents "What city would you like to live in, Timbuktu or Neverland?" Things like this can be woven into an evening's presentation.

With the topic of media—Begin the evening with silence, followed by humming or music, storytelling, and then a puppet play. Ask the parents about their experience during and after the puppet play. A presentation can then happen or the evening can simply be concluded by showing a video of *The Lion King* or whatever current video is being portrayed as child-friendly.

It has also been effective to have a high school teacher, remedial teacher or a teacher of the upper grades speak about his or her experience of seeing children who have been exposed to a lot of media. Having older students who have been protected from media describe their own experience is another option.

Inviting the parents to a meeting and having loud music blaring in the kindergarten can also portray the experience of how different the environment becomes when invaded by these sounds. Parents have become used to the sacredness of this child-centered space and can feel the violation that is happening.

On the topic of toys—Bring a bag of toys from a thrift shop to a parent evening. Parents feel inside the bag without looking and guess what each item is. Then the toys are taken out and the parents play with them. This can be done by breaking up into small groups. Then the groups can reassemble into the larger group and a lively discussion ensues. It is interesting for all to see what can or cannot be played with and for how long interest can be sustained.

Another idea is to ask the parents to imagine that they have the consciousness of the young child—filled with the urge to unite with everything. Then pass a Waldorf doll around the circle, asking the parents to unite with this image and to notice how they feel when doing this. Next pass a plastic action figure (spiky collar, green sneering face, muscle-bound—you know the type) around the circle and ask the parents once again to try to unite with this image (you may need to apologize first). Then ask, "Which image would you want your children to carry around within them?"

To illustrate the child's need for play and experiential learning rather than intellectual explanations—Bring to a parent evening some exotic fruits hidden under a cloth in a bowl. These fruits must be unfamiliar to the parents. Then tell the parents that you are going to describe something to them so that they will know it better. Do not show them what is under the cloth in the bowl but proceed to describe the fruits verbally and just assume that the parents will understand what is being described. It is likely that the parents will not be able to picture what they have never seen or experienced before. From this they can have the realization that they and their children need to touch and experience things in order to know them. Make the point that many things in this world are unfamiliar to their children and, rather than intellectual explanations, the children need to be given quality and quantities of time to sample appropriate things. And how do they do that? They play at it! (Thank you to Kim Hunter from Salt Spring Island, British Columbia for this idea about the fruits.)

Practicing observation and attention—Do an observation exercise at the beginning of each parent evening, and continue doing this at each meeting for one year. The hope here is that we learn together that slowing down to observe and take in our surroundings actually informs us about important things. This can be critical for our parenting. Often we don't realize how little we take in as we live our preoccupied lives. Here are some observation exercises:

- Draw something only felt with your hands and not seen.
- Draw something not seen but which another person describes to you.
- Describe what the person sitting next to you is wearing without looking at them again. Now describe what they are wearing after looking at them with this task in mind.
- Observe your child's eating habits—how she eats, food preferences, etc., and then inform the group at the next parent evening about what you observed.

After some of these experiences, it is explained that observation is a potent tool for teachers and can be for parents as well.

On the topic of movement—Offer experiences of movement, such as a circle time, a movement journey, a playful obstacle course, some circus-type movements. These experiences can help to illustrate to parents that they do not have to put their children in sports or a lot of extracurricular events in order to provide movement and playful experiences for their children. Encourage parents to help or allow their children to create a circus at home so they can see how children would rather do that than play in an organized sport. Through having experiences together, we can create a happening around which valuable conversations can emerge.

On the topic of nurturing—Invite the parents to school one evening. When they arrive they will be surprised to see that the kindergarten table is laid out for a meal. Serve the parents a meal of soup and bread, as the children would have at school, with a candle, the blessing, and a song, all in a mood of calm and warmth.

After the meal, tell a story to set the mood for bedtime, then describe how children may be put to bed. Better still, if you have a reliable volunteer, have her lay on a mat on the kindergarten floor, light a candle, rub her back or massage her feet with lavender oil, sing to her, and then say, "The angels are waiting for you. Time to go to their house." Blow out the candle and say, "I'll see you at the angel's house. I'll be there too." Have your volunteer say, "Mommy, don't go. I need a drink of water." Then you respond, "Oh, the angels are waiting for you. We'll have some more water in the morning."

Simple domestic chores such as washing dishes, wiping tables, sweeping, or making a bed can be demonstrated with conscious attention to the intent, meaning, and quality of the gesture. Parents can learn to appreciate how inspired children are by purposeful work and how children can become more absorbed and drawn into a task when the movements are slower and focused.

Nurturing through artistic activities—Hold a once-a-month meeting (perhaps in the afternoon, with childcare in another room) and share an artistic activity with the parents. This can be painting, drawing, singing, candle-dipping, felting, storytelling, creating a nature table, or a seasonal craft activity.

This can lead into many questions and further activities, such as plant-dyeing of cloth or wool. Setting up different seasonal scenes for the nature table stimulates questions about the seasonal rhythms, festivals, and the child's experience of the natural world. Often questions arising out of current discipline dilemmas come up at this time and many enthusiastic conversations ensue.

Festival experience—Prepare something for an upcoming festival with the parents. For example, they may come to make lanterns and learn songs in advance of the Martinmas or Lantern festival. While the parents are working with their hands, discussions can happen about the meaning and intention behind the festival. Parents could be asked to recount any other experiences, perhaps childhood memories, they have about this particular festival. The children, during kindergarten time, can then finish in the weeks ahead what the parents started on the night of the parent evening.

Coming to school on special occasions outside of class time has been very successful when parents and children come together with other families to prepare for festivals, for example to make dipped beeswax candles or lanterns. This can be done in the joyous mood of parents and children playfully creating together. Involving the parents in set-up for the festivals can be a rich and rewarding way for them to sample from the inside out what the meaning of a festival is.

Involve fathers—Hold a meeting for fathers only. Ask them what Waldorf education is like for them and what their questions are. Acknowledge that it is often the wives who choose the children's early childhood education. Fathers can be called on for a work bee—building a compost bin, tool shed, or creating something for the kindergarten. Fathers crave social interaction too and often feel more comfortable when they can be working alongside of someone else. Feeling that they have contributed to their child's education can bond them with the situation and help them to vocalize their questions and areas of interest.

Offer experiences that can weave the social fabric—All stand in a circle holding hands. A hula hoop hangs over the arms of two people. The group has to collectively pass the hoop around without breaking the circle and without letting go of hands.

Another idea is to have a big ball of yarn. Everyone sits in a circle and a question is asked. The teacher holding the ball of yarn says something pertaining to the question, holds on to the end of the strand of yarn, and then throws the ball of yarn off to another parent. The parent contributes something, holds on to the yarn, and tosses the ball to another. In this way the comments build and the ball is tossed, developing a picture of the web of ideas within this particular community pertaining to the question or theme that was expressed. An additional aspect of the game could be that everyone has to remember the contribution of the person who passes the yarn to them as well as their own response. Then at the end of the game, when everyone is holding on to their string, they retrace their patterns, throwing the ball of yarn back to the person who gave it to them and speaking out what that other person's contribution was to the theme. This allows a review of the question or theme and also builds rapport amongst the parent group.

There are many such social games available in books and on the Internet. Parents go away from a parent gathering feeling met and enlivened when they get to have "playful" times with others.

On the topic of child development—Have the parents sit in a circle according to the consecutive ages of their children. That is, if they have a baby, a three-year-old, and a six-year-old, they would sit at the beginning of the round and then they would move over to the place where the parents are sitting who have three-year-olds and then move again when it's time to talk about six-year-olds. Then tell the parents that we are going to create a story together about a child growing up. Each parent will speak in turn about the main character in the story by telling us one thing that is joyful and one thing that is a challenge about who or how their own child is right now. Each parent embellishes the story until it finishes with the parents of the oldest children. (The teacher who offered this exercise said that one evening she did this exercise with a group of parents who had children ranging in ages from three weeks to twenty-eight years. It was like having a course on child development! The parents expressed that it was an opportunity to bond and commiserate with others, and it was energizing to be part of the creative process of information sharing on what otherwise can be a very "dry" topic. The story they created definitely became a secondary part of the process.)

As mentioned, the above ideas are offered to assist you in strengthening your own inspired approaches. Please enjoy.

Scheduling Parent Meetings

Another consideration is when to hold parent meetings. One suggestion is to hold a monthly (or other rhythmic timing) series of evening meetings. This has worked well when the evenings are stimulating and consistently scheduled so that parents can count on planning them into their routines.

Some teachers found success in scheduling Saturday morning meetings. Ten to eleven-thirty a.m. was the suggested time frame. Childcare was arranged with high school students; $5 per child was the charge. The teacher who suggested this remarked that with these Saturday morning arrangements, couples tended to attend more. On a Saturday morning everyone was more rested and relaxed. These meetings were held in fall, winter, and spring. At the end of the year, parents expressed that they loved this opportunity to be together at the Saturday meetings and would have liked to do the same more regularly.

Friday evening (six-thirty to eight p.m.) has also worked well for some. With no school the next day, bedtime can be a little flexible ("We all knew we were compromising something"). Parents brought potluck snacks, and childcare was provided by older children for a modest charge. The evenings were always threefold:

1. Some experience from the children's day was shared—for example, part of circle time, a puppet play, or the painting activity.

2. The parents worked on something for the class—lantern preparation, preparing materials from which the children would make Valentine post-boxes, or sewing bells on ankle bracelets for May Day. The social time of chatting, in the second part of the evening, was important as well for strengthening class ties.

3. Finally the teachers presented a topic on development, parenting, bridging home and school life, festivals, and so on. The meeting finished promptly by eight o'clock. Finding ways to be succinct and economical with what is said during this last time was important. Sometimes less really is more.

Some teachers have had success holding their parent meetings after kindergarten, or later in the afternoon. Perhaps a conversation with the parents at the beginning of the school year can serve to help decisions to be made that work better for the whole group.

Encouraging Attendance at Parent Meetings

A final consideration is how can we support a full attendance at parent meetings? There is nothing more frustrating than low attendance at parent meetings when hours of preparation by the teacher have happened beforehand.

Here is some feedback from a group of parents who were polled on this topic:

✦ When the teacher looks me in the eye and asks me, "Are you coming to the meeting tonight?" I feel wanted and realize I am important to her.

✦ Giving me a task to do for the meeting helps me to feel more responsible.

✦ Make the meetings mandatory.

✦ Put a sign in your window saying, PARENT MEETING TODAY. PLEASE MAKE SURE YOUR CHILD IS REPRESENTED.

- ✦ Tell the parents that there is important information being discussed at the meeting tonight that you don't want them to miss.

- ✦ Parents are socially starved. Make sure there is a social element to it.

- ✦ Make time so that we can hear other parents' stories and then share creative ways of dealing with our children.

- ✦ Refer parents to other vocal parents who advocate going to parent meetings and value what they experienced there.

- ✦ Give reminders. Lots of reminders.

- ✦ Tell us in a newsletter that the meeting is coming up. Dangle a few carrots as to what will be discussed.

- ✦ Make available lists for reliable babysitters or have meetings when babysitting is available at school.

- ✦ Make the meetings fun and informative.

The above lists are by no means complete. Please enjoy these suggestions, which are the fruits of your colleagues' labor. And above all, add your own ideas to the list. A great venue for sharing your parent meeting successes is the *Gateways* newsletter published by WECAN. We look forward to reading about what has worked well for you.

Notes

1. Henning Kohler, *Working With Anxious, Nervous and Depressed Children* (Fair Oaks: The Association of Waldorf Schools of North America 2000), passim.

2. Devon Brownsey," Waldorf Education for the Child, and the Parent," in *You're Not the Boss of Me!*, Ruth Ker, ed. (WECAN 2007), p. 243.

3. Gudrun Burkhard, *Taking Charge—Your Life Patterns and Their Meaning* (Edinburgh: Floris Books 1997), p. 169.

Creating Partnerships with Parents in First Grade Readiness Decisions

Ruth Ker

From First Grade Readiness (WECAN 2009)

In my first years of teaching in a mixed-age kindergarten class I felt anxious about the challenge of making decisions around first grade readiness. Witnessing the grandness of the change that the six-year-olds experience on all levels left me confused as to what criteria I should consider when making decisions about their future placement. The ability to understand what I was observing was not living in me yet, and I relied heavily on my instincts and untrained observations. Many times I simply fell back upon the school's cut-off date for grade school entrance and hoped that the parents would support this.

Then I began to meet more and more mystery children whose development and future placement posed even larger questions to me and also more and more parents who wanted to know what was behind my recommendations. Many times I felt inadequate to meet the important questions of the parents. How I longed for skilled and informed local companions to accompany me in making these decisions!

Some Waldorf schools are fortunate to have school doctors, readiness committees, or remedial or curative teachers to assist them when it comes time to consider whether it's appropriate for a child to enter first grade, but in many schools the kindergarten teachers are on their own when determining whether the child is ripe for school. Results from the last extensive WECAN survey "Report on the Older Child in the Kindergarten"[1] show a variety of ways that schools in North America cope with the decision about first grade placement. Most established schools stated a definite procedure for shepherding the children into first grade—some more elaborate than others. Many kindergarten teachers reported using the cut-off date as the sole determinant. One school relayed that their assessment process and the subsequent report had become so stressful for the parents, children and faculty that they were questioning its benefits. This same teacher commented that she was going back to observing the children in their natural classroom setting rather than setting up separate out-of-class screening appointments. However, the majority of schools reported being at varying stages of establishing clear, effective assessment procedures and are still revising these practices. Many schools also stated that there is uneasiness about who gets to make the decision when the parents and the kindergarten teachers disagree about first grade placement. This survey also showed that even in schools that had extra professional support there seemed to be different understandings as to who should be responsible for this decision.

Here are some aspects of the question:

- Is it the responsibility of the remedial teacher or the child's kindergarten teachers or a care committee (comprised of the child's kindergarten teachers, the remedial teacher, grade school representatives, a member of the College of Teachers and/or an admissions person)? The answer to this question seemed to vary according to the personnel resources that the particular schools had.

- There was also the underlying question of whether it is best for the kindergarten teachers who have observed the child regularly to develop the skills of carrying the first grade readiness assessment, or are these teachers already too subjective?

- Another part of this question is the issue of how it affects the children's response to the assessment if they are taken out of a familiar environment to interact with someone, perhaps a remedial teacher or other school representative, who is unknown to them. One school reported that their remedial teacher had regular weekly contact with the kindergarten classes and teachers and this made it easier for her to do the assessments in consultation with the children's kindergarten teachers.

So we can see that there are a variety of perspectives and opinions on how to achieve recommendations for first grade placement.

One more observation that arose from the "Older Child in the Kindergarten" survey was that "Although the cut-off dates ranged from April to December, the majority (seventy-five percent) of the survey responses listed a May 31/June 1 cut-off date. Some schools said they also take a close look at March to June birthdays, especially those of boys."[2] Susan Howard, the coordinator of WECAN and someone who pays many mentor visits to schools in North America, comments: "Schools with cut-off dates that are flexible, and who use June for their cut-off date, as a general rule, seem to do well. Schools who hold children back longer (cutoff deadline in April or May) may have problems keeping the seven-year-olds involved in the kindergarten and may also have problems down the road when these truly older children go into the nine-year-change or into puberty before their classmates do. I have seen this happen in a few cases where it became really problematic later on. Schools who send children on to grade one who are just barely six (cutoff dates in September or later) may have different problems—a class not completely ready for full-day first grade. I also experience that there is confusion around developmental readiness/ripeness for first grade as opposed to developmental difficulties, including learning problems, emotional and family distress, health problems, etc. I wonder whether we are sometimes keeping troubled children back in the kindergarten who really need to go on with their peers and have their difficulties worked with along the way."[3]

So, we see that there is much to consider when we are establishing the future placement of our kindergarten children. If the readiness question is one of your deliberations, I would encourage you to visit the "Older Child in the Kindergarten" survey online at the Online Waldorf Library.[4] There are very many helpful suggestions and ideas from our North American colleagues within its pages.

At our school in British Columbia, Canada we do not have a curative or remedial teacher, a care group, or a readiness committee, and our first grade teacher often does not arrive until the summer before the next school year starts. Out of necessity, I have had to labor diligently to hone my observation skills and to develop my own process for determining the placement of the kindergarten children in the next first grade class. When I feel stumped I consult with my colleagues in the kindergarten and the grade school. Sometimes I consult with remedial teachers in other schools.

I owe much gratitude to a colleague who, through her own studies, began to share some of the ways in which she was beginning to gain fresh eyes through which to see the children. This opened doors to me and I began to realize that, through research and observation, I too could find ways to understand and look for developmental milestones. I began to determine what the common phenomena are that most children display at the transition between kindergarten and first grade. Some of these manifestations of the six-year change can be witnessed in the regular indoor and outdoor play of the children and are described in the book *You're Not the Boss of Me!* (WECAN 2007).

As time progressed, I also began to realize that some of the children's changes could not be witnessed easily by me while the children were engaged in their normal daily interactions with their peers. I began to wish for opportunities to be alone with the children in order to look more closely at other developments that are necessary for success in the first grade year. Memory, fine motor dexterity, fine balancing, crossing the midline, dominance, awareness of body geography, language development, stamina, and the child's ability to follow directions are just a few of the things that could not be easily observed while the distractions and needs of the group were ongoing. This is when I decided to begin a procedure of spending time alone with each one of the children who are candidates for the future first grade class, a time I refer to as "the first grade readiness games." (The children themselves do not know that this time has anything to do with first grade readiness. They only see that they have a chance to play games with their teacher.) This decision has served the children, the parents, and myself very well. For more about the games, which involve an objective process including a checklist with criteria for observation, please see "Developing Our Observation Skills for Understanding First Grade Readiness."[5]

As time has progressed, my initial clumsy observations have been replaced with a deepening of interest and understanding. Witnessing similar responses from the children as they played the games helped me to pinpoint the important milestones demonstrated before me. By repeating these experiences with different children over and over again I have been able to hone my own powers of observation and find my way into recognizing various nuances in the signs of readiness. The value of developing some concrete criteria that can be used year after year cannot be overestimated. There is an old adage that goes, "The journey of a thousand miles begins with one single step." I would encourage kindergarten teachers to take their initial steps upon this rewarding journey. Childhood and the six-year-old transformation came alive for me in a different way when I included the first grade readiness games in my yearly plan.

There has also been an added dimension of joyful interaction as I witness the enthusiasm with which the children look forward to the opportunity to play games with their teacher. Another bonus is the respectful response of the parents for the first grade readiness recommendations when they discover that it has a definite procedure and a set of observations behind it.

More importantly, these games have given me a venue in which I can make a deeper connection, a soul-spiritual link with the child and parent. I can't say enough about the value of this. There have been times when I have felt stumped by the placement of a child and, after playing the first grade readiness games with the children and consulting with the parents, I have known what my recommendations would be. I regard this time that I spend with the individual children as a time that supports a depth of observation so poignant that, in the evening when I carry the question of the child's placement into my sleep, I am able to present a truer picture of the child to his/her angel. Then I think that the child's angel, the parents' angels, and my own angel are able to find each other, draw closer, collaborate and inspire us all with the right decision.

Although my intent here is to share some ideas about being in this decision-making process with the parents, it seemed necessary for me to explain beforehand the benefit of having a first grade readiness assessment process that engenders the necessary respect from the parents, who have the potential to be some of our greatest allies and helpers. Below are some considerations that I implement in my work with the people who are most familiar with the children and tend to know them very well: their parents.

A very valuable piece of advice was given to our teacher training class by Joan Almon: "Before you begin to advise the parents, find a way to love them. When you strive to do this, then you will eventually be able to say what you need to say to them." Each year I take this up as my mantra right from the very beginning of my encounters with the children's parents.

Here are some ways that I develop this loving relationship through time:

✦ When I first meet a family I take interest in the parents as well as the child. What are the parents' hobbies, activities, and viewpoints? What are their concerns about their child? What were their childhoods like? This initial openness paves the way for a strong future connection.

✦ If there is a child that I sense may be in the position of needing another year in the kindergarten then I work very hard at creating this connection with his or her parents. I want trust, respect, and warmth to exist between myself and the parents when, later on, I know I will be advocating another year in the kindergarten for their child. At the initial interview when I meet the family I am very clear about stating our cut-off date for first grade readiness. If the child falls within this time then I explain the benefits of another year in the kindergarten.

✦ Engaging the parents in warm conversation by phone or taking them aside at drop-off or pick-up times is very helpful.

✦ Involving the parents in some kindergarten tasks can engage their interest and make the kindergarten year(s) more meaningful for them.

✦ Sometimes, I also incorporate the parents in my evening meditation by accurately seeing them in my mind's eye.

✦ When I sense that an issue is brewing in the parent group, newsletters can be an effective and neutral way to build group trust by addressing the issue and sharing living stories that are part of the kindergarten day. Sometimes it's easier to speak about an issue to the whole group, as if the topic just occurred to me, than it is to risk defensiveness or offending someone by approaching the person directly. Reading a newsletter gives parents the opportunity to read the idea and ruminate on it in freedom. Creating a vessel for the parents to get together and talk while I am present also paves the way for open discussion about parents' observations and questions. I host a monthly Parent Discussion and Craft Circle. During the school year there are several meetings with the parents. At each one of these events, the six/seven-year-old transformation and first grade readiness are mentioned, sometimes briefly and other times in greater detail (depending on what developmental manifestations we are witnessing in the older kindergarten children). Explaining common behaviors that can be witnessed at this age helps the parents to see the reason for their child's upheaval as being pertinent to the six/seven-year change and not the "fault" of the kindergarten.

VI. Working with Parents

As the year progresses and the children show more signs of the change, I speak directly to individual parents about it again. "Have you noticed Sarah's giggling and that she's racing around more lately? Have you noticed that Johnny has increased his appetite and is going through a growth spurt? Is Allison questioning your authority at home? Do you notice Nathaniel's fascination with teenagers lately?" By comparing observations the parents tend to be put at ease and feel more fellowship and support when their children are going through these changes. This can be a confusing time for parents and teachers alike. If this atmosphere of warmth, mutual respect and trust has been built and the parents have been properly informed beforehand, then it can be welcome news when the teacher recommends that a child have another year in the kindergarten.

The cutoff date for our school is June 1, although we often give May birthday children (especially boys) the opportunity to attend kindergarten for another year. As I look back over the past five years I see that we have been blessed with some March and April boys and girls turning seven during the end of their kindergarten year. Through time I have discovered some important ways to bring this possibility to the parents. The following suggestions are helpful when parents question the teacher's recommendation and are determined that they want their child to go on into first grade.

First, rather than using the language that the child is "staying back" (the connotation being that he or she is missing something), it works better to place the emphasis on the benefits of another year. The language I use is, "Let's give Sally the opportunity to have another year in the kindergarten."

Here are some of the benefits that can be mentioned to the parents:

✦ Rather than having to struggle to keep up with his peers, the child who has more time can have the opportunity to develop the self-esteem that comes with being fully ready to take on tasks with ease.

✦ A child who is the youngest in his or her family can have the opportunity to practice being an older "brother or sister" in the kindergarten.

✦ An only child or a youngest child in the family constellation can have an opportunity to nurture younger children, because in her second year in the kindergarten she will be in the position to be a helpful older child.

✦ If the child has just begun to show signs of the six/seven-year change then it can be helpful for him to have some consolidation time through more movement opportunities rather than sitting at a first grade school desk for longer periods of the day. It's often helpful to ask the parents if they can imagine their child managing her impulses and sitting contentedly for long periods of time.

✦ Having an extra year in the kindergarten can help a child who would have been the youngest in first grade to be one of the oldest in the kindergarten. Cultivating leadership qualities prepares the child for a successful future.

As well as discussing the benefits with the parents, there are also a few helpful strategies that can assist the decision.

- By far the most helpful strategy that I have found is to make a list, in order of age—oldest to youngest—of the children who will be going on into first grade, and then, in the same manner, a list of the children who will be staying back in the kindergarten. Then, with the parents present, plot where their child would be situated on these lists age-wise. Often when parents see that their child would be the very youngest in the first grade class and, as it often turns out, not even the oldest in next year's kindergarten class, they understand what that could mean for their child.

- Sometimes a decision can be assisted by the teacher saying "If I can let go of Johnny being in kindergarten next year, can you let go of him being in first grade next year and we'll just give this decision some more contemplation time?" If the parents agree, I ask them if we can keep this conversation open to future sharing of our observations. Then I often tell the parents about the importance of the child going on with his or her own peer group. I tell them that I will document daily whom the child plays with. Sometimes the parents invite over an older child and a younger child to their home (on separate occasions) and they can then witness how their child's play changes depending on the age of the playmate. It's important to keep in mind here that often the younger child becomes the slave of the older child, fetching things and so on. When we sensitively observe their play we can see that the younger child is not really playing as an equal with the older one.

- Handouts from parents expressing successful results from giving their child the opportunity for another year in the kindergarten are very helpful.

- Members of the parent body who struggled with this decision of first grade placement and whose children are in the grade school now can be a rich resource if they are willing to accept phone calls from a current questioning parent.

- Hosting a parent evening where the first grade readiness games are explained (after the games have been played with the children) eases the parents' concern that this decision be made by qualified professionals.

The warm bond that we make with the child's parents is essential for a healthy year in the kindergarten. The efforts we make to insure that the social fabric we weave together is abundant with the golden threads of love, trust, and respect are well-justified, forming a foundational garment that can be carried forward into the future.

Notes

1. Ruth Ker, ed., "Waldorf Early Childhood Association Report on the Older Child in the Kindergarten," http://www.waldorflibrary.org/articles/598-waldorf-early-childhood-assn-report-on-the-older-child-in-the-kindergarten (viewed December 27, 2016).
2. Ibid.
3. Ibid.
4. The Online Waldorf Library, www.waldorflibrary.org.
5. Ruth Ker, "Developing Our Observation Skills for Understanding First Grade Readiness" in *First Grade Readiness*, Nancy Blanning, ed. (WECAN 2009), p. 93.

VII. The Young Child and the Spiritual World

Rudolf Steiner's deep insights into the spiritual nature of the world offer a wellspring of insight to the early childhood teacher. Penetrating his work will deepen and broaden the teacher's work with children. His works on education and child development are invaluable for the kindergarten teacher, as are his works on many other subjects, including on fairy and folk tales, speech, painting, and so forth.

Steiner stressed again and again the spiritual nature of Waldorf education and of the kindergarten teacher's work. "Educational technique is of a different nature from the technique devoted to unspiritual things. Educational technique essentially involves a religious moral impulse in the teacher or educator." Waldorf education is an education based on deep spiritual truths and impulses.

In her essay "The Spiritual Foundations of Waldorf Education," Michaela Glöckler offers a synopsis of the spiritual significance of Waldorf education for the individual and for humanity.

Although inclusive and holistic, Waldorf education is based upon a spiritual Christ impulse. One way this can be understood is by reading Joan Almon's essay, "Festivals of the Year." Here she illuminates Waldorf education's connection to Christ as it is felt in nature and through the festivals of the year, in a way that can be inclusive of all religions and cultures. Stephen Spitalny's "The Name of 'John' and the Fairy Tales" illuminates another path to this understanding, as looking more closely at a small element of the stories we tell the children opens up vistas of spiritual evolution.

Nancy Foster's notes from lectures by Michaela Glöckler illuminate an understanding of the festivals which recognizes the universal and common spirit of humanity within them. According to these notes, festivals should include "admiration of nature, a spiritual relationship to the laws of nature; The magic of the social aspect— the joy of preparing a festival for one another; living with threshold experiences, making thresholds conscious, in a manner appropriate for specific developmental stages."

The task of a Waldorf early childhood educator calls upon a spiritual understanding of the young child and a deep commitment to inner development.

Spiritual Foundations of Waldorf Education

Michaela Glöckler

From *Working with the Angels* (WECAN 2004)

Editor's Note: While founded in a Christian and European culture, spirituality in Waldorf early childhood education strives for universality and to encompass many spiritual traditions. Some of the terms and concepts referred to by Michaela Glöckler in her essay can be further explored in Rudolf Steiner's works, including the series of lectures titled: *From Jesus to Christ.*[1]

Our times are characterized by a tremendous contradiction or discrepancy, which we can all feel, between two realities. One is the feeling of impotence in the face of outer circumstances and threats, such as terrible wars and the pollution of nature. The other is the possibility for individual freedom and responsibility for our own destiny. The times are no longer as they were when one person, such as Charlemagne, could rule large sections of the world. Today we have more freedom, including the possibility for individual thinking and for ruling ourselves.

As an indication of this new freedom in thought, every child today learns to read and write, which was never formerly the case. We each want to think individually, and we each feel a responsibility for our own destiny. Yet this individualism can go too far if we do not also have the idea that we share a common future as humanity. If our sense of autonomy grows too great, then each will pull against the other, and we will experience what Rudolf Steiner called the "all against all." It is necessary to develop a sense of community, seeing humanity as an organism, each one a part of the whole. We have a common future. This is the Christ impulse. This is a basic aspect of Waldorf education: respect for the development of the individual while at the same time cultivating a sense of responsibility for the whole. Developing a sense of responsibility requires reincarnation. We need to experience what we have done wrong. If we stand by and allow nuclear plants to be built and do not return in one thousand years to accept responsibility for these actions, we will not grow. We need reincarnation to gain responsibility.

What do we mean by the word "freedom?" It is a space in which one can grow and grow. In this space is the sum of all our abilities with which we can work. Freedom recognizes certain limitations. For example, one must study certain things to become an engineer. The freedom to act as an engineer comes after accepting the requirements and limitations of study and preparation. Thus in our lives, freedom is reached by working through the suffering and situations that meet us. We must reach the ability to offer our gifts, to decide in which direction we will work. Many incarnations are needed to develop more qualities and abilities and thus to experience greater freedom. This is linked with destiny and karma, which is an individual matter and cannot be shared. Yet at the same time, we as individuals are bound together through the Christian idea of the social future of mankind.

To find a personal connection with the reality of the Christ is most important for us in working with children and in going toward the future. We cannot get this from hearing about it. We must experience it ourselves. It is not true when people say, "You need to be clairvoyant to experience the Christ or to know the spiritual world." Clairvoyance is not necessary to be convinced of the Mystery of Golgotha.[2] You must be able to think and then feel whether your thoughts are true. Thoughts are a spiritual reality. In connection with this, Rudolf Steiner cites mathematical studies as training for spiritual development, for it helps develop pure thought, sense-free and exact. We must live and experience our own thoughts. We must find our own convictions about the Christ. This is not something we can learn from others, not even from the Gospel! This is something that we must experience.

When we look at Rudolf Steiner's statue of the Group, we look at the central figure, the *Representative of Man*,[3] and we have this feeling: Here is a being whose facial expression shows concentration and clarity. He is filled with light, with clear thoughts. If he opened his mouth, he would speak the truth. He cannot lie. I have faith in that which he would say. We look at his gesture and see that he is not standing still, but is in a position of striding. He fights against evil, and his arms are his swords. He is not aggressive, but has a calm, strong and sure gesture with which he holds evil in its place.

This being has three weapons in his struggle against evil:

✦ Clear thought—Thinking

✦ Ability to speak the truth—Speaking

✦ Forward movement—Walking

Today many people no longer know how to move forward. There is a paralysis in the will forces, and many people cannot inwardly move. They have a sense of a "dead end." Yet at the same time it is possible to catch glimpses of something higher. We are engaged in a constant search for balance, rather than in forming judgments that this is right or this is wrong. We must build on small things: humility, not egotism; the will to move ahead. With a goal, we can move toward the future and not be overwhelmed by a sense that life is unbearable.

We can look at the young child and see the similarities with the figure of the Representative of Man. The child has the same powers as those depicted in the statue. The two-year-old cannot lie. It is impossible. Only when self-knowledge enters can lying begin, only when we learn to hide ourselves as Adam and Eve did before God.

We come to the question of why Waldorf education is so important. The first lighting up of the ego, the I, comes in the third year while the child still needs much protection. The body is only slowly becoming an instrument for the I. The child is still carrying the gifts of the spiritual world, but he is being awakened intellectually at a very early age. There comes then a discrepancy for the child who cannot reconcile these things. Waldorf education must harmonize this discrepancy. For the young child, the will is developed through imitation. In the grades, the child is oriented through loving authority, but it is an objective love that goes beyond sympathy or antipathy. After adolescence, there is an emergence of clear thinking and intellectual growth.

The goal of Waldorf education is to help the consciousness of the self to develop slowly until the physical and soul organism is fully mature. Then the individual can act in freedom. If the necessity of acting comes too early, the discrepancy between willing and feeling will remain too great. There is also the question of how we can help the parents. Listen to their questions, and see where they are. Don't come at them dogmatically, but rather awaken development in them. The younger the child comes to us, the more possibility there is of reaching the parents.

When we look at the small child learning to walk, to speak, and to think we can experience three "wonders" in the child's development. First, the child is never angry that he has to learn so much. He is not angry that in one year he must learn to walk. Secondly, in learning to speak the child cannot lie. And thirdly, when the child is learning to think, he experiences a love of learning. Around the age of three, when the child begins to say I, he is using these qualities of walking, speaking and thinking. They are necessary for him if he is to say, "I."

As beautiful as this process of saying, "I" is, it can also come too early in the life of the child. There is a discrepancy between what the soul desires and what the individual can do. We must protect the unfolding self-consciousness of the child until the body is ready to be a vessel for the I. That is why Waldorf education must protect the child. In the early years this protection takes place through imitation. In the grades it takes place through authority. In adolescence intellectual thought develops after puberty at the end of the bodily ripening; then the Waldorf student develops his self-consciousness and says, "I go where I will." Now the young person is ready to say I, but if this comes too soon, he will have difficulty coming to the true living Christ. If his organs of perception are closed, he will not be able to achieve the higher possibilities described in *How to Know Higher Worlds*.[4]

The teacher must develop gestures that appear human, for example as in eurythmy. He or she must work out of an awareness of speech, and must educate thinking in such a way that it has clarity. Then the qualities of early childhood will be re-awakened in us. We will again have learned to walk, to speak and to think. Then we can develop an organ of perception for experiencing the Christ.

Every child shows us how to develop these qualities. Then later in our life we can truly say "I," see how much too soon the first I is, and how great the need is for protection if the recognition of the true I is to come.

In the cycle of the year, each festival has its own particular soul quality. At Easter, we experience the love that accompanies man's development. The resurrection forces are within us, and the face of helplessness there is a new strength that comes. Michaelmas has a different quality. Michael is there to be called on. He will not intervene; we must call on him and unite with him if we are to go forward. Then we come to know that the more possibilities we have to work in the world, the greater is our freedom, the greater our possibilities, the more we can do.

Notes

1   Rudolf Steiner, *From Jesus to Christ* (Great Barrington: SteinerBooks 2005).

2   Golgotha is Hebrew for "the Hill of the Skull," and refers to the location where Christ was crucified. The Mystery of Golgotha refers to Christ's death and resurrection.

3   The *Representative of Man* is a large wooden sculpture by Rudolf Steiner, currently kept at the Goetheanum in Dornach, Switzerland. Its central figure represents humanity as a balancing force between the polarity of Lucifer and Ahriman. See a further discussion of Lucifer and Ahriman in "Finding the Realm of the Spirit of Humanity" below.

4   Rudolf Steiner, *How to Know Higher Worlds* (Great Barrington: SteinerBooks 1994).

Festivals of the Year

Joan Almon

From *The Seasonal Festivals in Early Childhood* (WECAN 2010)
Originally published in *An Overview of the Waldorf Kindergarten* (WECAN 1993)

A growing question in Waldorf kindergartens and schools is to what extent Waldorf education is an expression of Christianity as a world religion or to what extent it is more broadly universal. Searching for the answer leads us towards the modern mysteries, for Waldorf education is centered around the Christ as a universal being who has helped humanity and the earth in their development from the beginning of time. Rudolf Steiner, the founder of Waldorf education, speaks of the Christ in the present time as dwelling in the etheric world surrounding the earth. The etheric world has much to do with the life forces of the earth, with nature and its seasons.

The Christ's presence, imbued with love and compassion, is felt more and more by human beings upon the earth, but it is a presence that is not limited to individuals of one particular religious persuasion. Waldorf education strives to create a place in which the highest Beings, including the Christ, can find their home, but it is not affiliated with one religion or another. For this reason one can find Waldorf kindergartens and schools in countries linked with all the religions of the world, yet all these schools feel themselves sharing a common understanding and approach.

The door to Waldorf education is open for all to enter, and early childhood educators have a special responsibility in representing this openness, for we are frequently the first teachers the parents come to know. Contemporary parents are often sensitive to the messages they receive as they first enter the life of the school. They want to know if this is simply another secular school, or a religious school promoting a particular religion, or a school that honors the spirit of all and nurtures the deepest and most universal elements of spirituality. Most, in my experience, are seeking the latter, and it is the festivals that most clearly communicate to parents our approach to spiritual experience and understanding.

My international work for Waldorf education took me to schools that celebrate festivals from many different religions. I found that one of the common elements was a deep relationship to the world of nature and its rhythms. On that foundation the teachers were developing a new understanding of how the spiritual and earthly elements of life interpenetrate and how this relationship manifests in the festivals.

As teachers we tend to live from season to season, from festival to festival, but it is also wonderful to carry a picture of the breathing rhythm of the year as a whole, including the way that the northern and southern hemispheres breathe together in an annual rhythm. Rudolf Steiner's Soul Calendar[1] is a means of sensitizing ourselves to the inner moods of the year and our soul responses to them. Working with the current verse and relating it to the verse for the opposite time of year is one approach to the Soul Calendar which may develop a consciousness for the year as a whole and for its powerful rhythms as experienced in the northern and southern hemispheres at the same time.

I also found that working year after year with Rudolf Steiner's lectures, *The Four Seasons and the Archangels*,[2] deepened my appreciation of the festivals through the great imaginations alive in each of them. The pictures of how the spirit of the festivals is passed from one Archangel to another and of how different aspects of a festival live in the two hemispheres at the same time contributed to a view of the earth as a living, breathing being. All of this wove together in my classroom on the season table in wool felt pictures, through changing colored cloths on tables, in the seasonal activities we did and the foods we ate, through the songs and verses of the seasons, and in the stories I chose, both fairy tales and simple nature tales, some offered as puppet plays.

Each season was a rich experience, and the high point was the festival celebrations that we observed with the parents. I learned that the festival celebrations needed to be meaningful for the children, for the parents, and for me, and it was possible to create such festivals by entering more deeply into their spirit and meaning each year. I also discovered over the years that as my understanding grew deeper, the celebrations themselves seemed to grow simpler. Like a homeopathic drop which is small but potent, a well-prepared festival need not be elaborate to be meaningful to those present.

One starting point for approaching the festivals is to look outward at the ever-changing face of nature as the earth breathes in and out through the course of the seasons. The farther away from the equator we live, the fuller are these breaths, so that the contrast between winter's in-breath and summer's out-breath can be very great. In the town of Barrow, Alaska, for instance, residents see the sun rise in the afternoon in mid-November and an hour later watch it set. For the next sixty-four days they will not see the sun again. Of course, in the summer they have an abundance of sunlight, and all the growth of nature, which for most of us stretches over six or more months, is compressed into just two months.

Being used to an array of seasons and the shift from the short chill days of winter to the long dreamy days of summer, it was hard for me to imagine life near the equator where the sun rises and sets at the same time each day and the temperatures fluctuate only narrowly. Visiting Ecuador twice was eye-opening, for my Ecuadorian friends assured me they were very aware of the passing seasons and that the rhythm of the year was of great importance to them. When I asked a Waldorf kindergarten teacher how she reflected these changes on the season table, she said it was through the fruits, for during each month different fruits ripen. I have heard similar examples from colleagues in Hawaii, where seasonal changes are also present but not always obvious to the visitor. In such surroundings we can see how strongly the human being longs to experience time as an annual journey, not only as a daily or a monthly rhythm. It is wonderful that nature provides us with rhythmic changes, both quiet and dramatic, to meet this need.

There is another aspect to experiencing the yearly rhythm. We usually think of the similarities from one year to the next as the seasons unfold. We take delight and even comfort in seeing certain flowers bloom in the same spot each year. But gradually we may also develop a sensitivity to the differences between nature's work from one year to another. No two springs are ever quite the same, in part because some are warmer or wetter than others, but also because of subtler differences we may sense as we watch the seasons progress year after year. Evelyn Capel, a priest in the Christian Community, expresses this beautifully in the following passage from *The Christian Year*, which inspires a new relationship to the seasons and how they may live in us and in our classroom.

> *The background to the drama of human existence is the changing scenery of the earth's seasons. Winter changes to spring, spring to summer, summer to autumn, in much the same way each year. Their magical transformations can be relied upon but the wonder of the magic never grows stale with repetition. Spring has come before, it will come again, but there is a particular note, a subtle effluence, a shade of feeling in this spring that has never been quite the same before and which will haunt the expectation of next spring, though it will not be realized again. A particular season can be lost to one's experience if, in the midst of the pleasure in finding again its well-known, often repeated character, the heart does not catch the inner quality that can only be apprehended this once. It is a joy to find in spring the crocuses coming into blossom under the same tree where they have been growing for years, to catch in the height of summer the familiar scent of new-mown hay, to catch in the autumn the blue smoke of a bonfire rising past the bronzed leaves still fast in the branches and to sense in winter that tang of a clear frosty morning. Yet there is, amidst the familiar joys, the thrill of the unrepeatable element that makes each season in its own year an event of a lifetime, if only one is awake enough not to miss it.*[3]

So many elements weave together in creating a festival: our attunement to the season and the inner qualities or outward expressions of the season in that year compared to another year; our own evolving consciousness; and our relationship with the individual children and families in our class that year. All of these work together so that each festival celebration is unique, even if the stories and circles appear to be basically the same from year to year. Nature is different, we are different, and the children themselves are different. We can deepen this living approach to the festivals through our own meditative activity, through artistic work on the seasons and festivals, and through the study of written works that have grown out of Waldorf education and anthroposophy and speak of the festivals. Then the pathway through the year becomes a living journey that we celebrate with each other and dare to share with the highest spiritual Beings.

Notes

1   See, e.g., Rudolf Steiner, *The Calendar of the Soul* (Great Barrington: SteinerBooks 1988).

2   Rudolf Steiner, *The Four Seasons and the Archangels* (Great Barrington: SteinerBooks 1996).

3   Evelyn Francis Capel, *The Christian Year* (Edinburgh: Floris Books 2012).

The Name of "John" and the Fairy Tales

Stephen Spitalny

From *Gateways* Newsletter Issue 51 (WECAN 2006)

> *There is nothing of greater blessing than for a child than to nourish it with everything that brings the roots of human life together with those of cosmic life. A child is still having to work creatively, forming itself, bringing about the growth of its body, unfolding its inner tendencies; it needs the wonderful soul-nourishment it finds in fairy tale pictures, for in them the child's roots are united with the life of the world.*[1]

As an underlying thought to give context to the following, the author's perspective is that a fairy tale, a true fairy tale, is a picture of the human being, of each one of us. The characters depict various aspects of the human organism and psyche and all the characters are contained within each of us. The stories offer guidance through life's challenges and a path toward the reconnecting of one's soul and spirit as carried by the physical body during life on earth.

For many years I have thought about the following question: why is the name John so common in fairy tales? Or any of the many variations of the name; Johannes, Hans, Hansel, Evan, Ivan, Vanya, Ian, Giovanni, Jean, Juan, Sean or Jack. In the Grimms' tales: "The Griffin," "Iron Hans," "The Miller's Drudge and the Cat," "Faithful John," "Hansel and Gretel," "Hans in Luck." Or the Russian tales: "The Crystal Mountain," "The Three Kingdoms and Ivan the Simpleton." "Jack" stories abound in English and American tales. The name John and its many variations are widespread in fairy tales from around the world.

The John character in the fairy tales is faithful, giving and honest. He is sincere, gentle and patient. Usually though, he is described as simple and lazy and unlikely to succeed in the world. Yet it is John, out of his purity and selflessness, who meets success when others do not. John bears a natural, innocent wisdom that carries him where the old wisdom no longer holds true.

Often the third son, the simpleton, can be a picture of the working of the Consciousness Soul, the newest, youngest aspect of the human soul to develop and the part of the individual human being where soul and spirit meet. One could then think of the two older brothers as Sentient and Intellectual Soul members of the human being. The Consciousness Soul brings a new capacity into humanity, a capacity to discover one's own individuality and an inner freedom to create new community. These capacities can seem unimportant and impractical at first, even lowly qualities, to others. The youngest son has innocent wisdom and a pure heart, as opposed to his clever brothers. With a warm heart, the youngest son comes to truth and facilitates deep transformation of the human psyche. It is with this aspect of the human soul that spiritual reality is perceivable. John is quite frequently the name of that third son in the stories.

> *Then she took her faithful John by the hand and led him to the carriage. They drove away together and went straight to the little house John had built with the silver tools. It was a big castle now, and everything in it was silver and gold. Then she married him, and he was rich, so rich that he had enough to last him the rest of his life.*[2]

The deep knowledge and golden wisdom of true fairy tales is palpable. As one carries the fairy tale images inwardly, more and more the underlying spiritual truths can reveal themselves. In ancient times, initiates at the various mystery centers experienced true knowledge of the spiritual world. This information was embedded in images as stories that could speak of these truths, not to the intellect but to the heart of the listener. In long-ago times, the intellect was not as developed as it is today, and so for the average person to have access to that truth, it had to be woven into story. The stories spread from the mystery centers out into the diverse cultures of the earth. Troubadours, minstrels and storytellers carried the stories on their travels and shared them throughout the lands as they wandered and told the tales.

One can try to picture a sheath of spiritual knowledge surrounding the earth, and anyone who could access that sheath was privy to the spiritual wisdom available there. The initiates and shamans and various wisdom-bearers throughout the world shared access to this etheric sheath. When they "received" information in this way, it was cloaked in the trappings of the culture familiar to the recipient. This is why there is an archetype behind the story, but the actual stories have differences in the details. Those archetypes live in the etheric sheath, and as they incarnate into culture, they take on details and trappings from that surrounding culture. The true fairy tale gives information of the path an individual can take to unite the various aspects, the bodies of the human being, so a balanced path in life can be attained. Fairy tales are a guide to the uniting of souls and spirit and body in the individual, given as story. In our time this information would be offered as a book, perhaps *How to Marry Your Own Soul and Spirit*, or a lecture, "Overcoming the Sentient Soul by Allowing the Consciousness Soul Its Voice." In olden times, when the intellect was in its infancy, the guide to becoming a more evolved human being was story. This fairy tale character was able to see the goddess that was hidden to others.

> *Said Thandiwe, "You may be clothed in torn zebra skins and covered with ashes, but those cannot conceal your splendor. In your eyes I see the bright gleam of rivers, ponds, lakes and seas. In your eyes I see one who greens the earth and nourishes the crops. Such beauty far surpasses the charm of well oiled skin and the jingling of bracelets and cowry shells. You are my bride. You are the Rain Goddess."*

When the Rain Goddess heard these words, she knew she had chosen wisely. "Let the ceremonies begin," she said. Soon the villagers were dancing and feasting, celebrating the marriage of Thandiwe and the Rain Goddess. When the sun dipped behind the hills and the stars sparkled silver beads in the night sky, the heavens shone their blessings on the marriage.

Thandiwe and the Rain Goddess rose up into the heavens, hand in hand. They journeyed to the Rainbow House, high up in the heavens. And there they live to this day and will always live.[3]

As the stories incarnated into the cultures of humanity, various esoteric groups adapted the details to help refine the process of individual development. One of the last groups to adapt these ancient spiritual stories were the Rosicrucians. As early as the seventh century, they brought in the element of esoteric Christianity to widespread fairy tales. One can look to Rudolf Steiner for more background about the Rosicrucians.[4] The true Rosicrucians have worked outside the mainstream of the Church, yet they are connected to the deepest truths of the working of the Christ Being on earth. Their inner teachings were about the possibility of awakening the higher ego in each individual, by which one is connected with the guiding spirit of humanity.

In historical Christianity, there have been two widely known streams. Peter began the Catholic stream, and we can see Paul as connected to the various Protestant churches. One could name a third stream: the John stream, to which the Rosicrucians belong. This could also be called Johannine Christianity, the streaming of the future. This youngest stream has yet to come to maturity and be recognized for the deep truth and conscience it represents. So from this angle, we can see John as the youngest brother to Peter and Paul, not yet valued for the capacities he brings.

Says the fairy to Jack at the end of "Jack and the Beanstalk":

"If you had looked at the gigantic beanstalk and only stupidly wondered about it, I should have left you where your misfortune had placed you, only restoring her cow to your mother. But you showed an inquiring mind, and great courage and enterprise, therefore you deserve to rise; and when you mounted the beanstalk you climbed the ladder of fortune."

And thus Jack was able to rise into and see the spiritual world.

What does the name John offer about the role of this character in the human being? Who is John?

Two famous beings named John immediately come to mind, both playing major roles in the biblical stories of Jesus Christ. Rudolf Steiner has offered profound insight on the subject of the two biblical Johns and their connection with each other. Further, Steiner explained that John was evolved to a level that allowed him in full consciousness to experience his own connection to the Christ Spirit and become the representative for all humanity in that connection. John showed the path that is possible for any one of us to undertake, the path of true awakening and connection. Through initiation, John became the bearer of cosmic wisdom, the Divine Sophia, and his task was to tell the truth to those who had ears to hear. (That in itself harkens to the essential role of story, to bring the truth to those who are ready to receive it.) Thus the name John grows from a proper name to a symbol characterizing he who has become or is to become the herald of the Ego.[5]

John is one who is able to cross the threshold to the spiritual world consciously, to truly awaken and see and recognize the spiritual within the material world. He has developed a spiritual organ, and its name is conscience.

Ivan found the water of life and sprinkled it on his brothers. They rubbed their eyes. "How long have we slept?" they asked. "Without me you would have slept forever," said Ivan Goroh, pressing them to his heart.[6]

The more ancient name for John offers some interesting insight into the name itself. In Greek, IOANNES, and phonetically in Hebrew, Jehohannen, and also in the German Johannes, we hear a particular order of vowel sounds contained in the name; the sounds ee, oh and then ah. In the last lecture in a series entitled "The Festival of Easter,"[7] Steiner described how the pupils and initiates of the Ephesus Mysteries experienced the cosmos as a form of light, and within the light of the sun, the sounds J O A (ee, oh, ah), which had effects on the pupil.

And in this feeling of the [sounds] J O A one felt oneself as the very sound J O A within the light. Then one was truly HUMAN—resounding 'I,' resounding astral body, clothed in the light-radiant etheric body. One was sound within the light. And so indeed one is as cosmic Human Being and as such one is able to perceive what is seen in the surrounding Cosmos, just as here on Earth one is able to perceive through the eye what takes place within the physical horizon of the Earth.[8]

So one can see the ancient power which still lives in the very sounding of the name John whether or not we are even aware of its possible effects on the children we work with.

From other perspectives, Rudolf Steiner spoke about the relation of cosmic activity and the formative quality of spoken sounds. Steiner articulated that certain sounds are connected to particular planets. In reference to the vowel sounds in the more original forms of the name for John, ee is connected to Mercury, oh to Jupiter and ah, Venus. Our Earth phase of evolution began under the rule of Mars. At the turning point of time, the Mercury phase began. That is where our earth is at present. Next will be the Jupiter and then Venus phases. Ioannes is a name sounding us from the present moment toward the future, when deep spiritual mysteries will be awake in the consciousness of all human beings, and humanity as a whole will become the tenth hierarchy. So we can consider the name John as a picture of the archetypal human being after spiritual awakening by the highest spiritual beings. He has the possibility of healing the earth and transforming it into the star of love.

John lives within all of us as a potential, and it is our birthright in this time. Yet it can only be awakened individually out of our own freedom and will-engaged activity. Fairy tales offer a roadmap to our own awakening and hence to the transformation of our world.

Steiner quotes Ludwig Laistner (1848-1896) in his lecture "The Poetry and Meaning of Fairy Tales."

The fairy tale is like a good angel, given us at birth to go with us from our home to our earthly path through life, to be our trusted comrade throughout the journey and to give us angelic companionship, so that our life itself can become a truly heart-and-soul enlivened fairy tale.[9]

Notes

1. Rudolf Steiner, *The Poetry and Meaning of Fairy Tales*, Ruth Pusch, trans., ed. (Spring Valley: Mercury Press 1989).
2. "The Poor Miller's Boy and the Cat," from The Brothers Grimm, *The Complete Grimm's Fairy Tales*, no. 106.
3. From an African tale, "The Marriage of the Rain Goddess." Perhaps Thandiwe (tahn-dee-way) is another variant of John?
4. See Sergei O. Prokofieff, *The Cycle of the Year as a Path of Initiation* (UK: Temple Lodge Publications 2014); see also Sergei O. Prokofieff, *The Mystery of John the Baptist and John the Evangelist at the Turning Point in Time* (UK: Temple Lodge Publications 2005).
5. Karl König, "The Two Disciples John" (1909), cited in *Jesus, Lazarus, and the Messiah* by Charles S. Tidball (Great Barrington: SteinerBooks 2005).
6. From the Russian tale "Ivan Goroh and Vasilisa Golden Tress."
7. Rudolf Steiner, "The Festival of Easter," Lecture given on April 22, 1924. The only known English translation is availble at the Rudolf Steiner Archive (http://wn.rsarchive.org/Lectures/GA/GA0233a/19240422p04.html).
8. Ibid.
9. Steiner, *The Poetry and Meaning of Fairy Tales*.

Finding the Realm of the Spirit of Humanity

Notes from lectures by **Michaela Glöckler** at the 2006 WECAN East Coast Childhood Conference on "The Spirit of Humanity in Early Childhood Education," recorded by Nancy Foster

From *The Seasonal Festivals in Early Childhood* (WECAN 2010)

On Friday evening and Saturday morning, Dr. Michaela Glöckler read to us a quotation from Mahatma Gandhi:

There are times when you have to obey a call which is the highest of all, that is, the voice of conscience, even though such obedience may cost many a bitter tear, and even more, separation from friends, from family, from the state to which you may belong, from all that you have held as dear as life itself. For this obedience is the law of our being. (1919)

This quotation was the keynote for her theme of becoming peacemakers, following our conscience as we establish a new identity with our higher Self in the realm of the Spirit of Humanity. Through the Goethean approach to the young child, we can observe the developmental steps toward the awakening of the "I." Trust is the underlying necessity for these three steps:

- *Self-initiation into the mystery of space*: In this sacred ground of self-teaching, the child orients the self in the three dimensions and comes into the upright.
- *Self-initiation in speaking*: The child enters into soul-to-soul communication through the vehicle of language, by means of three components: genetics, environment, and the Self. Initially the child is open to whatever language(s) are offered in the environment.
- *Self-initiation in thinking*: There is no imitation involved in thinking; rather, the child "wakes up" to realize he has thoughts and learns to express them. To say "I" to the Self is the awakening of thinking. This "I" indicates the spiritual reality that is in all of us; I share the ability to say "I" with all of humanity. The "I am" is the Spirit of Humanity, and the child finds it out of his own striving.

The Spirit of Humanity is the crown of nature, but it is still in its infancy. Animals are wiser: they cannot be evil. Only human beings disturb the ecological balance.

We call nature divine because it is so complete. Only the human being has the possibility and the need to develop, to improve. What the human being has to learn is beyond nature; it is from the spiritual realm. For example, the infant has a walking reflex, but true walking does not arise from this reflex. The baby must overcome this reflex and develop his own walking through sensory-motor learning—that is, he must bring nature under his own will-control. As human beings, we are not the slaves of our instincts.

This first experience of overcoming instinct gives us self-trust, the realization, "I can learn; I can develop." Thus the steps of development above are humanizing principles, with trust as the prerequisite.

As developing human beings, we must learn to be homeless in order to find our higher Self. In his 1910 lecture cycle *The Mission of the Individual Folk Souls*,[1] Rudolf Steiner describes the necessity of entering consciously into our Folk Soul identity to see what it can contribute to humanity, thus also learning to see the mission of other Folk Souls. We must strengthen our ego and establish a new identity independent of the Folk.

Dr. Glöckler pointed out that babies are truly "homeless" in this sense: the younger the child, the more open and the less bound to a particular Folk Soul. Therefore, we do not want to offer a "museum of religions" in the kindergarten by celebrating festivals of every family's religion. Instead, in early childhood education we can lay the basis for an independent self-identity through keeping the realm of common humanity alive in the young child and developing a strong sense of the Spirit of Humanity. The ideal in the kindergarten is that all festivals meet the challenge to address the common Spirit of Humanity.

The elements of such festivals might be the following:

✦ admiration of nature, a spiritual relationship to the laws of nature;

✦ the magic of the social aspect—the joy of preparing a festival for one another;

✦ living with threshold experiences, making thresholds conscious, in a manner appropriate for specific developmental stages.

Without the spiritual in education, children would be cut off from the source of their humanity, yet religion is a private matter. What we bring into the early childhood classroom must be that which is beyond a personal religion. Rudolf Steiner said that Christianity began as a religion but has become something more. By bringing it into the thought realm, it transcends the sectarian. In *How to Know Higher Worlds*, we find concepts from many religions, because Rudolf Steiner was seeking to formulate a universally human path of development so that nearly any human being could participate. "There slumber in every human being faculties by means of which he can acquire for himself a knowledge of higher worlds." This idea that each human being can find the spirit is also found in the Gospels. (Religious traditions often do not reflect this; we have to go to the source.)

Dr. Glöckler ended by giving a picture of human nature in the context of the challenge of the adversarial beings. In the Old Testament, there are two creation stories. In the first, the human being is portrayed as a spiritual being, encompassing all realms, and is declared by God to be "very good." In the second, the human being is portrayed as a physical being, with each kingdom of nature placed beside the others. Here, there is the possibility of evil. The very young child belongs with the first picture. Once ego-consciousness has dawned, the second picture is added, and so we have both possible views of our humanity.

The anthroposophical understanding of this paradox is found in the qualities of Lucifer and Ahriman.[2] Lucifer represents the ancient paradigm of fanaticism: "You will know what is good and what is evil." This ignores the reality that good and evil are in all of us, and denies the possibility of development, of becoming.

Ahriman intends that we forget good and evil and view the human being as an animal which can be formed and directed. This is the modern paradigm, in which freedom is seen to cause trouble and human beings are treated as automatons.

Our challenge is to develop moral intuition, the ability to discern in the moment what is good or evil. We must not fall into either of the above paradigms, but find our way forward as human beings on a path of development to the realm of the Spirit of Humanity. Another verse from Gandhi speaks to us of strength of heart and the power of everlasting spirit:

> *Power invariably elects to go into the hands of the strong. That strength may be physical or of the heart, or, if we do not fight shy of the word, of the spirit. Strength of the heart connotes soul force. Let it be remembered that physical force is transitory. But the power of the spirit is permanent even as the spirit is everlasting.* (1942)

Notes:

1 Rudolf Steiner, *The Mission of the Folk Souls* (London: Rudolf Steiner Press 2005). Rudolf Steiner's term Folk Soul can be understood as referring to the culture of a people.

2 Lucifer and Ahriman represent a polarity: Lucifer represents the spiritual pole; Ahriman represents the material pole. As with all polarities, each represents an extreme. For further interest, see Rudolf Steiner, *Lucifer and Ahriman* (London: Rudolf Steiner Press 1954).

Contributors

Joan Almon is the co-founder of the Alliance for Childhood and currently works with the Alliance as a consultant. She is a former Waldorf kindergarten teacher, was co-founder of WECAN, and has worked internationally as a consultant to Waldorf educators and training programs.

Nancy Blanning has taught within Waldorf education for twenty-five years as a lead kindergarten teacher and presently serves as a therapeutic and remedial teacher at the Denver Waldorf School. Her special focus is on developing movement enrichment for young children. With her colleague, Laurie Clark, she has co-authored the book *Movement Journeys and Circle Adventures*. She also does consulting work with Waldorf schools in North America, teacher training and mentoring. She is a member of the WECAN board. She was also a member of the WECAN Working Group on the Older Child in the Kindergarten and a contributor to the book *You're Not the Boss of Me!* (WECAN 2007).

Rune Bratlann is an educator at Nøkken, a mixed-age early childhood program in Copenhagen, Denmark.

Tim Bennett, born in England, came to America when he was ten years old. Living in the Pacific Northwest, he took full advantage of experiencing the wilderness around him, camping, skiing and hiking. He graduated from the University of Washington with a BFA in Fine Arts, concentrating on ceramics and painting. Through art, he came to working with children. After assisting for three years in the Waldorf kindergartens of the Seattle Waldorf School, he became a lead teacher. He has been teaching kindergarten since 1990. Tim also graduated in the first class of Spacial Dynamics taught in the USA, back in 1994. His interest in young children and movement led him to meet Helle Heckmann and visit her school in Copenhagen. His own kindergarten incorporated a love of nature and joy in movement.

Margret Constantini, fascinated by art from earliest childhood, studied music at the Musikhochschule in Hannover. She worked as a music teacher for two years in Munich after her studies. She met her husband while visiting Italy, and they had four sons. Later the family moved to southern Germany, where Margret was commissioned to found a kindergarten, which she then directed for twelve years, also studying in Öschelbronn with art professor Fritz Marburg. As a final work, Margret helped to design the interior of a kindergarden. In 1986 Margret became a lecturer for pedagogy and art at the Waldorf kindergarten seminar in Hanover, and worked there for fifteen years.

In the year 2000 Margret met the African sand painter Epaphrodite Binamungu from Kigali in Rwanda, who introduced her to the various techniques of sand painting that fascinated her and with which she works today.

Louise deForest, as an independent consultant to Waldorf schools, travels the world offering lectures on early childhood education, mentoring support and early childhood teacher training. She is a WECAN Board member and is one of two representatives of North America to IASWECE. She has edited two story collections for WECAN: *For the Children of the World* (2012) and *Tell Me a Story* (2013).

Dora Dolder was an early childhood educator from Germany.

Nancy Foster taught children and parents at Acorn Hill Waldorf Kindergarten and Nursery in Silver Spring, Maryland, for over thirty years, and taught in the early childhood teacher education program at Sunbridge Institute. She also served as the Membership Coordinator of the Waldorf Early Childhood Association of North America. Now retired, she continues to be active in mentoring early childhood teachers, and has also edited several books for WECAN, most recently *The Mood of the Fifth* (2013).

Michaela Glöckler, MD is currently the head of the Medical Section of the School of Spiritual Science in Dornach, Switzerland. She has been active as a pediatrician and school doctor in Germany and is the co-author with Wolfgang Goebel of *A Guide to Child Health* (Floris Books 2013).

Shannon Honigblum was born in Florida, growing up there and in Colorado, Michigan, and New York. She has lived in France, Germany, and South Africa. A Waldorf alum, She graduated from Green Meadow Waldorf High School. After receiving a B.A. in Classics from the University of Florida, she was a Peace Corps Volunteer in Niger. She has an M.A. in Literary Cultures from New York University and an M.S. in Early Childhood Waldorf Education from Sunbridge College. Shannon has experience teaching all ages of students. She taught high school English in Brooklyn and in Garden City, New York, and she taught in the middle school at the Austin Waldorf School in Texas. Currently she teaches kindergarten at the Austin Waldorf School. She is the author of *Making a Family Home* (SteinerBooks, 2010).

Susan Howard is Coordinator of the Waldorf Early Childhood Association of North America (WECAN). She has been teaching and directing the Sunbridge Early Childhood Teacher Education program since 1984. She is also a co-founder and board member of the Research Institute for Waldorf Education and is a member of the WECAN Teacher Education Committee and the IASWECE Working Group on Early Childhood Teacher Training. She is the editor of *The Developing Child* (WECAN 2012), *Working with the Angels* (WECAN 2011), and *Love as the Source of Education* (WECAN 2016).

Freya Jaffke is a master Waldorf kindergarten teacher and teacher trainer from Germany who has lectured and offered workshops for educators and parents in many different countries. Her books have sold over a quarter of a million copies worldwide; *Play With Us!* and *Let's Dance and Sing!* have recently been published in English by WECAN.

Ruth Ker has been a teacher of early childhood education for over thirty years, first in mainstream education and then at Sunrise Waldorf School in British Columbia, Canada. Ruth is presently in the mixed-age kindergarten classroom with her beloved six-year-olds, is a member of the WECAN board, and a teacher trainer and mentor for the early childhood teacher training program of the West Coast Institute for Studies in Anthroposophy. Ruth was also a facilitator for the retreats attended by the WECAN Working Group on the Older Child in the Kindergarten, and editor of the resulting book *You're Not the Boss of Me!—Understanding the Six/Seven-Year-Old Transformation* (WECAN 2007).

Barbara Klocek taught a mixed-age kindergarten for over twenty years at the Sacramento Waldorf School. During that time she also worked professionally as an artist and art therapist. Her love of art early in life led her to a Master of Fine Arts degree from Temple University. Her three sons, now grown, were Waldorf educated and inspired her to become a Waldorf teacher. She completed her teacher training studies at Rudolf Steiner College. She has offered many workshops for kindergarten teachers at Rudolf Steiner College, as well as teaching nationally and internationally. She currently enjoys mentoring teachers in the art of teaching and research. Her other interests include music and gardening.

Kimberly Lewis teaches in the nursery at the Tucson Waldorf School in Arizona. She is the co-editor of *Creating Connections: Perspectives on Parent-and-Child Work in Waldorf Early Childhood Education* (WECAN 2014).

Renate Long-Breipohl holds a doctorate in theology and a degree in early childhood education. In 1985 she and her family migrated to Australia where she became the co-founder of the Samford Valley Steiner School, Brisbane, and taught there in the kindergarten from 1987–1997. In 1997 she moved to Sydney to join the Sydney Rudolf Steiner College as coordinator and lecturer for Steiner early childhood education and was a member of the Council of IASWECE for until 2009, representing Australia. Renate has lectured widely in Steiner early childhood training courses in Southeast Asian countries and in Australia. She has been invited as keynote speaker at early childhood conferences in New Zealand, the United States, China, and at the Goetheanum/Switzerland.

Nancy Macalaster holds a degree in child development from Connecticut College and a master's degree in counseling psychology from Antioch University New England. She is a graduate of Sophia's Hearth Family Center's professional development course for early childhood professionals, "The Child and the Family in the First Three Years," and has completed advanced training at the Pikler Institute in Budapest, Hungary. She has completed training in maternal and infant mental health in Boston at the Jewish Family and Children's Services. She teaches at the Early Childhood Education Center at Sophia's Hearth in New Hampshire.

Claudia McKeen, MD is a general practitioner and school and kindergarten doctor. She is also a lecturer at Waldorf teacher trainings and conferences in Germany and South America.

Eldbjørg Gjessing Paulsen was born in Trondheim, Norway. She completed her Waldorf teacher training in Stuttgart, Germany. With three children of her own, she started Stjerneglimt Waldorfkindergarten in Arendal, Norway in 1984 and has been there ever since. For twelve years, Eldbjørg was the representative for Norway in the International Association of Steiner-Waldorf Early Childhood Education. She has taught various models at the Seminar in Oslo, Norway, and has been a board member of the Norwegian Association for many years. She spends time in Cape Town, South Africa every year helping with mentoring and teaching in the Townships, focusing mainly on children under the age of three years, and began running birth-to-three courses in Beijing and Chengdu, China, in 2015.

Margaret Ris taught early childhood classes at the Waldorf School, Lexington, Massachusetts, for seventeen years. She has completed advanced training at the Emmi Pikler Institute in Budapest, Hungary, and studies with the Infant Parent Training Institute of the Center for Early Relationship Support at Jewish Family and Children's Services in Waltham, Massachusetts. She has served on the board of directors for Sophia's Hearth Family Center in Keene, New Hampshire, for three years and offers parent-child classes at the Cambridge YMCA.

Claus-Peter Röh is co-leader of the Pedagogical Section of the School of Spiritual Science, based at the Goetheanum in Dornach, Switzerland. He was a class teacher for many years in Germany.

Ingeborg Schöttner was an early childhood educator in Germany. A long-standing member of the Anthroposophical Society, she passed on in 2013.

Stephen Spitalny is a former editor of the WECAN *Gateways* Newsletter. He teaches kindergarten at the Waldorf School of Santa Cruz, California.

Helmut von Kügelgen (1916-1998) was a champion of the Waldorf early childhood movement and a steadfast supporter of its growth in North America.

Susan Weber has been a public school teacher and administrator, Waldorf early childhood teacher, and Waldorf early childhood teacher training coordinator at Antioch University New England, where she also previously earned a certificate in Waldorf early childhood education. She was among the founding circle of Sophia's Hearth Family Center in Keene, NH, and is presently the Center's director. Susan has completed RIE Level I training in Los Angeles and introductory and advanced training at the Pikler Institute in Budapest, Hungary. She presented the work of Waldorf education in developing parent-infant and parent-toddler programs at the Pikler Institute's Sixtieth Anniversary Symposium in Budapest, Hungary, in April 2007. She is the co-editor of *Creating Connections: Perspectives on Parent-and-Child Work in Waldorf Early Childhood Education* (WECAN 2014).

Bronja Zahlingen, born of a Jewish family in Poland in 1912, began teaching Waldorf kindergarten in Vienna, Austria, in 1932. After escaping Austria during World War II, she returned in 1955 and was instrumental in re-establishing the kindergarten that grew into the Rudolf Steiner School. Bronja was well-known for her beautiful dolls and puppets, taught doll-making, created magical puppet shows for festivals, and developed circle games based on fairy tales such as "The Queen Bee," "The Miller's Boy and the Cat," and "The Turnip," which continue to influence early childhood teachers today.

Recommended Further Reading

The early collections of material from the Waldorf Kindergarten Newsletter, *An Overview of the Waldorf Kindergarten* and *Deeper Insights into the Waldorf Kindergarten*, are now out of print. They can still be downloaded from the Online Waldorf Library (waldorflibrary.org), which also offers PDF versions of the *Gateways* newsletter and of many other resources.

The main contents of these two classic volumes have been preserved in this introductory reader and in the following WECAN publications:

> *The Developing Child: The First Seven Years*
> *The Young Child in the World Today*
> *Working with the Angels: The Young Child and the Spiritual World*
> *The Seasonal Festivals in Early Childhood*
> *A Lifetime of Joy*

All are highly recommended as a starting place for your further explorations of Waldorf early childhood education, along with the other sources from which the essays in this book have been taken.

The following is a list of additional recommended resources from WECAN and other publishers. It can also be found in slightly different form on the WECAN website at www.waldorfearlychildhood.org/bibliography.php

I. An Introduction to Waldorf Early Childhood Education

Baldwin, Sarah. *Nurturing Children and Families: One Model of a Parent-Child Program in a Waldorf School* (WECAN, 2013, second edition).

Foster, Nancy. *In a Nutshell: Dialogues with Parents at Acorn Hill, a Waldorf Kindergarten* (Acorn Hill Waldorf Kindergarten and Nursery, 2005; distributed by WECAN).

Grunelius, Elizabeth. *Early Childhood Education and the Waldorf School Plan* (Rudolf Steiner College Press, 1991).

Heckmann, Helle. *Nøkken: A Garden for Children* (WECAN, 2015, second edition).

Jaffke, Freya. *Work and Play in Early Childhood* (SteinerBooks, 1996).

Lewis, Kimberly and Weber, Susan, eds. *Creating Connections: Perspectives on Parent-and-Child Work in Waldorf Early Childhood Education* (WECAN, 2014).

Long-Breipohl, Renate. *Under the Stars: The Foundations of Steiner Waldorf Early Childhood Education* (Hawthorn Press, 2012).

Nicol, Janni and Taplin, Jill. *Understanding the Steiner Waldorf Approach: Early Years Education in Practise* (Routledge, 2012).

Oldfield, Lynne. *Free to Learn: Introducing Steiner Waldorf Early Childhood Education* (Hawthorn Press, 2012, second edition).

Patterson, Barbara and Bradley, Pamela. *Beyond the Rainbow Bridge: Nurturing Our Children from Birth to Seven* (Michaelmas Press, 2000).

Patzlaff, Rainer, et al. *The Child from Birth to Three in Waldorf Education and Child Care* (WECAN, 2011).

Paulsen, Eldbjørg Gjessing. *Trust and Wonder: A Waldorf Approach to Caring for Infants and Toddlers* (WECAN, 2011).

Raichle, Bernadette. *Creating a Home for Body, Soul and Spirit: A New Approach to Child Care* (WECAN, 2008).

Ris, Margaret and Atchison, Trice, eds. *A Warm and Gentle Welcome – Nurturing Children from Birth to Age Three* (WECAN, 2008).

von Kügelgen, Helmut. *Love as the Source of Education* (WECAN, 2016).

II. The Development of the Young Child

Aeppli, Willi. *The Care and Development of the Human Senses: Rudolf Steiner's Work on the Significance of the Senses in Education* (Floris Books, 2013).

Blanning, Nancy, ed. *First Grade Readiness: Resources, Insights and Tools for Waldorf educators* (WECAN, 2016, second edition).

Dancy, Rahima Baldwin. *You are Your Child's First Teacher: Encouraging Your Child's Natural Development from Birth to Age Six* (Ten Speed Press, 2012, third edition).

Udo de Haes, Daniel. *The Creative Word: The Young Child's Experience of Language and Stories* (WECAN, 2014).

Howard, Susan, ed. *The Developing Child: The First Seven Years* (WECAN, 2004).

Howard, Susan, ed. *Working with the Angels: The Young Child and the Spiritual World*, Gateways Series, WECAN Books.

Howard, Susan, ed. *The Young Child in the World Today* (WECAN, 2003).

Goebel, Wolfgang, and Glöckler, Michaela. *A Guide to Child Health* (Floris Books, 2013, fourth edition).

Jenkinson, Sally. *The Genius of Play: Celebrating the Spirit of Childhood* (Hawthorn Press, 2003).

Jaffke, Freya, ed. *On the Play of the Child: Indications by Rudolf Steiner for Working With Young Children* (WECAN, 2012, second edition).

Ker, Ruth, ed. *You're Not the Boss of Me! Understanding the Six/Seven-Year-Old Transformation* (WECAN, 2007).

Köhler, Henning. *Working with Anxious, Nervous and Depressed Children: A Spiritual Perspective to Guide Parents* (Waldorf Publications, 2000).

König, Karl. *The First Three Years of the Child: Walking, Speaking, Thinking* (Floris Books, 2001).

Lievegoed, Bernard. *Phases of Childhood: Growing in Body, Soul and Spirit* (Floris Books, 2005, third edition).

Long-Breipohl, Renate. *Supporting Self-Directed Play in Steiner Waldorf Early Childhood Education* (WECAN, 2010).

Pedagogical Section of the Goetheanum. *School Readiness Today* (WECAN, 2014).

Schoorel, Edmond. *The First Seven Years: Physiology of Childhood* (Rudolf Steiner College Press, 2004).

Steegmans, Johanna. *Cradle of a Healthy Life: Early Childhood and the Whole of Life* (WECAN, 2012).

Strauss, Michaela. *Understanding Children's Drawings: Tracing the Path of Incarnation* (Rudolf Steiner Press, 2008).

von Heydebrand, Caroline. *Childhood: A Study of the Growing Soul* (SteinerBooks, 1988).

III. Activities for Young Children

Bryer, Estelle. *The Rainbow Puppet Theatre Book* (WECAN, 2013).

deForest, Louise, ed. *For the Children of the World: Stories and Recipes from the International Steiner Waldorf Early Childhood Association* (WECAN, 2012).

deForest, Louise, ed., *Tell Me a Story: Stories from the Waldorf Early Childhood Association of North America* (WECAN, 2013).

Ellersiek, Wilma. Gesture games book series: *Giving Love – Bringing Joy* (WECAN, 2003); *Gesture Games for Spring and Summer* (WECAN, 2005); *Gesture Games for Autumn and Winter* (WECAN, 2007); and *Dancing Hand, Trotting Pony* (WECAN, 2010). A Spanish translation of several of the games is available in *Juegos de Gestos de Mano* (Editorial El Liceo/WECAN, 2012).

Foster, Nancy. *Let Us Form A Ring: An Acorn Hill Anthology* (Acorn Hill Waldorf Kindergarten and Nursery, 1989; distributed by WECAN).

Foster, Nancy. *Dancing As We Sing: Seasonal Circle Plays and Traditional Singing Games* (Acorn Hill Waldorf Kindergarten and Nursery, 1999; distributed by WECAN).

Foster, Nancy, ed. *The Seasonal Festivals in Early Childhood: Seeking the Universally Human* (WECAN, 2010).

Foster, Nancy, ed. *The Mood of the Fifth: A Musical Approach to Early Childhood* (WECAN, 2013).

Jaffke, Freya. *Toymaking with Children* (Floris Books, 2012).

Jaffke, Freya. *Play With Us!* (WECAN, 2016).

Jaffke, Freya. *Let's Dance and Sing!* (WECAN, 2017).

Loescher, Margaret, *A Year in the Woods: Reflections on Leading an Outdoor Parent-and-Child Group* (WECAN, 2016).

Lonsky, Karen. *A Day Full of Song: Work Songs from a Waldorf Kindergarten* (WECAN, 2009).

Mellon, Nancy. *Storytelling with Children* (Hawthorn Press, 2013, second edition).

Müller, Rudolf. *Painting with Children* (Floris Books, 2003).

Udo de Haes, Daniel. *The Singing, Playing Kindergarten* (WECAN, 2005).

Willwerth, Ilian. *Merrily We Sing: Original Songs in the Mood of the Fifth*, WECAN Books.

The Wynstones Anthologies: *Summer, Autumn, Winter, Spring, Spindrift,* and *Gateways* (Wynstones Press, 1999, revised edition).

Zahlingen, Bronja. *A Lifetime of Joy: A Collection of Circle Games, Finger Games, Songs, Verses and Plays for Puppets and Marionettes* (WECAN, 2005).

IV. Lectures and Writings by Rudolf Steiner on Education

In the German edition of Rudolf Steiner's complete works (*Gesamtausgabe*), each volume has been given a unique "GA" number. Because this can be useful in navigating various translations and editions, we have included this number in the citations below.

The Education of the Child and Early Lectures on Education (SteinerBooks, 1996). The title essay, from GA 34, was originally written in 1907 and gives a short introduction to Waldorf education and child development. Other lectures in this volume are taken from GA 31, 33, 55, 60, and 96.

The Essentials of Education (GA 308; SteinerBooks, 1998). Five lectures given in Stuttgart, Germany, April 1924. Contents include the development of the child, the task of the teacher, the "bodily religion" of the young child, relationship of teacher and child.

The Foundations of Human Experience (GA 293; SteinerBooks, 1996). Also available as *The Study of Man* (Rudolf Steiner Press, 1995). These fourteen lectures were given in Stuttgart in August and September of 1919, just prior to the founding of the first Waldorf School. They are fundamental and challenging lectures on the physical, soul, and spirit organization of the child, and on the psychology of education.

The Kingdom of Childhood (GA 311; SteinerBooks, 1995). Seven lectures given in August 1924, in Torquay, England, to a small group of pioneers planning to open a new Waldorf school. They give an excellent introduction to child development and Waldorf education, including the incarnation process, the child as a sense organ, imitation, development of fantasy, and the kindergarten, as well as teaching main lessons, numbers, plants and animals.

The Roots of Education (GA 309; SteinerBooks, 1998). Five lectures given in Bern, Switzerland, in April 1924. Topics include the change of teeth as the end of the first stage of childhood, the child as a sense organ, memory, moral development, and the power of spiritual perception for understanding children and adults.

Soul Economy: Body, Soul, and Spirit in Waldorf Education (GA 303; SteinerBooks, 2003). These sixteen lectures were given in Dornach, Switzerland, during Christmas 1921-22. Lectures on phases of child development, health and illness, aesthetic, physical, religious and moral education. Includes "The Child Before the Seventh Year."

Spiritual Insights, compiled by Helmut von Kügelgen (WECAN, 2013, revised edition) gives spiritual content primarily from the work of Rudolf Steiner chosen specifically for the educator. Additional titles in this series include *Christmas*; *Easter*; *Michaelmas*; *Seeking the Spirit*; *Love*; and *Working with the Dead*.

V. Books on Organizational Development

Foster, Nancy, ed. *Mentoring in Waldorf Early Childhood Education* (WECAN, 2007).

Koteen-Soulé, Holly. *Professional Review and Development in Waldorf Early Childhood Education* (WECAN, 2008).

Schaefer, Christopher. *Partnerships of Hope: Building Waldorf School Communities* (Waldorf Publications).

Smit, Jörgen. *The Child, the Teachers, and the Community* (Waldorf Publications).

Tautz, Johannes. *The Founding of the First Waldorf School in Stuttgart* (Waldorf Publications).

Publishers

Waldorf Publications, formerly AWSNA Publications, Chatham, NY – waldorfpublications.org

Floris Books, Edinburgh, UK – florisbooks.co.uk

Hawthorn Press, Stroud, UK – hawthornpress.com

Mercury Press, Spring Valley, NY – mercurypress.org

Rudolf Steiner College Press, Fair Oaks, CA – rscbookstore.com

Rudolf Steiner Press, London, UK – rudolfsteinerpress.com

Steiner Books, formerly Anthroposophic Press, Great Barrington, MA – steinerbooks.com

WECAN Books, Spring Valley, NY – store.waldorfearlychildhood.org

Other Resources

The Alliance for Childhood, Annapolis, MD – allianceforchildhood.org

International Association for Steiner/Waldorf Early Childhood Education – iaswece.org

The International Play Association – ipausa.org and ipaworld.org

The Online Waldorf Library – waldorflibrary.org

Pikler/Loczy USA, Tulsa, Oklahoma – pikler.org

Resources for Infant Educarers (RIE), Los Angeles, CA – rie.org

The Rudolf Steiner Archive and e-Lib – rsarchive.org

For more information about Waldorf early childhood education, please contact:

The Waldorf Early Childhood Association of North America

285 Hungry Hollow Rd.

Spring Valley, NY 10977

waldorfearlychildhood.org

Made in the USA
Middletown, DE
17 September 2024